"HOW DO YOU
KNOW
YOU'RE NOT
WRONG?"

"HOW DO YOU KNOW YOU'RE NOT WRONG?"

RESPONDING TO OBJECTIONS THAT LEAVE CHRISTIANS SPEECHLESS

PAUL COPAN

BakerBooks

Grand Rapids, Michigan

Published by Baker Books
a division of Baker Publishing Group
P.O. Box 6287, Grand Rapids, MI 49516-6287
www.bakerbooks.com

Printed in the United States of America

Library of Congress Cataloging-in-Publication Data

Copan, Paul.
    How do you know you're not wrong? : responding to objections that leave Christians speechless / Paul Copan.
        p.   cm.
    Includes bibliographical references and index.
    ISBN 0-8010-6499-6 (pbk. : alk. paper)
    1. Apologetics. 2. Skepticism. I. Title.
BT1212.C665 2005
239—dc22   2005007932

To my sister Lil,
whose good humor, compassion, loyalty, and sacrifice
continue to bless and encourage.

CONTENTS

INTRODUCTION

An electrician was doing some wiring in our home. When he found out that I teach philosophy, he asked, "So who's your favorite philosopher?" I told him, "Jesus Christ." He was taken aback. "That just blows my mind! I've never thought of Jesus as a philosopher." Well, a lot of people don't think of Jesus as a philosopher, which is a tragedy.

Philosophers have gotten a bad name as those who think about and discuss obscure and irrelevant topics. The satirist H. L. Mencken said, "Philosophy consists largely of one philosopher arguing that all the others are jackasses. He usually proves it, and I should add that he also usually proves that he is one himself."[1] However, when done rightly, philosophy can be an immensely useful tool, and being a philosopher doesn't have to mean being a jackass! Philosophy is "the love of wisdom," and it involves hard thinking about things.

In his brief, readable book *On Jesus* (in the Wadsworth Philosophers Series), Douglas Groothuis presents Jesus of Nazareth as a rigorous philosopher. He defines a "philosopher" as one having a "strong inclination to pursue truth about philosophical matters." These philosophical matters include "life's meaning, purpose, and value as they relate to all the major divisions of philosophy"—especially the areas of knowledge (epistemology), ultimate reality (metaphysics), and ethics. A philosopher's task is accomplished "through the rigorous use of human reasoning and . . . with some intellectual facility."[2]

Philosopher Dallas Willard calls Jesus the smartest man in the world and a master at using logic.[3] In fact, the apostle Paul said that in Christ "are hidden all the treasures of wisdom and knowledge" (Col. 2:3). Christ not only spoke wise words—offering wise teaching—but is himself Wisdom incarnate. Of course, Jesus was more than a philosopher, but certainly not less.

The point I want to make here is this: *Jesus discussed topics that were publicly accessible and knowable.* For any who had ears to hear him, Jesus presented truths—indeed, he claimed to be the *embodiment* of truth (John 14:6)—that weren't just enclosed in some private or subjective "realm of faith" or reserved for some elite few. In fact, what Jesus said has always had a bearing on societal life, politics, economics, and business. Now some will disagree. For example, the atheist Michael Martin calls Jesus's approach to poverty "unrealistic" and "simplistic."[4] But as New Testament scholar R. T. France observes, Jesus didn't proclaim a specific socioeconomic program for society. Rather, he addressed underlying attitudes such as greed, generosity, industriousness, and contentment. Surely these topics have huge economic ramifications.[5] Just think of how the Enron, Worldcom, and Adelphia financial scandals of 2001 could have been avoided had Jesus's advice been heeded!

So often when it comes to the topic of God or ethics, people see these categories as completely different from physics or chemistry in this sense: God or ethics deals with opinion or feeling, not facts or publicly available knowledge. But that's incorrect. As in astronomy or geology, we can make actual *truth*-claims in theology or ethics. People can make *incorrect* claims about God or morality.

I repeatedly tell my philosophy and theology students not to write "I feel" in their papers. Using this kind of language shifts the discussion from the realm of truth-claims to that of inner states—mere private opinions and preferences. Instead, I tell them to use phrases such as "I think" or "There is good reason to believe" to reflect that we're dealing with truth-claims, not mere inclinations or likings—comparable to a favorite pizza topping or ice cream flavor.

Christians can't afford to assume that they can just "give people the gospel" in a day when many want to know *why* Christianity should be believed. In fact, a lot of Christians are intimidated in their outreach to non-Christians because they're afraid non-Christians will bring up objections to the Christian faith. So Christians tend to clam up or shy away from telling others the Good News. Thankfully, there's another alternative. C. S. Lewis astutely wrote: "Good philosophy must exist, if for no other reason, because bad philosophy needs to be answered."[6] The gospel offers answers to key questions that non-Christian worldviews can't answer. We can familiarize ourselves with basic answers from available resources (I've tried to make some important answers accessible in my popular-level books, *True for You, But Not for Me, That's Just Your Interpretation*, and the one you happen to be holding).

With a simple but clear understanding of the key issues, we can become a bolder witnessing community of loving believers. When we look at the alternatives, the good news of the gospel offers answers for the whole person—including its intellectual defensibility. Being equipped with basic answers and a gracious spirit will enable us, by God's Spirit, to bring greater light to a culture that's losing its way. As Lewis beautifully put it: "I believe in Christianity as I believe that the Sun has risen, not only because I see it, but because by it I see everything else."[7]

In my previous writings, I've mentioned a basic threefold strategy for defending and dealing with objections to the Christian worldview. First of all, we can't escape the objectivity of *truth* and the *reality*, to which truth-claims correspond. If people deny objective truth, they're actually affirming the existence of truth ("It's true that there's no truth"). If people deny that there's an objective *reality* to which our thinking should conform (e.g., "There's no reality—only appearances"), then they're admitting something that they take to be real and to which our minds should conform (at least the *appearances* are real)!

Second, if, with God's help, people see that truth and reality are inescapable, then we can deal with the next level—*worldviews* (theism, naturalism, and Eastern monism or pantheism being the leading contenders). At this stage, we seek to show that naturalism and Eastern monism are inadequate and that theism does the best job of explaining features of the *universe* (its origin, its fine-tuning, the emergence of first life and consciousness, the existence of beauty). Theism also does a better job of helping us understand our *humanity* (we have rights and dignity; we're morally responsible agents who are capable of reasoning and making free choices and who have the capacity for great evil).

Theism offers the best explanation to help us put the pieces together and connect the dots.

Third, if theism is the best option among competing worldviews, then *which* theistic option is the most viable—Judaism, Islam, or Christianity? After all, *if there is a God, then has he done anything to reveal himself within human history and to rescue us from the miserable, fallen condition in which we find ourselves?* At this stage, we deal with *Christian apologetics.* This addresses God's special revelation to us (especially in Christ) and covers topics such as the Bible's reliability and authority, the unique claims of Christ and his resurrection, and so on. So we move from (a) the broad discussion of truth to (b) the more specific topic of worldviews to (c) the even more specific topic of the Christian faith as offering answers for a wide range of questions. Despite our many questions and puzzling mysteries in our earthly pilgrimage, we also find much hope in the gospel to help us along the way. In this book, I deal with a host of issues that fit within these three broad categories—skepticism, science, animal rights, the soul, and much more. This book is like a handbook of self-contained chapters, each ending with summaries and recommended resources for readers who want to pursue that specific topic further. (At the back of the book are lots of explanatory endnotes; so check those out too.)

It's my hope that this material will encourage Christians in general, but particularly Christian students in high schools and universities (and their parents!) who regularly face skeptical challenges to their faith. I trust this book will be a resource for believers to be built up in their own faith and to become better equipped to help others, by God's Spirit, to come to faith in Christ. The Christian shouldn't only be prepared with wise and informed *answers.* She should also be prepared both to *listen* as well as ask probing *questions.* More often than not, Jesus himself responded to questions *with* questions. As Randy Newman points out in his fine book, *Questioning Evangelism*, this approach can better help the *believer* discover where a non-Christian is coming from and the *unbeliever* understand his worldview's foundations and deal honestly with its inadequacies.[8] Dallas Willard reminds us that questions such as "Would I *like* there to be a God?" or "Would I *like* it if Jesus turned out to be Lord?" may help unbelievers (and believers as well!) "realize the extent to which what they *want* to be the case is controlling their ability to *see* what is the case."[9]

In addition to all this, the believer's winsome *character* and the support of a loving Christian *community* must increasingly characterize our witness in the marketplace of ideas.

FURTHER READING

Groothuis, Douglas. *On Jesus*. Wadsworth Philosophers Series. Belmont, CA: Wadsworth, 2003.

Moreland, J. P. *Love Your God with All Your Mind*. Colorado Springs: NavPress, 1997.

Moreland, J. P., and William Lane Craig. *Philosophical Foundations for a Christian Worldview*. Downers Grove, IL: InterVarsity, 2003.

Newman, Randy. *Questioning Evangelism: Engaging People's Hearts the Way Jesus Did*. Grand Rapids: Kregel, 2004.

Willard, Dallas. *The Divine Conspiracy*. San Francisco: HarperSan-Francisco, 1998.

P A R T   I

SLOGANS RELATED TO TRUTH AND REALITY

1

How Do You Know You're Not Wrong?

While driving on an asphalt road on a hot, sunny day, you'll see what appears to be wet pavement. As you draw closer, though, you see the pavement isn't wet after all. Because of the sharp temperature difference between the hot pavement and the cooler air several feet above it, the blue light rays from the sky bend (refract) and create a "mi-ra-gee," as Bugs Bunny once called it.

Or what about our dreams, which, while we're having them, seem to be so real? Lao-Tzu, the purported founder of Taoism, asked, "If, when I was asleep, I was a man dreaming I was a butterfly, how do I know when I am awake, I am not a butterfly dreaming that I am a man?"

These examples of being fooled (at least temporarily) in our perceptions have led to interesting philosophical questions. A more sophisticated one is raised by Hilary Putnam. He suggested the logical possibility that I might be a "brain in a vat."[1] Perhaps some mad scientist gives me a tranquilizer, brings me to his lab, removes my brain from my body, and hooks it up by electrodes to a computer. The brain experiences a *virtual* reality—things are real only in *effect* but not in actual *fact*. Electronic impulses to the brain create the *impression* that I have a body and that

17

I am eating chocolate, driving my Honda Accord, playing soccer, or reading a book on the Civil War. But in the end, I'm nothing more than a brain in a vat with these virtual experiences.

Or consider these questions: How do we *know* that the world *really* is older than five minutes? How do we *know* that other minds exist? And how do I *know* that there is a world "out there," independent of my mind? The skeptic plays upon these illusions and questions to challenge the trustworthiness of our minds/senses—and whether we can come to true, knowing conclusions on a regular basis. His question is, "How do you *know* that you're not being deceived?" The assumption is that *if you can't perfectly prove that you're not being deceived, then you can't claim knowledge of something. Or if you can't have 100 percent certainty about something, then knowledge is up for grabs; one view is just as legitimate as another.*

French (Catholic) philosopher René Descartes (1596–1650) was troubled by the *theological* uncertainty (brought on by the Protestant Reformation) and *philosophical* skepticism of his day. In response, he wanted to establish knowledge with unshakable certainty. He asked: What if an evil genius, or demon, might be deceiving me? What if things only *seem* to be one way, but in reality *aren't* that way because of the influence of this being who constantly distorts my thinking? This question has given many philosophers much grief over the centuries. Descartes' solution was that even if he doubted everything, he couldn't doubt that he was doubting. And since doubting is a form of thinking, he concluded, "I think; therefore, I am [*cogito, ergo sum*]."

Now there are different types of skepticism. For example, there's a *total* (global) skepticism that denies knowledge altogether. Another is a *partial* (local) skepticism that denies that we can have knowledge in certain areas (such as moral knowledge or knowledge of God). Pyrrhonian skepticism (named after Pyrrho of Elis [ca. 365–ca. 270 BC]) recommends that we suspend judgments about most matters rather than hotly argue about them.[2] We can't tackle individual species of skepticism here. Rather, we'll have to treat skepticism in a general way, addressing basic concerns related to the question "How can you really be sure you know?" The following points offer a more plausible and believable alternative to skepticism, which often trips over its own skeptical methodology.

First, skepticism isn't always bad: one kind can be healthy, another unhealthy; one constructive, another destructive; one enriching, another

corrosive. Perhaps you've heard the joke that the word *gullible* isn't really in
the dictionary. Of course, the person who actually checks the dictionary
(or simply responds, "Really?") serves as a living example of gullibility!
Well, gullibility may be bliss, but it isn't a virtue. A healthy skepticism
can help us be discerning rather than naïve in our beliefs. It can also help
clarify and properly nuance what we believe. Or perhaps we're overly
dogmatic in some aspects of our thinking; in that case, another's skepticism can prompt us to reinvestigate our assumptions and better move
us toward the truth of the matter.[3] (Encouraging humility is also another
fringe benefit of skepticism!)

Jesus himself was skeptical of the religious elite of his day and many
of their theological assumptions. He reminded them that they shouldn't
expect God to conform to our puny—and often misguided—human
categories: "That which is highly esteemed among men is detestable
in the sight of God" (Luke 16:15). In the spirit of the Old Testament
prophets, Jesus challenged the status quo—that is, by eating with pros-
titutes and other social outcasts and challenging the Jewish nationalism
and religious elitism of his time. We too must take the challenge of
Jesus seriously: if we are open to God's Spirit, we are always going to be
learning and growing. Like the untamable Aslan of Narnia, we should
be prepared for God to revise our faulty—and even idolatrous—theological perspectives and categories. And as we interact with our fellow
human beings, we must be "shrewd as serpents" and "innocent as doves"
(Matt. 10:16). Jesus himself knew the limitations of human beings and
didn't place his full confidence in them (John 2:24–25).

So a *healthy* skepticism is necessary. We shouldn't be gullible. In the
rest of this chapter, however, we'll be looking at an *un*healthy, corrosive
skepticism.

*Second, the Bible takes for granted a "critical realism"—that a world
exists independently of human minds ("realism"); however, intellectual
and even moral discernment or sifting ("critical") is often required in the
knowledge process.* Scripture takes for granted a view known as *realism*—that is, it acknowledges that real entities exist on their own and
aren't dependent upon human minds or language or society's categories
or constructs. Also, this realism is *critical* because it acknowledges
cultural and historical influences—not to mention sin's distorting and
further limiting our thought processes.

Furthermore, the Bible assumes that *sense perception* is a means of arriving at knowledge ("perceptual realism" or "direct realism"). Jesus tells us, in Matthew 6, to look at the lilies of the field and the birds of the air. Paul, in Romans 1, makes clear that evidence for God's existence is available to all humans through what can be *seen*. In fact, Scripture assumes that *miracles* have certain observable effects (a voice from heaven, a lame man walking, a leper being cleansed) and that our senses are generally reliable. The Christian worldview assumes that God is *truthful*. He isn't a deceiver. This enables us to affirm the general reliability of our senses. We can rightly assume we're not regularly being fooled by our senses. *There's no reason to deny what seems so obvious to us* ("common sense realism"). And as Douglas Groothuis correctly observes, Jesus was "a common sense realist."[4]

Our senses can give us *direct* access to the physical world around us. Now I may *perceive* the color of a table differently from another individual (say, if I'm a color-blind person). Or I may be looking at the table in pitch darkness and then suddenly in bright light—which may distort my perception. But such differences of perception don't suggest that the table has no real, enduring color. The table has *real* properties, and the different perceptions individuals have of that table (based on different conditions such as keenness of eyesight or available lighting) only mean that *one or more persons might not know the real properties of the table*. A cherry-wood coffee table may not *appear* reddish at night (we could call its apparent black coloring a "transient" property). However, the table *is* dark red even at night (we could call this a "standing" property). The "standing" color remains the same even if the "transient" color varies in perception from person to person (based on various conditions). So the properties of the table (color, size, shape, texture) *exist independently* of our minds. Tables, chairs, trees, and stones (and their properties) must be distinguished from how we may perceive them. We can say that *direct perception of these sense-objects takes place when there's no difference between a property and how it impinges upon/affects the sense organ. Any difference between them means there isn't an accurate ("veridical") perception. We know truly when the properties we perceive match up with the properties in the object under consideration.*[5]

Along these lines, we could also add that we can know *God* directly and immediately through Christ by his Spirit. God isn't unknowable;

rather, he is self-revealing and freely gives us genuine knowledge of himself. As the late theologian Colin Gunton argued in his *Act and Being*, "The gospel assures us that we can know God as he truly is."[6] So when we are told that because God so *loved* us, we ought to *love* one another (1 John 4:11), we are talking about the same category of love. Although God's love is dependable, nonarbitrary, and steadfast, we fallen human beings can still identify this as love because we have been made in God's image. We don't have to be skeptical about our knowledge of God. The gospel message inspires confidence that we can know God *truly*—even if not *exhaustively*.

Third, our pursuit of knowledge involves both embracing as many true beliefs as possible and rejecting as many false ones as possible. We can't engage in one without the other. If my goal is to accumulate as many true beliefs as possible, I should just believe *everything* I hear, and in doing so, I'm bound to pick up new, true beliefs. Someone reading *MAD* magazine might learn some interesting facts and insights in an attempt to acquire as many true beliefs as possible; however, he'll pick up a lot of nonsensical beliefs along the way too. The problem with our only trying to gather as many true beliefs as possible is that *we'll pick up lots of false ones too*. That's not good.

On the other hand, what if we take the opposite approach—rejecting all beliefs and refusing to believe *any* claims or authorities on any topic? We'll certainly cut down on the number of false beliefs we hold. *But* we'll also be rejecting plenty of true beliefs in the process. That's not good either. So the appropriate goal in pursuing knowledge is twofold: *embrace what's true* and *reject what's false*.

Fourth, a global or total skepticism is impossible since it rejects knowledge or the possibility of knowledge—which is itself a knowledge-claim and therefore makes the rejection of knowledge incoherent. I've seen a bumper sticker that reads, "Militant Agnostic: I don't know and you can't know either." Of course, this kind of statement is problematic; after all, it's a *knowledge*-claim: "I *know* that no one can *know* (that God exists)." And how does he know this? Perhaps there are skeptics who simply want to suspend judgment altogether about whether we can know (the Pyrrhonian or tentative kind). But *why* is this? Presumably, they *know* something that serves as the basis for their skepticism—that error exists, that people make mistakes, and so on.

In the spring of 2001, I was speaking at Worcester Polytechnic Institute. (I like to tell people that it's near—believe it or not—Lake Chargoggagogg-manchauggagogg-chaubunagungamaugg in Webster, Massachusetts!) After I was done speaking, there was time for questions from the floor. Some of the students were out for blood! One student shot out of his seat and protested, "You've talked a lot about truth and knowledge. Now the truth may exist, but I don't see how you can say that you *know* the truth."

I replied, "It sounds to me as though you *know* you're *right* and I'm *wrong*; that your position is the *superior* one and that mine is *inferior*; that *you* have a virtue that *I* don't have. It sounds like you *know* that you *can't know* the truth." Despite his skepticism, this student was another militant agnostic. Despite his doubts about being able to know, he was very dogmatic about his position! To say we can't or don't know at all is to make a knowledge-claim.

Fifth, a chief motivation for skepticism is the fact that human beings make errors and get a lot of things wrong. But this very realization assumes that we already have some knowledge about the way things are so that we can discern error. Philosopher Josiah Royce (1855–1913) observed that recognizing error assumes an awareness or knowledge of the way things really are. Skepticism claims to *know* that an error has been committed; it *assumes* that there has been a deviation from the truth.[7] Error presupposes truth, and the skeptic's arguments have some punch to them only because knowledge of the truth is taken for granted.

Furthermore, when the skeptic suggests, as did Descartes, that an evil mastermind may be misleading us, she implies that she *knows* or *assumes* that *there's a difference between knowing and being deceived*. Even though we've been mistaken in our sense perceptions, we still know there's a difference between dreams and nondreaming states. If we didn't recognize a difference between the two, why would the topic of dreams even arise? It's *hindsight* that enables us to see the difference between dreaming and not dreaming. If we never realized the difference between truth and error, how could the issue ever emerge?

Also, our awareness of illusions or dreams forces us to conclude that it's *true* that they take place. Even if I'm on medication, it's *true*, at least, that I'm hallucinating about an elephant in pink tights (even if there is no actual elephant in the room). It's true that I'm being appeared to "elephantly." Clearly, it's a *fact* that sticks *appear* to bend in the water. So we can even draw true and firm conclusions from our individual experiences of illusions and misperceptions.

Sixth, the skeptic doesn't question (a) inescapable logical laws and (b) a reliably functioning mind in order to do his skeptical questioning; he assumes them, which allows him to draw skeptical conclusions. Clearly the skeptic draws the conclusion that skepticism is justified. But *how* did he come to conclude this? Hasn't he used certain fundamental laws of *logic* to draw such an inference? Doesn't he take his conclusion to be *nonarbitrary?* But the skeptic isn't skeptical about these laws of logic. He uses them all the time and places great confidence in them to do a decent job of reasoning. He believes he *knows* the difference between what's logical and illogical.

But the skeptic isn't just assured of the necessity and inescapability of these logical laws. The skeptic also assumes his *mind* is working just fine and that his skeptical conclusions are trustworthy! But, ironically, taking for granted the reliable operations of the mind is a *denial* of the very *skepticism* that's being concluded!

Seventh, if the standard for knowledge is 100 percent certainty, then we're aiming too high. Such a high standard for knowledge can actually lead to skepticism where there doesn't need to be any; we do know many things even if we aren't absolutely certain about them, and this is legitimately called "knowledge." Furthermore, if we assume "100 percent certainty = knowledge," we'll be denying lots of things that we really do know. So we should embrace a more modest kind of knowledge—that of a "high degree of plausibility," "greater likelihood," or a "belief (or set of beliefs) that does the best job of explaining." In his quest for certainty, Descartes wrongly assumed that *knowledge* equals *absolute certainty.* The problem is that there are *plenty* of things that we can know even if we aren't absolutely certain of them—that the universe is expanding, that time (the succession of events) won't cease, that I have certain childhood memories that are accurate, and so on. We just find ourselves knowing *particular* things.[8] But if we could "know" only those things that are 100 percent certain, we'd have to remove huge chunks from our belief structure that we're reasonably confident about but don't reach that "certainty" level.

So we can *truly know* that Siddhartha Gautama was the founder of Buddhism, and that England and France fought the Hundred Years' War (1337–1453), and that the body of Ulysses S. Grant is buried in

Grant's Tomb. Do we know these things with *absolute* certainty? No. It's conceivable or logically possible that we could be in error—even if this is highly unlikely. We truly *can* claim that these beliefs are true with a high degree of confidence; that is, we can *know* them even if we aren't *absolutely certain* about them. *The high degree of plausibility of these beliefs qualifies them to count as "knowledge."* So we can reject Descartes' view of knowledge (as absolute certainty) and still truly know things.[9] *Descartes raised the bar for knowledge much too high.* (He didn't want to admit that one could *know* something while there was an outside chance of being wrong.) If we adopted Descartes' approach, we would have to reject beliefs that we *already* and *truly* know.

Also, we can question the person who says knowledge involves 100 percent certainty: "How can you be 100 percent certain that knowledge must involve 100 percent certainty?" It's just not obvious that knowledge necessitates 100 percent certainty.

*Eighth, to choose between 100 percent certainty and doubting everything/not knowing anything is a false choice. There are degrees of belief in between, many of which can legitimately be called knowledge—even if this knowledge isn't exhaustive or absolutely certain. This know-everything-or-nothing dichotomy results in the unfortunate consequence of having to hold that (a) the **plausible** (though not 100 percent certain) and (b) the **ridiculous** can't be differentiated, which is silly. Also, certain beliefs may require further investigation before they can legitimately be considered knowledge.*

In the movie *Hannah and Her Sisters*, Woody Allen is asking about God's existence and demands certainty on the topic. "I want certainty or nothing." After all "maybe" is "a slim reed to hang your life on."[10] Some people give the impression that if you don't know something with absolute certainty (whether about God's existence or some other topic), then you can't know anything at all. But this is a false dichotomy. There are *degreed* beliefs ranging between certainty and doubt. One philosopher has listed thirteen categories of knowledge, ranging from certainty to doubt ("certainly false"):[11]

    6   Certain
    5   Obvious
    4   Evident

3 Beyond reasonable doubt
2 Epistemically in the clear
1 Probable
0 Counterbalance
-1 Probably false
-2 In the clear to disbelieve
-3 Reasonable to disbelieve
-4 Evidently false
-5 Obviously false
-6 Certainly false

Certain beliefs may be far more plausible or likely than others. We can know *truly* even if we don't know *exhaustively* or with *absolute certainty*. We must reject the either-or of 100 percent certainty or doubt and allow for knowledge to exist between these extremes.

Furthermore, the problem with being skeptical about *all* claims (global skepticism) is that it is so unreasonable: it allows for no degrees or levels of knowledge-claims. Consider two beliefs: (a) the earth is round and (b) there are elves in the cypresses in my backyard. *Shouldn't even the most radical skeptic have greater doubts about (b) than (a)?* The problem with being skeptical about *everything* is that it fails to differentiate between more and less reliable beliefs. Global skepticism must treat a well-established theory in the same way as the most ridiculous theory.[12]

Also, there are times when an initial observation needs further investigation for a true belief to be warranted and therefore considered knowledge. If I see a nonworking clock that *happens* to show the correct time of day when I look at it, I can't call this knowledge (*warranted* true belief). My belief might require further investigation to be "upgraded" to the level of knowledge,[13] or it might require certain "truth-sustaining conditions" to justify the claim to knowledge.[14] The upshot is that propositional knowledge will be sustained (and not undermined) by all relevant truths taken together.

Ninth, we should assume our senses are innocent until proven guilty (the "credulity principle"). This is part of the "common sense realism" we typically live by—there's no reason to reject what seems so obvious to us in favor of less obvious alternatives. Sometimes seriously ill patients may take medications that cause hallucinations of spiders crawling up the walls or wolves attacking. Of course, when patients take these prescribed drugs, they should rightly question their ability to see correctly. Under normal circumstances, though, we commonsensically assume our senses are not systematically misleading us. I'm wise to accept the testimony of my senses unless I have good reason to doubt them (e.g., when I am tired, drugged, brainwashed, hypnotized, etc.). If there is nothing that leads me to suspect my senses are unreliable, then they should be regarded as innocent until proven guilty. That is, *some things are so basic and common-sensical that the burden of proof would be on those who question them.*

Besides the evil genius or illusion question, we've noted other skeptical questions philosophers raise: "How do I know that the external world exists? How do I know that other minds exist? How do I know the world is older than five minutes?" An appropriate response is that there are some basic beliefs we have and that there is no good reason to deny that we know them to be true. Now, it's *logically possible* that we could be wrong on some of these beliefs. And it may be that we have to *adjust* or *refine* these views to be more precise. But *rejecting* plausibly held beliefs as items of knowledge (though there's not 100 percent certainty) would do serious damage to the belief-structure in our minds. *Why go against all these basic beliefs and embrace a skeptical view that doesn't even seem to be true?* We have very good reason to claim that we have knowledge; this is based, for example, on evidence through our senses and reasoning processes (whose reliable function we regularly assume) *and* the absence of anything to overturn our beliefs.[15] The skeptic must explain why we don't know that such evidence is reliable.

The Scottish philosopher Thomas Reid (1710–1796) captured it nicely:

> The sceptic asks me, Why do you believe the existence of the external object which you perceive? This belief, sir, is none of my manufacture; it came from the mint of Nature; it bears her image and superscription; and, if it is not right, the fault is not mine. I ever took it upon trust, and without suspicion.[16]

The very fact that skeptics *ask* whether or not an external world exists is probably good evidence that it does exist. Otherwise, it's hard to know why the question would even come up.

*Tenth, the very real **possibility** of my being wrong doesn't warrant the conclusion that I **am** wrong. The first doesn't necessarily lead to the second.* What if someone says, "An evil mastermind could be deceiving you" (or "How do you know you're not being deceived by an evil mastermind?"), and then asks, "*Therefore,* how can you say you know something?" You can point out that it *doesn't logically follow* that *if it is possible* that I am being deceived (or am a brain in a vat), that I actually *am* being deceived or that I cannot know something. This is a *non sequitur.* The burden would be on the skeptic to show why I can't take my experiences as generally reliable in the face of what seems quite obvious to me. *The skeptic has to do more than suggest the possibility that I'm wrong; he must give reasons for believing I'm wrong in this particular instance.* The skeptic wrongly thinks he must be *refuted first* before we can claim to know. But we can seek, with God's help, to *rebut* the skeptic by saying, "You haven't convincingly shown that I'm wrong." Why think that we have to bear the burden by showing that the *skeptic's* position is false? As one philosopher put it:

> It would be simply ridiculous to insist, despite the complete absence of evidence, that nevertheless the earth *might* still be a giant spaceship, and until we show that it is not, we cannot be sure that our lives are not being controlled by somebody from within the earth. But this is just what we do with the problem of skepticism.[17]

We could even ask the skeptic: *What makes you think I even **need** to give justification or warrant for my beliefs?* Doesn't this assume that we are knowers by nature and that the knowing process is at work?

Eleventh, skepticism doesn't take seriously "the inference to the best explanation"—that is, determining which worldview does a better job of explaining (in a more simple, powerful, and sweeping way) why certain important features of existence are the way they are.[18] You've probably had this experience: a skeptic approaches you with the presumed demand that you be able to answer, to her satisfaction, any and all objections before she will even begin *considering* the Christian faith as a viable belief-option. However, in responding to skeptics, it's not necessary that we answer *all* the questions they raise (a pretty tall order). But we should discuss *which worldview does the best job* of explaining key questions or beliefs we take for granted (the beginning and fine-tuning of the universe, the emergence of consciousness, the existence of objective moral values, the reliability of our rational faculties, etc.). Which view provides a better or more "natural" basic framework of explanation?

So we can ask the skeptic: *Why should we take a skeptical view of things?* Skeptics themselves believe that skepticism has greater power to explain the way things are. They believe they *know* how things *really* operate, how the knowledge process really works. While this point doesn't refute skepticism, it reflects the common commitment skeptic and nonskeptic have to the value of best explanation. And as we've seen, it's highly doubtful that skepticism does the better job of explaining various features of the world.

Twelfth, skepticism—like relativism—tends to eliminate personal or moral responsibility since truth (which is part of the very definition of knowledge) is systematically ignored or evaded. (Even this skeptical approach can be carried out only with partial success; one can't be a complete skeptic.) We shouldn't ignore the personal motivational factors that may be driving the skeptical enterprise—even if one's motivation doesn't disprove an argument. Radical skepticism is a condition that needs curing rather than a rational ground for one's worldview. Knowledge necessarily includes *truth*. Well then, what is *truth*? It's like the attachment on a socket wrench that fits or matches the bolt the mechanic is trying to tighten. Similarly, truth is a *matchup between beliefs and reality; a belief fits or corresponds to what actually is the case.* There is an *authenticity about* and a *correspondence/fit between* beliefs/claims and the way things are. So to say that the moon is made of cheese is *false* because it doesn't match up with what the moon is really made of (silicon dioxide, aluminum, calcium, titanium, etc.).

Now if the skeptic admits that a belief or worldview is *true*, he's no longer a skeptic (on that matter at least). He therefore claims to have *knowledge* of something. If, however, the skeptic avoids making *truth*-statements (and thus claims to *knowledge*), then why take personal responsibility for our actions? Why be committed to anything? Skepticism would be undermined if one is committed to fundamental truths and objective moral values. It seems that skepticism is a position that *eliminates any kind of personal responsibility or accountability*; it's legitimate to query if an underlying *resistance* to truth is motivating this approach. Philosopher Dallas Willard rightly argues that a comprehensive skepticism is *an affliction of the mind that needs curing*, but it can't be advanced as a *rational* ground for anything.[19]

Thirteenth, much of our contemporary crisis in knowledge stems from taking skepticism too seriously. While skeptical questions have their place, they are dependent upon the confident assumption that we are creatures who can know.[20] We don't have to despair of ever having knowledge since it doesn't require 100 percent certainty. We can ask the question: *Why take seriously radical skeptical questions (e.g., Descartes' evil genius or Putnam's brain-in-a-vat) that cast massive doubts upon our ability to know? What good reasons are there for doing so?* If we have no good reasons, then it seems perfectly legitimate to dismiss the possibility. It's *logically* possible that I could jump to the moon or swim across the Atlantic, but it's *practically* impossible. So we should tell the skeptic that *practical possibilities* should receive more of his attention since we don't have any real basis for taking brains in vats seriously. It's not *vat* big a deal! Sure, such bizarre, nonsensical, and practically impossible scenarios may be logically possible, but so what? We shouldn't take skepticism seriously unless we have excellent or serious reasons to doubt what we appear to know reasonably and confidently.

SUMMARY

- Skepticism isn't always bad: one kind can be healthy, another unhealthy; one constructive, another destructive; one enriching, another corrosive.

- The Bible takes for granted a "critical realism"—that a world exists independently of human minds ("realism"); however, intellectual and moral discernment ("critical") are often required in the knowledge process.

- Our pursuit of knowledge involves both embracing as many true beliefs as possible and rejecting as many false ones as possible. We cannot engage in one without the other.

- A global or total skepticism is impossible since it rejects knowledge or the possibility of knowledge—which is itself a knowledge-claim and therefore makes the rejection of knowledge incoherent.

- A chief motivation for skepticism is that human beings make errors and get a lot of things wrong. But this very realization assumes that we already have some knowledge about the way things are so that we can discern error.

- The skeptic doesn't question (a) inescapable logical laws and (b) a reliably functioning mind in order to do his skeptical questioning; he assumes them, which allows him to draw skeptical conclusions.

- If the standard for knowledge is 100 percent certainty, then we're aiming too high. Such a high standard for knowledge can actually lead to skepticism where there doesn't need to be any; we know many things that we aren't absolutely certain about, and this is legitimately called "knowledge."

- Furthermore, if we assume "100 percent certainty = knowledge," we'll be denying lots of things that we really do know. So we should embrace a more modest kind of knowledge—that of a "high degree of plausibility," "greater likelihood," or a "belief (or set of beliefs) that does the best job of explaining."

- It's just not obvious that knowledge necessarily involves 100 percent certainty. Can you *really* be 100 percent certain that knowledge requires 100 percent certainty? It's highly doubtful.

- To choose between 100 percent certainty and doubting everything/not knowing anything is a false choice. There are degrees of belief in between, many of which can legitimately be called knowledge—even if this knowledge isn't exhaustive or absolutely certain. This know-everything-or-nothing dichotomy results in the unfortunate consequence of having to hold that (a) the plausible (though not 100 percent certain) and (b) the ridiculous can't be differentiated, which is silly. Also, certain beliefs may require further investigation before they can legitimately be considered knowledge.

- We should assume our senses are innocent until proven guilty (the "credulity principle"). This is part of the "common sense realism" we typically live by—there's no reason to reject what seems so obvious to us in favor of less obvious alternatives.

- The very real possibility of my being wrong doesn't warrant the conclusion that I am wrong. The first doesn't necessarily lead to the second.

- Skepticism doesn't take seriously "the inference to the best explanation"—that is, determining which worldview does a better job of explaining (in a more simple, powerful, and sweeping way) why certain important features of existence are the way they are.

- Skepticism—like relativism—tends to eliminate personal or moral responsibility since truth (which is part of the very definition of knowledge) is systematically ignored or evaded. (Even this skeptical approach can be carried out only with partial success; one can't be a complete skeptic.) We shouldn't ignore the personal motivational factors that may be driving the skeptical enterprise—even if one's motivation doesn't disprove an argument. Blanket skepticism is an affliction of the mind that needs curing.

- Much of our contemporary crisis in knowledge stems from taking skepticism too seriously. While skeptical questions have their place, they are dependent upon the assumption that we are creatures who can know.

FURTHER READING

Clark, David K. *To Know and Love God: A Method for Theology*. Wheaton: Crossway, 2003.

Clark, David K., and Jim Beilby. *Why Bother with Truth?* Norcross, GA: Ravi Zacharias International Ministries, 2000.

Moser, Paul K., et al. *The Theory of Knowledge: A Thematic Introduction*. New York: Oxford University Press, 1998.

Wood, W. Jay. *Epistemology: Becoming Intellectually Virtuous*. Downers Grove, IL: InterVarsity, 1998.

2

WHATEVER WORKS FOR YOU

Americans tend to be pragmatic.[1] Why repair a windup toy when you could save time by going out and getting another one? Why pull out the china for dinner when you could use disposable paper plates instead? It's not at all uncommon to hear, "Hey, whatever works for you," "That'll work," or "Whatever floats your boat."

The pragmatist says that *truth is what's useful. If it "works," brings good results, helps us to cope, or contributes to human well-being,* then it's true. For the pragmatist, true beliefs are those that encourage actions with desirable results and benefit human beings. Historically, pragmatists have wanted to avoid getting stuck in abstract theories and ivory towers—a noble ideal. The pragmatist William James (1842–1910) emphasized the *concrete* ("the *verified*") as opposed to the abstract ("the *verifiable*").

An extreme pragmatist like Stephen Stich says that we don't need to know or care whether our beliefs are true or false. The real question is *whether these beliefs enable us to achieve happiness and well-being.*[2] Another notable pragmatist of our day is Richard Rorty. He's known for having said that *truth is what your peers let you get away with say-*

ing.[3] That is, we basically justify our beliefs within and to our peer groups and conversation partners ("fellow inquirers")—with people who have basically the same outlook on life as we do. This enables us to *cope*.

In science, the famous Cambridge physicist Stephen Hawking takes a pragmatic (or "instrumentalist") approach to his discipline. He's merely concerned that theories work: "I . . . am a positivist who believes that physical theories are just mathematical models we construct, and that it is meaningless to ask if they correspond to reality, just whether they predict observations."[4] In this case, a scientific theory is "true" if it works. So pragmatists aren't very concerned that their view *mirrors* the world (or corresponds to the way things are); they're concerned with how to *manage within* the world.

Before looking at some problems with a full-blown pragmatic approach to truth, we should remember that *there's an element of truth in pragmatism.* For several reasons, pragmatism reminds us of important considerations.

Consideration 1: "Whatever works" is a perfectly appropriate approach when truth (or right and wrong) isn't at stake. This kind of pragmatism (non-epistemic or non-alethic) poses no problem. In a number of areas, we make decisions based on pragmatic considerations because we have certain goals in mind. We might choose to buy a snowblower over a snow shovel (or a chain saw over an ax) because of the time and energy we'd save. On the other hand, if we want the exercise, we could go with the snow shovel (or the ax) instead.

Here, choosing one over the other is legitimate and appropriate because the consequences aren't *truth*-making or *truth*-constituting. (It's not as though "The snowblower brings better consequences than a snow shovel." = "It's *true* that a snowblower is better than a snow shovel.") Nor are the consequences *right*-making or *right*-constituting. (We're not saying, "One *ought* to use a snowblower rather than a snow shovel.") The "whatever works" approach is fine with certain equally legitimate goals and their outcomes in mind. This approach *isn't* appropriate *when the consequences constitute truth.*

Consideration 2: Pragmatism rightly reminds us of the dangers of getting stuck in the ivory tower of abstract ideas and theories. Lofty ideas might sound great in a textbook or on paper, but it's often important to ask: What do these ideas actually *do*? The book of James reminds us that mere orthodox belief can't save; even the demons are solid monotheists (2:19). True saving faith is a living and active one.

Consideration 3: Pragmatism reminds us of the importance of humility and that knowledge is a gift to be received, not an object we control. Let's move from St. James to William James. This philosopher opposed the idea that we can somehow find the truth and arrogantly sit back as though we have arrived intellectually and have no further work to do.

Unfortunately, this can be a problem for Christians. Often we can be quick to give "answers" but slow to listen to and understand the concerns and backgrounds of others. Christians face the danger of smugness—giving the impression that they've completed their spiritual or personal pilgrimage and have learned all they need to know. They become puffed up and arrogant from a knowledge detached from love, as Paul reminds us (1 Cor. 8:1). But even what we come to discover and know is a gift from God to be humbly and gratefully received: "What do you have that you did not receive? And if you did receive it, why do you boast as if you had not received it?" (1 Cor. 4:7).

Again, as Christians we can affirm aspects of pragmatism. As we saw, *given certain legitimate goals* (e.g., efficiency or exercise), it's appropriate to consider whether one method or approach works better than another. The problem comes when pragmatism is made into a comprehensive philosophy of life—and when *truth* or *morality* is reduced to "whatever works" or "whatever promotes the greatest good for the greatest number." At this point, pragmatism becomes not only counterintuitive but a danger as well.

What then are some problems with a pragmatic view of truth?

First, something can be true even if it's detrimental to a this-worldly sense of well-being or success; "well-being" and "success" can be very subjective, easy-to-bend standards. The pragmatist wouldn't say he's speaking of what makes one or a few persons happy or successful; he's speaking generally. But even if pragmatism pertains to whole cultures or civilizations, we still run into problems. It seems that large groupings of people (e.g., the people of Nazi Germany) could, in the name of "success," suppress the truth and cling to false, immoral beliefs. Believing Aryans to be superior, many Germans thought that getting rid of

Jews would make Germany more successful or increase its happiness and well-being.

Even today across Western "civilization," abortion and euthanasia may seem to "work" or "help people" to engage more freely in certain pursuits. (Of course, abortion and euthanasia don't "help" the *victims* of these "procedures"—just the ones who should be caring for them!) But what "works" or "brings success" can be a very *subjective and pliable* standard.

After making it to the finals in the 2000 Sydney Olympics, British 400-meter hurdler Tasha Danvers-Smith won gold and silver medals in several European competitions and had her sights set on medaling at Athens in 2004. But a few months before the Athens Games, she discovered that she was expecting a child. This would mean Tasha would have to drop out of the competition at the prime of her athletic career. And noting that she and her husband-coach depended financially on that career, she said, "When my body is my business, then if my body is not functioning, there is no business."

This conflict prompted Tasha to contemplate having an abortion. But she thought of Luke 9:25, which asks: What does it profit you to gain the whole world and lose your soul? Tasha couldn't rationalize away her moral obligation to preserve the human life within her body. *That* was a higher moral priority than competing in the Olympics. Yes, something may "work" (e.g., having an abortion to get an Olympic medal), but it may contradict what's true—including what's morally true.[5]

Second, we'd have to consider contradictory points of view true if they prove to be useful for opposing "peer groups," but this is obviously problematic. What if an abortionist believes he's helping "unexpectedly expecting" women to uphold their "right" to "control their own bodies" and their "freedom of choice"? And what if the abortionist claims he finds the work of killing unborn babies satisfying and useful for the upward mobility of women in society? Well, pragmatism bumps up against the "problem of the other side": What about volunteers at a pro-life counseling center who are richly rewarded and gratified by counseling women considering abortion to keep their babies in the face of challenging circumstances—or to give them up for adoption? These volunteers are also aware of postabortion trauma and the psychological (and physiological) havoc that abortion wreaks on women; so they show concern for the well-being of the mother as well.

Of course, the abortionist usually isn't pro-*choice* but pro-*abortion*; he wants to stay in business! So he *doesn't* want to encourage women to *freely choose* to keep their babies or freely choose to give them up for adoption. But *what if* the abortionist views his work as useful and promoting human well-being? On the other hand, what if the pro-life counselor finds *her* work useful and promoting human well-being? So to say "whatever works for you" leads to a deep conflict. Both cannot be true, however well they may "work" for each party. But pragmatism would lead to this kind of incoherence.

Third, the "whatever works" philosophy is counterintuitive since it may demand holding a view that's in conflict with what's inescapably obvious—a clear denial of reality. During the 2003 Gulf War, many of us witnessed from our living rooms the toppling of Saddam's statue in the heart of Baghdad. We had seen the remarkable advance of coalition troops into Iraq, leading to the end of Iraq's ruling Baath party and Saddam Hussein's reign of terror. But as the troops neared Baghdad, we received televised "updates" from Iraq's information minister Mohammed Saeed al-Sahhaf. In attempting to reassure the Iraqi people, he denied that coalition troops were even in Iraq! We shook our heads in disbelief at such desperate measures to save face and rally the Iraqi people.

But here's a question for the pragmatist: What if a cover-up or propaganda campaign actually "worked" in an attempt to deny what was *really happening*? What if, say, denying the Holocaust ever took place and suppressing the evidence of death camps could have helped postwar Germany prevent a shattering identity crisis? Wouldn't this have benefited the Germans?

Or what about historical revisionism? For example, references to the deep religious belief in early America has been suppressed in students' textbooks, giving the impression of a secular American history. In his 1986 book *Censorship: Evidence of Bias in Our Children's Textbooks*, Paul Vitz writes of this kind of revisionism: "One social studies book has thirty pages on the Pilgrims, including the first Thanksgiving. But there is not one word (or image) that referred to religion as even a part of the Pilgrims' life." Another textbook said, "Pilgrims are people who take long trips"—without any mention of religion and why they came to the New World. Another reference mentions the first Thanksgiving: the Pilgrims "wanted to give thanks for all they had"—and God is left out altogether.[6] Yes, this revisionism may "help" the secularist cause of church-state separation (removing from view and memory historical reminders or markers of America's Judeo-Christian heritage *and* turning the Christian faith into a private hobby that has no bearing on public policy). Nevertheless, we recognize that such revisionist attempts rest on false premises and distortion.

*Fourth, even though pragmatism emphasizes the practical while denouncing the merely abstract and theoretical, this view is itself a **philosophical theory**; it is an abstract and theoretical philosophy loaded with assumptions.* I've been in discussions before with people who are concerned about "being practical." Of course, many an absentminded professor has greatly benefited from a practically minded spouse. However, the determination to reject the theoretical for the sake of the practical is itself a theoretical position. It is theory-laden and presupposes theoretical commitments.[7] *Why* should one prefer the practical over the theoretical? What is the *goal* in doing so? How can we evaluate the legitimacy of starting with the practical? Presumably, some abstract, theoretical, philosophical answers will be given in response to these questions!

One can be a *thoughtless activist* just as one can be an *ivory-tower, impractical theoretician.* We must do our best to bring both together rather than make theory and practice mutually exclusive.

*Fifth, what is useful or promotes well-being may be **person-relative** or **culture-relative**; what is true may not necessarily be of much use or benefit to certain persons but may be to others.* A western physicist may find Einstein's $E = mc^2$ formula or Maxwell's equations of electromagnetism very useful. A Tuareg nomad from Niger would likely consider them worthless and of no great benefit at all. What's useful is not always the same as what's true.

Sixth, in its strong form, pragmatism leads to relativism ("That's true for you, but not for me")—a view which is incoherent and self-contradictory. Although we've already hinted at this point of pragmatism leading to relativism, let's explore this a bit further here.

Richard Rorty, we've noted, has said that truth is what your peers let you get away with saying. Now Rorty denies he's a relativist. Except for some naïve freshmen, "one cannot find anybody who says that two in-compatible opinions on important topics are equally good."[8] Of course, since Rorty wrote those words in 1982, relativism has been steadily on the rise.[9] But despite Rorty's protestations, it's hard to avoid the rela-tivism that flows from his system of pragmatism. After all, someone in North Korea or Saudi Arabia will have certain peers while I have completely different peers—with a different set of beliefs. Or someone's peers *today* may be different than the peers of a person who lived in Nazi Germany or Stalinist Russia. If these radically opposed peer-group views somehow "worked," they would have to be true, according to the pragmatist. But how could this be? How could it be (as the Nazis claimed) that Jews are subhuman *and* that Jews are fully human (as you and I believe)? How could it be that Communism is historically and philosophically sound *and* that it is historically and philosophi-cally problematic? Once the relativist declares that no universal truth exists, he's just shot himself in the foot. He's asserting a universal truth; he believes its denial by anyone would have to be false.

Rorty believes that an "ideal democratic community"—which pro-motes "freedom"—demands our loyalty.[10] But *why think freedom and democracy are good?* Rorty assumes these are undeniable goods, that they are good for all people, and that they transcend culture and peer-groups. This sounds quite different than Rorty's claim that truth is what your peers let you get away with saying. Rorty thinks that Nazism is *wrong*, but doesn't he mean it's wrong because it's a false, immoral philosophy? Doesn't he hold this in some absolute, nonpragmatic sense? Rorty's denial of relativism ends up being inconsistent with pragmatism. If we take Rorty's strong pragmatism to its logical conclusion, relativism is around the corner.

Seventh, some belief or view could be true, but it may be practically worthless or irrelevant for virtually everyone: it may not help us to cope or get along better in our lives. But this doesn't negate its truth (the fact that it matches up with or mirrors reality). Today's temperature at the South Pole is, practically speaking, irrelevant. The color of my Cleveland Indians shirt is gray, but it's not that big of a deal. These facts would be trivial to everyone who knows them, but they'd still be true.

Richard Rorty says that there's no need to worry about what's real or about measuring our beliefs against reality to see if they match up.

Rather, the pragmatist is only concerned about what "just plain enables us to cope."[11] But *surely it's important to distinguish between "what works" and "what's true"* since there are truths that just don't seem to serve any useful function, and what makes them true is that they match up with or correspond to the way things really are.

We can't escape the view of truth as corresponding to or mirroring the way things really are. The better our views approximate reality, the more accurate or true they are. If I say, "There's a computer screen in front of me," it's true because there is, in fact, a computer screen in front of me. Truth is like the fit of a socket wrench: the *socket attachment* represents our *belief*, and the *bolt* to be (un)tightened represents *reality*. When a belief "fits" or corresponds to reality, then it's true. When it doesn't fit, it's not. As we'll see below, pragmatism can't escape this very basic understanding of truth.

Eighth, pragmatism is self-refuting because this view assumes that it corresponds to the way things are; pragmatism itself assumes a correspondence view of truth. On the one hand, pragmatists generally deny truth as correspondence (this correspondence view maintains that a belief or proposition is true because it corresponds to reality—to the way things really are). On the other hand, however, *pragmatists believe that **their** view best corresponds to the way things really are.* So pragmatists assume a correspondence view of truth that, they claim, we shouldn't follow! They *deny* that truth as correspondence reflects the way things really are! Yet in their very denial, they admit to truth as correspondence. And this is another problem with the philosophy of pragmatism.

*Ninth, what if a society's believing in a correspondence view of truth **helped** people in society better cope, succeed, or get along than if they held a pragmatic view? In this case, pragmatists shouldn't mention their view of truth as a viable alternative if a correspondence view of truth creates a greater sense of well-being.* We have something of a paradoxical or ironic scenario for the pragmatist: *What if we observe that when people in society believe in truth as correspondence, this helps them better cope with life?* What if societal order started to slip because people held to a pragmatic view of truth? Perhaps the societal "herd" should be taught truth as correspondence by the "philosopher-kings"—the rulers and idea-shapers of society. If teaching truth as correspondence brought about better results, then why not *ban* the teaching of pragmatism? After all, this tactic might be pragmatically justified! The pragmatist should allow this "noble lie" to be believed so that society could flourish. This suggests that there's more to truth than "whatever works."

Tenth, the pragmatist's concern that truth can be abstract, detached, impersonal, or impractical is addressed by the Christian faith, in which truth is located in the persons of the divine Trinity. And while a proposition is true because it corresponds to the way things are, we must be careful about reducing everything about the Christian story to mere true propositions. When Jesus says, "I am . . . the truth" (John 14:6), or when John says of the Holy Spirit, "The Spirit is the truth" (1 John 5:6), we see that truth isn't merely propositional (a matter of true or false statements). Many evangelicals see theology as an attempt to discover the true propositions or truth-statements "behind" Scripture's parables or figures of speech in order to classify and systematize them. The late—and indeed great—theologian Carl Henry, despite his remarkable contribution to evangelical thought, remarked of the biblical authors that "regardless of the parables, allegories, emotive phrases and rhetorical questions used by these writers, their literary devices have a logical point which can be propositionally formulated and is objectively true or false."[12] But more and more evangelical Christians are starting to realize that this kind of propositionalizing can lead to a *propositional reductionism*—reducing the truth as articulated in Scripture to mere truth-statements. This methodology encourages a more abstract and detached approach to the Scriptures.

Don't get me wrong. We *do* need propositions to help us formulate important biblical truths that are necessary for identifying key doctrinal dimensions of orthodox Christianity ("Jesus died for the sins of the world" or "God raised Jesus from the dead"). The Apostles' and Nicene Creeds are examples of this important endeavor. True propositions help anchor the biblical text to the real world.

However, we can't capture the power, majesty, and inspiration of the biblical *narrative* and the Triune God's *revelation* in mere truth-statements. To reduce the beautiful verse "The heavens are telling of the glory of God; and their expanse is declaring the work of His hands" (Ps. 19:1), to "God's creation attests to His greatness" does a great injustice to this majestic text. Or when Paul writes, "Rejoice in the Lord" (Phil. 4:4), or "Remember Jesus Christ, risen from the dead, descendant of David" (2 Tim. 2:8), there's more here than just propositions.[13] Many biblical passages aren't simply meant to *say* something (that is, communicate truth in propositional form). They're often meant to *do* things ("speech-acts"). When Paul says, "Remember Jesus Christ," he means to inspire a certain mindset in Timothy that will shape his attitudes and actions. "Remember Jesus Christ" *isn't* a truth-statement or a description; it's a meaningful *command* written to inspire courage and perseverance in Timothy.[14]

Furthermore, *questions* are often asked in Scripture (e.g., God calling to Adam, "Where are you?"). Although such questions aren't really describing something or making a truth-claim, they are still meaningful. Or sometimes words in Scripture *bring about* something. By simply speaking (e.g., "Let there be light"), someone accomplishes or does something (*performative utterances*—such as our declarations of "I baptize you . . ." or "I nominate her . . ."—in which the words spoken actually perform something). This can't be reduced to mere propositions.

Scripture also meaningfully communicates *emotion* or *passion* with the intent to help persons draw near to God so that they may be transformed to become more loving, humble, and wise. When Paul writes that Demas has left him for the love of the world and that only Luke is with him (2 Tim. 4:10–11), these are more than just descriptive facts that Paul is recounting. There's a sense of loneliness and sorrow—despite Paul's confidence about his ultimate destiny. Or take the Psalms: they weren't written and compiled just to inform us of facts but to help us identify with the emotions, circumstances, and attitudes of the psalmists. They enable us to connect with God, to have our attitudes transformed, and to deepen our faith. Again, the Psalms can't be boiled down to mere true propositions. Propositions *don't tell the whole truth* about the biblical text.[15]

Eleventh, the pragmatist's legitimate concern that truth not be an object to be handled is overcome by the believer's attitude of receiving the truth as a gift and willingly humbling oneself before God's Word to receive it rightly. Christians shouldn't just be interested in the *text* of the Bible. Here again we can learn something from the pragmatist. We shouldn't be content with knowing abstract truths, but we should come to God's Word humbly and with an open heart. The divine Trinity communicates God's truthful and richly meaningful revelation—especially in the

Word who became flesh and lived among us (John 1:14). In response, we should approach God's Word with a willing reverence and openness to listen to the voice behind the text that says, "Hear me." Within us must lie the devotion of the disciple, who gladly hears Christ's voice saying, "Follow me."

Rather than seeking to master the *text*, we, by God's Spirit and through communion with Christ, must let it master *us*. Augustine reminds us that we should be more concerned with what Scripture signifies (what it points or refers to) rather than becoming fixated on the biblical text (the "sign") and not moving beyond it:

> He is a slave to a sign, who uses or worships a significant thing without knowing what it signifies. But he who uses or venerates a useful sign divinely instituted whose signifying force he understands does not venerate what he sees and what passes away but rather that to which such things are to be referred.[16]

Theologian Karl Barth said that God's "word" isn't to be abstracted from God's own loving, self-revealing, and holy presence: "God's word is itself God's act."[17] While interpreting *the text* is important, the biblical text must interpret *us*. Scripture, if we allow it, should shape our identity as persons and transform us within.[18]

So (as we've seen) for all the faults and inadequacies of their views, pragmatists helpfully remind us that truth must be embodied or lived out; truth isn't simply a matter of abstract entertainment or an object we control.

SUMMARY

- The pragmatist says that truth is what's useful. If it "works," brings good results, helps us to cope, or contributes to human well-being, then it's true.
- Some elements of pragmatism should be taken seriously: (1) "Whatever works" is a perfectly appropriate approach when truth (or right and wrong) isn't at stake. This kind of pragmatism (non-epistemic or non-alethic) poses no problem. (2) Pragmatism rightly reminds

us of the dangers of getting stuck in the ivory tower of abstract ideas and theories. (3) Pragmatism reminds us of the importance of humility and that knowledge is a gift to be received, not an object we control.

- Something can be true even if it's detrimental to a this-worldly sense of well-being or success; "well-being" and "success" can be very subjective, easy-to-bend standards.

- We'd have to consider contradictory points of view true if they prove to be useful for opposing "peer groups," but this is obviously problematic (e.g., the abortionist vs. the pro-life counselor).

- The "whatever works" philosophy is counterintuitive since it may demand holding a view that's in conflict with what's inescapably obvious—a clear denial of reality.

- Even though pragmatism emphasizes the practical while denouncing the merely abstract and theoretical, this view is itself a *philosophical theory*; it is an abstract and theoretical philosophy loaded with assumptions.

- What is useful or promotes well-being may be *person-relative* or *culture-relative*; what is *true* may not necessarily be of much *use* or *benefit* to certain persons but may be to others.

- In its strong form, pragmatism leads to relativism ("That's true for you, but not for me")—a view which is incoherent and self-contradictory.

- Some belief or view could be true, but it may be practically worthless or irrelevant for virtually everyone: it may not help us to cope or get along better in our lives. But this doesn't negate its truth (the fact that it matches up with or mirrors reality).

- Pragmatism is self-refuting because this view assumes that it corresponds to the way things are; pragmatism itself assumes a correspondence view of truth.

- What if a society's believing in a correspondence view of truth helped people in society better cope, succeed, or get along than if they held a pragmatic view? In this case, pragmatists shouldn't mention their view of truth as a viable alternative if a correspondence view of truth creates a greater sense of well-being.

- The pragmatist's concern that truth can be abstract, detached, impersonal, or impractical is addressed by the Christian faith, in which truth is located in the persons of the divine Trinity. And while a proposition is true because it corresponds to the way things are, we must be careful about reducing everything about the Christian story to merely true propositions.
- The pragmatist's legitimate concern that truth not be an object to be handled is overcome by the attitude of receiving the truth as a gift and willingly humbling ourselves before God's Word to receive it rightly.

FURTHER READING

Clark, David K., and Jim Beilby. *Why Bother with Truth?* Norcross, GA: Ravi Zacharias International Ministries, 2000.

Hinkson, John, and Greg Ganssle. "Epistemology at the Core of Postmodernism: Rorty, Foucault, and the Gospel." Chap. 4 in *Telling the Truth: Evangelizing Postmoderns*. Edited by D. A. Carson. Grand Rapids: Zondervan, 2000.

Schmitt, Frederick F. *Truth: A Primer*. Boulder, CO: Westview, 1995.

PART II

SLOGANS RELATED TO WORLDVIEWS

3

Naturalism Is a Simpler Explanation Than Theism

Atheist philosopher David Papineau declares that "nearly everyone nowadays wants to be a 'naturalist.' "[1] British philosopher John Lucas tells us that philosophical naturalism is the "orthodox" view among Western intellectuals.[2]

What *is* naturalism? Carl Sagan captured it in his book *Cosmos*, stating, "The cosmos is all that is or ever was or ever will be."[3] The *gist* of naturalism is this: *The space-time universe—which can be studied by the physical sciences—is all the reality there is.* Naturalists argue that this is a "simpler" worldview than theism because it requires fewer entities to explain the way things are. God becomes unnecessary—a metaphysical fifth wheel, a mere appendage. It's not so much that naturalists are *opposed* to God's existence; they may claim that God simply isn't *required* in order to explain things. Science will do just fine.[4]

The same applies to the human soul. Why think that there is an *immaterial* aspect to the human being, some ask, when the body's operations can account for any "soulish" activities? Naturalism seems simpler here too.

Before responding to naturalism's claim to being simpler, we should first look at three key characteristics of naturalism.

1. *Knowledge (epistemology)—the increasing tendency to see knowledge as nothing more than what contributes to survival rather than requiring a belief to be true.* We intuitively recognize that knowledge involves *truth.* I can't *know* that the earth is flat or that the sun orbits the earth. Why not? These are false beliefs. While I can know that it's *false* that the earth is flat, I *can't* know *that* the earth is flat—because it isn't! There's an increasing temptation among naturalists to deny that *truth* is a vital and necessary aspect of knowledge.

Not all naturalists take this view, but an increasing number are taking this route (called "naturalized epistemology"). After all, if we're just physical beings who respond to our environment and whose thoughts are determined by our nervous systems, then why think that we are freely choosing agents who can reflect about our beliefs and then reject falsehoods and embrace truths? Humans are just surviving beings who form beliefs to survive—even if they happen to be false. For example, we might *believe* that humans have intrinsic dignity and rights, and this may help us as a species to survive, but this belief may be completely *false.* We might, in actual fact, have no value at all.

According to this recent approach of naturalized epistemology, we shouldn't talk about how we *ought* to think (*prescriptively—namely, to reject as many false beliefs as possible and to embrace as many true ones as we can*). Rather, our focus should be on how human beings actually *do* think (*descriptively*). *Philosophy* (or "first philosophy") is reduced to *psychology* (how humans happen to think).

2. *Causal explanations (etiology)—the tendency to explain all events mechanistically (from the Big Bang to the choices we make each day), suggesting a rigid determinism.* Naturalism's grand story of origins is that our universe had physical, impersonal, mechanistic beginnings, and this physical cause-and-effect scenario describes all events since the Big Bang.

This physical causation from the Big Bang until now implies an underlying *determinism.* There's no room for *libertarian agency,* where an agent can *rise above purely physical influences* since he is free and not determined by physical causes that go all the way back to the Big Bang. If we allow for such a libertarian agency, then we have another kind of cause—not simply one that is physical and mechanistic.

3. *Entities that exist (ontology)—the assumption that only physical things exist; if anything not strictly physical exists, it at least depends upon the physical for its existence.* Naturalism, generally speaking, is rigid in its physicalism. God or angels, who are spirit beings, don't fit anywhere on the naturalist's radar screen of reality. What about souls or minds? Some naturalists, like Paul and Patricia Churchland, say that there's no true mental life. The Churchlands charge that those who claim otherwise are engaging in "folk psychology"—what the everyday person holds but should be rejected by the thoughtful and scientifically minded. They declare that human thinking skills can be understood in terms of "neural networks and neurochemical concentrations."[5] Now other naturalists will admit that the mental and the physical are different. They claim, however, the mental/subjective emerges from and is dependent upon the physical. And once the physical body dies, the mind goes with it. (These are called property dualists—that is, the body has two properties: the mental and the physical.)[6]

By biting the bullet and embracing naturalism, one takes a very bold step. Many commonsense beliefs—that evil exists; that we have free will, a soul, moral obligations—will have to be thrown out because this is what naturalism requires. Naturalist philosopher of mind Jaegwon Kim notes that naturalism is "imperialistic; it demands 'full coverage' . . . and exacts a terribly high ontological price."[7]

With this background of naturalism in mind, we should ask the question: Compared to theism, is naturalism the simpler—and therefore, preferred—explanation? Perhaps we can get some insight from the movie *Groundhog Day*. In this film, the arrogant, self-centered weatherman Phil Connors (Bill Murray) is trying to get to know Rita (Andie MacDowell) as they cover the Groundhog Day festivities in Punxsutawney, Pennsylvania. At the Tip-Top Diner, Phil asks Rita, "So what do you want out of life, anyway?" When Phil starts to get too personal, Rita asks Phil about what he wants. Here's how their exchange goes:

PHIL: What I really want is someone like you.

RITA: Please!

PHIL: Well, why not? What are you looking for? Who's your perfect guy?

RITA: Well, first of all, he's too humble to know he's perfect.

PHIL: That's me.

RITA: He's intelligent, supportive, funny.

PHIL: Intelligent, supportive, funny—me . . . me . . . me.

RITA: He's romantic and courageous.

PHIL: Me also.

RITA: He's got a good body, but he doesn't have to look in the mirror every two minutes.

PHIL: I have a *great* body, and sometimes I go *months* without looking.

RITA: He's kind, sensitive, gentle. He's not afraid to cry in front of me.

PHIL: This is a *man* we're talking about, right?

RITA: He likes animals and children. . . . Oh—and he plays an instrument, and he loves his mother.

PHIL: Whew! I am *really* close on this one—really, really close.[8]

Although Phil *was* quite funny, he was too full of himself to be humble, supportive, fond of animals and children, and so on. What's funny is that "me . . . me . . . me" doesn't describe Phil at all!

However, when it comes to determining which view—naturalism or theism—best explains various phenomena, we can go through a large list of items and say, "God . . . God . . . God." God makes better sense than naturalism when we talk about the origin and fine-tuning of the universe, the emergence of first life and consciousness, the existence of human rights/dignity, objective moral values, free will, rationality, beauty, and even the existence of evil.[9] For example, which scenario is more plausible—that *consciousness* came from *nonconscious* matter or from a supremely *self-aware* Being? Or that *personhood* emerged through *impersonal* processes or by way of a *personal* Creator? Or that *free will* emerged from *deterministic* processes or from a Being who *freely chose* to create? Or that the universe *just popped into existence*, uncaused, a finite time ago out of nothing or that a powerful Being *brought it into existence*?

If these arguments support the existence of a supernatural realm, then at least we can say that we live in an "ontologically haunted universe."[10] That is, if these arguments succeed, then there's a reality beyond nature that's worth taking seriously and investigating with diligence.

Take a look at the chart below to see how theism and naturalism compare, given certain features of the created order and our existence/experience:

Phenomena We Recognize/ Observe/Assume	Theistic Context	Naturalistic Context
(Self-)consciousness exists.	God is supremely self-aware/-conscious.	The universe was produced by mindless, nonconscious processes.
Personal beings exist.	God is a personal Being.	The universe was produced by impersonal processes.
We believe we make free personal decisions/choices.	God is spirit and a free Being, who can freely choose to act (e.g., to create or not).	We have emerged by material, deterministic processes and forces beyond our control.
We trust our senses and rational faculties as generally reliable in producing true beliefs.	A God of truth and rationality exists.	Because of our impulse to survive and reproduce, our beliefs only help us *survive*, but a number of these could be completely *false*.
Human beings have intrinsic value/dignity and rights.	God is the supremely valuable Being.	Human beings were produced by valueless processes.
Objective moral values exist.	God's character is the source of goodness/moral values.	The universe was produced by nonmoral processes.
First life emerged.	God is a living, active Being.	Life somehow emerged from nonliving matter.
Beauty exists (e.g., not only in landscapes and sunsets but in "elegant" or "beautiful" scientific theories).	God is beautiful (Ps. 27:4) and capable of creating beautiful things according to his pleasure.	Beauty in the natural world is superabundant and in many cases superfluous (often not linked to survival).
The universe (all matter, energy, space, time) began to exist a finite time ago.	A powerful, personal Being, God, caused the universe to exist, creating it out of nothing.	The universe popped into existence, uncaused out of nothing (or possibly self-caused). Being emerged from nonbeing.

Phenomena We Recognize/ Observe/Assume	Theistic Context	Naturalistic Context
The universe is finely tuned for human life (known as "the Goldilocks effect"—the universe is "just right" for life).	God is a wise, intelligent designer.	All the cosmic constants just happened to be right; given enough time and/or many possible worlds, a finely tuned world eventually emerged.
Real evils—both moral and natural—exist/take place in the world.	Genuine evil assumes (a) some *design plan* (of how things *ought* to be but are not) or even (b) a standard of goodness (a corruption or absence of goodness, by which we judge something to be evil). God is the Intelligent *Designer* of the universe. God's good character provides a moral *standard* or moral context to discern evil.	Atrocities, pain, and suffering just happen. This is just how things *are*—with no "plan" or standard of goodness to which things *ought* to conform.

As we compare the contexts, we see that theism ("God . . . God . . . God") makes better sense and offers a better fit than naturalism. The theistic explanation is more natural than naturalism!

But some might claim that naturalism is "simpler." How so? Well, naturalism is simpler in that it claims that *fewer* entities exist—that is, the *physical cosmos* is all there is. But the theist says, "That's not all. God *also* exists." Does this mean that, all things being equal, God is a metaphysical "fifth wheel" that isn't required for explaining things? Perhaps the following points might be helpful.

First, whenever possible, we should use the principle of simplicity or economy to get rid of unnecessary explanations. This is certainly true when it comes to eliminating polytheism (*many* gods) in favor of monotheism (*one* God): Why involve extra entities when just one will suffice? Polytheism—the belief in many gods—isn't really required if one God (monotheism) is adequate for the task of creating and sustaining the universe, furnishing a moral standard for humans, and so on. As stated in the principle known as "Ockham's razor," there's no reason to multiply additional entities beyond necessity. Extra deities can be plausibly eliminated on the basis of explanatory simplicity. All things being equal, polytheism becomes unnecessary or superfluous as an explanation. One God will do just fine.

Second, while atheism (no God) is theoretically simpler than theism (one God), this is true only in a numerical sense. To eliminate God as an explanation leaves us with massive conundrums and huge gaps in our knowledge. Getting rid of God doesn't enhance our power to explain. In fact, removing God from our explanatory resources *reduces* our explanatory power dramatically. Naturalism is simply inadequate to account for a number of different features of the universe and our human existence.[11] Philosopher Alvin Plantinga correctly observes that theism—or more specifically, the Christian worldview—"offers suggestions for answers to a wide range of otherwise intractable questions."[12] That is, without God, we would just be left with "that's just the way it is" explanations regarding how the universe began, how it came to be finely tuned, how humans came to have rights or moral obligations, and so forth.

*Third, if we apply the principle "the fewer entities the better" without exception, then why not just say, "**No** explanatory entities are better than **one**"? We know that "spontaneous generation" (e.g., flies simply emerge from rotting meat) is an inferior explanation to the principle that whatever begins to exist has a cause. If atheists do hold to the emergence of something from nothing, this goes against what science affirms every day.*

In 1668, Francesco Redi, an Italian scientist, tried to show that maggots didn't simply appear spontaneously from rotting meat. Although it was popularly believed that maggots spontaneously arose from meat, Redi tried to show that maggots came from flies' eggs. To test his hypothesis, he put some meat into a sealed jar and laid out other meat that was accessible to flies. Obviously, the meat in sealed jars didn't produce maggots; the meat exposed to flies, which laid their eggs in it, ended up with maggots.

This raises an interesting question: Why not believe in "spontaneous generation" since it involves fewer entities? That is, why not think that life just popped into existence from nonliving matter? Or why not say that the rabbit *really* popped into existence from nothing and suddenly appeared in the magician's hat? Surely something coming from *nothing* is "simpler" (i.e., requires fewer entities) than something coming from *something*.

As surprising as it seems, there are atheists who *are* willing to accept that something can come from nothing at several levels. (Of course, we shouldn't be surprised at this, given the obvious theistic implications of Big Bang cosmology.) Although he says a lot of things I disagree with, the atheist philosopher Kai Nielsen gets it right when he asks us to consider the following scenario: "Suppose you hear a loud bang . . . and you ask me, 'What made that bang?' and I reply, 'Nothing, it just happened.' You would not accept that. In fact you would find my reply quite unintelligible."[13] We can readily agree. This makes perfect sense, and science supports the idea that something cannot come out of nothing. Of course, it's *numerically* simpler to say that *nothing* caused something than *one* thing caused something. *One* entity is not as simple as *zero* entities. But to explain events *without any sufficient reason*—that they "just happened"—is clearly inadequate.[14]

Some atheists, such as Michael Martin, will still argue that something (like the universe) can pop into existence, uncaused out of nothing.[15] This does prompt the question: *Are there any scientific findings that would give us reason for believing that something can come out of nothing?* There's nothing promising on the horizon. Based on Kai Nielsen's example, we suspect that if the Big Bang didn't strongly suggest a Creator, there wouldn't be any good reason to think that something could come out of literally nothing. *The findings of science, to which naturalists standardly appeal, constantly confirm the obvious intuition that something can't come out of nothing.*[16] Martin can appeal all he wants to scientists who believe the universe came from nothing (scientists who, not surprisingly, happen to be naturalists and—take note—have certain theological motivations themselves). But this "free lunch" idea is really metaphysical nonsense. As Dallas Willard rightly observes, the chances that something could come into existence from nothing are exactly *zero*.[17] Philosopher John Locke (1632–1704) wisely argued that "man knows by an intuitive certainty, that bare nothing can no more produce any real being, than it can be equal to two right angles."[18]

The metaphysical bankruptcy of the "something from nothing" idea doesn't just apply to the beginning of the universe. It applies to the emergence of first life, consciousness, and moral values. It makes better sense to say that *life came from life*, that *consciousness came from consciousness*, and that *moral values came from a supremely valuable Being*. Now atheist Michael Martin says there's no reason why objective moral values can't be comprised of matter.[19] There's a big problem here. We'll search in vain for

any physics textbook identifying "moral value" as one of matter's properties. But perhaps we shouldn't be surprised that Martin believes moral
values *could* emerge from valueless matter. After all, Martin believes
that the universe could emerge from literally nothing! The fact is that
for Martin *value* somehow emerges from *valueless* processes. But doesn't
it make more sense to hold that moral values are rooted in a supremely
valuable Being? Value comes from value—not valuelessness.

Practically speaking, we should ask: Do we really want to bite the
bullet and face the stark implications of naturalism and its leveling (or
reduction) of reality? Nobel laureate Steven Weinberg put it this way:
"The reductionistic worldview *is* chilling and impersonal. It has to be
accepted as it is, not because we like it, but because that is the way the
world works."[20]

So we've seen that naturalism, while "simpler" in terms of involving fewer entities within its system, doesn't help us account for a lot of
things. Getting rid of God means getting rid of significant explanatory
power. A theistic context helps us make sense of many important features of the created order. But to resort to beliefs such as *the universe
came from nothing* flies in the face of the very "scientific method" the
naturalist so heartily applauds. Theism guides us to a clearer explanation of things. To quote C. S. Lewis again: "I believe in Christianity as
I believe that the Sun has risen, not only because I see it, but because
by it I see everything else."[21]

SUMMARY

- Naturalism maintains that the space-time universe—which can
  be studied by the physical sciences—is all the reality there is.
- There are three core elements of naturalism: (1) Seeing *knowledge* as how humans typically think (involving only beliefs that
  contribute to survival) rather than how they ought to think (requiring a belief to be true). (2) Seeking *causal explanations* of all
  events (from the Big Bang to the choices we make each day) in a
  mechanistic manner, suggesting a rigid determinism. (3) Assuming that *only physical things* exist; if anything not strictly physical
  exists, it at least depends upon the physical for its existence.

- The price to be paid for being a naturalist is high, as it will mean rejecting a number of commonsense beliefs (that we have free will, that knowledge includes truth, that genuine evil exists, etc.).
- All things being equal, we should use the principle of simplicity or economy to get rid of unnecessary explanations. This is certainly true when it comes to eliminating polytheism (many gods) in favor of monotheism (one God): Why involve extra entities when just one will suffice?
- While atheism is theoretically simpler than one God, this is true only in a numerical sense. To eliminate God as an explanation leaves us with massive conundrums and huge gaps in our knowledge (see the theism-naturalism chart).
- If we apply the principle "the fewer entities the better" without exception, then why not just say, "*No* explanatory entities are better than *one*"? We know that "spontaneous generation" (e.g., flies simply emerge from rotting meat) is an inferior explanation to the principle that whatever begins to exist has a cause. If atheists do hold to the emergence of something from nothing, this goes against what science affirms every day.
- In the case of the universe's beginning, all that nothing can produce is nothing. The chances of something coming into existence from nothing are exactly zero.

FURTHER READING

Beckwith, Francis J., William Lane Craig, and J. P. Moreland. *To Everyone an Answer: A Case for the Christian Worldview*. Downers Grove, IL: InterVarsity, 2004.

Boa, Kenneth D., and Robert M. Bowman Jr. *20 Compelling Evidences That God Exists*. Tulsa: River Oak, 2002.

Copan, Paul, and Paul K. Moser, eds. *The Rationality of Theism*. London: Routledge, 2003.

Moreland, J. P., and Kai Nielsen. *Does God Exist? The Great Debate*. Nashville: Thomas Nelson, 1990; Amherst, NY: Prometheus, 1993.

Wallace, Stan W., ed. *Does God Exist? The Craig-Flew Debate*. Burlington, VT: Ashgate, 2003.

4

UNLESS YOU CAN SCIENTIFICALLY VERIFY OR FALSIFY YOUR BELIEF, IT'S MEANINGLESS

In 1956, C. P. Snow, who had established himself as both a scientist and a novelist, wrote of "two cultures"—the literary and the scientific. Snow observed that literary culture was declining whereas scientific culture was expanding. These scientists were the "new men" and "the directing class of a new society."[1]

There's a certain authority that scientists carry. They've been called the "high priests" of modern culture. If anybody gets a hearing these days, it's the scientist. If we want to appeal to credible sources, we cite the findings of "scientific" studies or research. If there's a scientist on a TV talk-show panel, she's the one with "definitive answers." When television commercials or magazine ads present persons in white lab coats with clipboards in their hands, the message is clear: you can trust the scientific research that backs this product.

Not only does public trust in science appear to be on the increase, but many assume that doing science and believing in God are *opposed* to each other. After all, we're asked, what about the Catholic Church's opposition to the scientist Galileo? (As we'll see later, there's a lot of misunderstanding and historical revisionism surrounding this issue: Galileo was committed to harmonizing his scientific research with a *true* understanding of Scripture.) In our day, Oxford zoologist Richard Dawkins declares, "Scientific beliefs are supported by evidence, and they get results. Myths and faiths are not and do not."[2] Science and belief in God, we're told, are inherently at odds. The reasonable person travels along the road of "science"—the safest route to go.

Such an approach, though called "science," is actually the *philosophical view* of *scientism*, which *goes beyond the actual study of the world of nature.* There are various types and hues of scientism, and we won't go into the details here.[3] We can speak of two versions of it—the *strong* and the *weak*—that seem to capture what scientism is all about. The strong version declares that *only* science can tell us what is meaningful or true. The weak version declares that science gives us the *best* and *surest* path to knowledge and truth—even if some other disciplines are able to contribute to our knowledge. Or perhaps one could say that we're only *rationally entitled* to believe what's scientifically knowable. If scientism is the correct approach to take, then theological statements, *at best*, have to be subjected to scientific scrutiny if they're to have any intellectual credibility (*weak* scientism). *At worst*, theological or philosophical statements are either wholly irrelevant or just simply false (*strong* scientism).

The strong version—our focus in this chapter—suggests that *there aren't any limits to science*, or that *science alone will solve virtually all human problems*, or that *science will eventually explain or describe everything*. As Cambridge physicist Stephen Hawking confidently asserts, science can help us answer "why we are here and where we came from . . . And the goal is nothing less than a complete description of the universe we live in."[4] The message from many in the scientific community is this: Something is true and reasonable to believe if and only if it's scientifically testable or part of an accepted scientific theory. If a belief isn't "scientific," then it's meaningless or even false. Theology as well as philosophy are suspect. *They* can't help you settle any questions. Only science can definitively do so. Harvard biologist Richard Lewontin has declared that the "social and intellectual apparatus, Science, [is] the only begetter of truth."[5] A bit more moderate is the position of the late

Stephen Jay Gould of Harvard. He said that the "magisterium [authoritative domain] of science" is a "magisterium of fact." The "magisterium of religion" deals with "meaning" and "morality" (which isn't really factual). Science tells us the ages of rocks while religion tells us about the Rock of Ages. Science tells us how the heavens go while religion tells us how to go to heaven.[6] So the origin and fine-tuning of the universe or the emergence of first life and consciousness *don't* have anything to do with God. God takes a backseat to "science."

As we'll see, these statements by Lewontin and Gould *aren't* scientific. They are philosophical statements expressing a worldview—namely, that *the material world is all that exists and that science is the only (or best) means of verifying truth-claims; all claims of knowledge have to be scientifically verifiable.* This is scientism. What are some problems with scientism—particularly its strong form? We'll look at some of them below and in the following chapter.

*First, the viewpoint of scientism is both arbitrary and self-refuting (and thus incoherent). It demands that all truth-claims have to be scientifically (empirically) verifiable. However, this viewpoint is simply **arbitrary**. Furthermore, there's no way to verify **scientifically** that all truth-claims must be scientifically verifiable. This viewpoint isn't the result of scientific research (a **scientific conclusion**); it's a **philosophical assumption**.*

In the classic story *A Christmas Carol*, the ghost of Ebenezer Scrooge's late business partner, Jacob Marley, appears in Scrooge's home on Christmas Eve. Scrooge wonders what the Dickens is going on. At first, he refuses to believe he's being visited by a ghost. He tries to explain away his visitation by some purely naturalistic cause that has affected his senses: "You may be an undigested bit of beef, a blot of mustard, a crumb of cheese, a fragment of underdone potato. There's more of gravy than of grave about you, whatever you are!" But in the end, Scrooge can't deny Marley's presence: "Dreadful apparition, why do you trouble me?"

"Man of the worldly mind!" replied the Ghost, "Do you believe in me or not?"

"I do," Scrooge is forced to admit. "I must. . . ."[7]

Within the walls of the academy are persons "of the worldly mind" who don't acknowledge anything nonphysical or supernatural. They claim that "science" enables us to understand anything that can be known. Paul Horwich, a prominent philosopher at City University of New York, has written: "It is now widely believed that the sciences exhaust what can be known, and the promise of metaphysics [the study of ultimate reality] is an intellectually dangerous illusion."[8] Vanderbilt University philosopher (emeritus) John Post claims that there can't be a cause of the origin of the universe, since "by definition the universe contains everything there is or ever was or will be."[9] Or consider John J. O'Dwyer's once-popular textbook, *College Physics*, which defines science this way: "[Science] seeks to understand *the world of reality* in terms of basic general principles . . . involving observation, intuition, experimentation, debate, and reformulation."[10]

These sorts of statements are commonly heard today in many of our universities. This kind of strong scientism is a view historically known as *logical positivism*, which exerted a surprising influence in the first part of the twentieth century. Even before this, David Hume (1711–1776) made contemptuous remarks about special revelation or nonnaturalistic explanations: Any volume of "divinity or school metaphysics" should be consigned to the flames since "it can contain nothing but sophistry and illusion."[11]

Logical positivism had its heyday but has taken a severe philosophical beating for some of the reasons I'll give below.[12] When Horwich says that the sciences exhaust what can be known, he's speaking *not* as a scientist but as a philosopher. When O'Dwyer claims that science studies "the world of reality," he's making an arbitrary philosophical claim: *he's assuming that the physical world is the only reality there is.* God, objective moral values, the soul, free will—these are outside the realm of "science." So they aren't real.

This scien*tistic* (not scien*tific*) view—that everything must be empirically verifiable to be meaningful knowledge—can't itself be empirically verified. It's a self-refuting view since it *doesn't measure up to its own standards*. The very *articulation* of the statement actually *undermines* the statement—like saying, "I can't speak a word of English," or "I don't exist."

This viewpoint of logical positivism makes a statement *about* science (i.e., a *philosophical* statement)—not *of* science (i.e., a *scientific* statement). *We can't validate science by appealing to science.* To claim that all genuine knowledge is scientifically verifiable has been severely discredited because it's simply a *philosophical* claim.

Philosophical	Scientific
A statement *about* science (i.e., an assumption about what counts for reality or what can be known)	A statement *of* science (i.e., the result of scientific research)

Second, science is different from scientism; the scientific is different from the scientistic. **Science** *studies the natural world;* **scientism** *tends to reduce or limit (all) legitimate knowledge to scientific methodology (epistemology). Scientism tends to assume that only the physical world is real (ontology) and is therefore the only realm of knowledge.* The Christian philosopher of science Del Ratzsch suggests that we can understand *science,* roughly, as *the attempted objective study of the natural world/ natural phenomena whose theories and explanations do not normally depart from the natural realm.*[13] There isn't any need for science to despise or disallow philosophical or theological explanations when they are warranted—for example, God being the explanation for the origin of the universe (through the Big Bang), the fine-tuning/delicate balance of the universe, or the emergence of first life. Science must recognize its limits—that an explanatory metaphysical viewpoint (e.g., naturalistic or supernaturalistic) will have to enter into the discussion at important points to help give the bigger picture.

Third, what about the criterion of falsification—that unless something is falsifiable somewhere along the way, then it's meaningless? Like the verification criterion, when this falsification criterion is absolutized, it becomes arbitrary and self-refuting—and faces other problems as well. The philosopher Karl Popper (1902–1994) claimed that a scientific theory must, in principle, be experimentally or scientifically falsifiable; otherwise, the theory isn't rationally believable. For example, Marxism isn't falsifiable. Marxism claims that history is inevitably moving past a *feudal* economic system (with lords of the manor and serfs/peasants working for them) to a *capitalist* one, reaching, eventually a *communist* stage. Here the common people (the *proletariat*) rather than the privileged, leading elite (the *bourgeoisie*) own "the means of production" (the instruments that produce economic goods). Popper's argument was that *no matter what history looks like—no matter how much counterevidence the historian can give—Marxism could never be falsified or overturned.* For example, the Marxist could say that the collapsed Soviet

Union wasn't really communistic anyway. Popper rightly saw this lack of falsifiability as the undermining credibility of Marxism.

Some people have applied this criterion to belief in God. The former atheist Antony Flew once formulated the falsification principle: *a statement is meaningful if there's empirical evidence one can give that could count against it.* If there's no empirical evidence that could potentially disprove a belief, then it's just not meaningful. Flew gave the example of evil in the world. He asked: At what point should a theist stop saying, "A good God exists"? Flew claimed: "Now [for] an assertion, to be an assertion at all, [it] must claim that things stand thus and thus; *and* not *otherwise.* Similarly an explanation, to be an explanation, must explain why this particular thing occurs; *and not something else.* Those last clauses are crucial." If you can't point to what evidence would *falsify* a claim, then the claim isn't really worth believing. If my belief always needs to be adjusted and qualified when faced with evidence that appears to undermine it, then it dies a "death by a thousand qualifications."[14]

Now falsifiability—just like verifiability—has its place. The apostle Paul made the claim that if Christ hasn't been bodily raised from the dead, then our faith is worthless and pathetic (1 Cor. 15:14, 17, 19). He suggests that if it could be shown that Christ hasn't been raised (say, by asking some of the five hundred witnesses about it; see 1 Cor. 15:6), then the Christian faith could be falsified and undermined. So far so good. The problem comes when we lean too heavily on falsifiability and make it an all-encompassing criterion. Here are some considerations:

1. The principle of falsifiability—like verifiability—is limited and shouldn't be absolutized. Otherwise, it becomes self-refuting: the claim that "only what is falsifiable is meaningful" isn't itself falsifiable; therefore it's incoherent and undermines itself. No right-thinking believer in God should say that falsifiability (or verifiability) has no merit at all. We see throughout the New Testament that signs and wonders were graciously provided to encourage belief. Jesus said, "Though you do not believe Me, believe the works, so that you may know and understand that the Father is in Me, and I in the Father" (John 10:38; see also John 20:30–31). Jesus's deeds *give evidence to or offer empirical support for* his authoritative claims.

However, verifiability and falsifiability are limited criteria in the pursuit of knowledge. When falsifiability (or verifiability) is made to be an ultimate criterion, it ends up becoming self-refuting. That is, how can we falsify the principle of falsifiability? What inevitably happens is that the principle isn't subject to its own standard: every statement must be falsifiable—except for the falsifiability principle.

2. *At certain points, falsifiability just won't be helpful as a criterion to follow, and we must be wise to see its limits.* Some people assume that if God exists, he shouldn't allow certain kinds or amounts of evils to exist. How could a good God allow *this much* evil to exist? A common assumption by some critics is this: "If you can't say *how much* evil is too much, then you're just making meaningless claims." The problem with the critics' charge is that *we creatures simply aren't in a good position to say how much evil is too much.*

In addition, falsifiability doesn't make room for trusting God's good character in the face of horrendous evils. Falsifiability doesn't really have a place for trusting God in light of our previous spiritual experiences or in his sending his Son, out of love, to die for us. In such a case, falsifiability doesn't work as a criterion to distinguish between what is meaningful and what is not. So however helpful this criterion might be in some contexts, we can't use it as a sweeping universal criterion to determine what is meaningful.

3. *Another problem with the falsifiability criterion is known as the Quine-Duhem thesis: any theory can be adjusted in the face of conflicting evidence by adjusting secondary aspects (or auxiliary hypotheses) rather than tossing out the entire hypothesis.* When Isaac Newton's observations about motion and gravitation failed to support certain predictions, Newton didn't throw out his fundamental assumptions. He made some adjustments that eventually led to a more successful model.[15] It would have been unfair to say that since *one aspect* of a theory is proven false, then the *whole thing* is meaningless. So to apply a rigid standard of falsifiability to the main point of Newton's hypothesis would be overkill. Only minor modifications were necessary to accommodate minor glitches. Revising one *segment* of the theory was all that was needed—not an overhaul of the entire system.

4. *One could insert unobservable mechanisms or forces into a theory that enable us to make the same predictions with the same observable consequences, and the criterion of falsifiability wouldn't be much of a guide to help choose between them.* Henri Poincaré (1854–1912) and

Ernst Mach (1838–1916) argued this point: we can have two distinct theories with the very same identical observational predictions with the same observational consequences.

Aristotle, for instance, believed that heavenly bodies moved or orbited in perfect circles. His work had a profound influence on medieval theologians and philosophers. But as science progressed in the West, the perfect-circle hypothesis didn't really work. As a desperate measure, some astronomers proposed that the perfect circular motion of planets would be interrupted by "epicycles"—perfectly rounded minicycles *on top of* the larger orbits. But the astronomer Johannes Kepler (1571–1619) helped eliminate the epicycles theory by proposing a simpler solution in his first law of planetary motion: *planets move around the sun in an elliptical or oval-like pattern.* Now, at a certain level, the epicycle hypothesis (to preserve Aristotle's perfect circular orbits) and the elliptical hypothesis have the same results. Inserting epicycles was an attempt to preserve Aristotle's perfect circles. That is, an additional (ad hoc) factor was added to the hypothesis in order to smooth out the wrinkles in the Aristotelian view of the universe. The point is this: The falsification criterion, by itself, proves inadequate to help decide *which* view should be preferred; after all, extra entities or forces could be inserted into a hypothesis to help prop it up in the face of certain glitches. So falsification doesn't give us the guidance we need in deciding between rival hypotheses.

5. *This falsifiability criterion ultimately denies probable (inductive) conclusions that are based on observation: it incorrectly assumes that all theories are on the same level when it comes to falsifiability.* Sunrise and sunset have been part of the earth's history from the beginning. Christians assume that—unless Christ returns and the new heavens and earth are established—the sun will continue to rise and set. *The steadfast regularity of past events suggests the strong probability of similar future events.* (Of course, if God exists, then miracles are possible. The regularity of nature doesn't rule them out.) Now the criterion of falsifiability basically assumes that *past evidence shouldn't really affect how we'll formulate theories or beliefs in the future.* All beliefs are on the same level when it comes to falsifiability; we must take each theory as it comes.

So it would be *just as rational*, according to Popper's theory, to believe that I will die if I jump off the Empire State Building as to believe that I would float gently to the ground. But we have excellent reasons for *not* waiting to discover whether the gentle-float hypothesis is falsifiable! For obvious reasons, the falsifiability criterion is inadequate here.

So we've seen that tests for meaningfulness such as verification and falsifiability—while helpful to some degree—can't be absolutized. Otherwise, they become self-contradictory, incoherent, and problematic.

SUMMARY

- The viewpoint of scientism is both arbitrary and self-refuting (and thus incoherent). It demands that all truth-claims have to be scientifically (empirically) verifiable. However, this viewpoint is simply *arbitrary*. Furthermore, there's no way to verify scientifically that all truth-claims must be scientifically verifiable. This viewpoint isn't the result of scientific research (a *scientific conclusion*); it's a *philosophical assumption*.

- Science is different from scientism; the scientific is different from the scientistic. *Science* studies the natural world; *scientism* tends to reduce or limit (all) legitimate knowledge to scientific methodology (epistemology). Scientism tends to assume that only the physical world is real (ontology) and is therefore the only realm of knowledge.

- What about the criterion of falsification—that unless something is falsifiable somewhere along the way, then it's meaningless? Like the verification criterion, when this falsification criterion is absolutized, it becomes arbitrary and self-refuting—and faces other problems as well.

- Some other problems with falsifiability are as follows: (1) The principle of falsifiability—like verifiability—is limited and shouldn't be absolutized. Otherwise, it becomes self-refuting: the claim that "only what is falsifiable is meaningful" isn't itself falsifiable; therefore it's incoherent and undermines itself. (2) At certain points, falsifiability just won't be helpful as a criterion to follow, and we must be wise to see its limits. (3) Another problem with the falsifiability criterion is known as the Quine-Duhem thesis:

any theory can be adjusted in the face of conflicting evidence by adjusting secondary aspects (or auxiliary hypotheses) rather than tossing out the entire hypothesis. (4) One could insert unobservable mechanisms or forces into a theory that enable us to make the same predictions with the same observable consequences, and the criterion of falsifiability wouldn't be much of a guide to help choose between them. (5) This falsifiability criterion ultimately denies probable (inductive) conclusions that are based on observation: it incorrectly assumes that all theories are on the same level when it comes to falsifiability.

FURTHER READING

Moreland, J. P. *Christianity and the Nature of Science*. Grand Rapids: Baker Academic, 1989.

Pearcey, Nancy R., and Charles B. Thaxton. *The Soul of Science: Christian Faith and Natural Philosophy*. Wheaton: Crossway, 1994.

Ratzsch, Del. *Science and Its Limits*. Downers Grove, IL: InterVarsity, 2000.

5

You Can't Prove That Scientifically

Haeaving spoken many times on university campuses, I've been asked about "proving" the existence of God, the soul, or objective moral values "scientifically." Once you start to ask what exactly is meant by "scientifically," you find there's a lot of baggage that goes along with it. There are lots of philosophical assumptions people tend to make when they ask such questions.

In the last chapter, we saw that verification or falsification, while helpful at important places in scientific inquiry, can't be absolutized. We observed that once science imposes arbitrary or all-consuming assumptions about the domain of science, it becomes *scientism*. In this chapter, we'll respond to this "prove it scientifically" demand and explore further problems with scientism.

First, there's no clear or obvious criterion that helps us differentiate between science and nonscience ("lines of demarcation"). Rather, science has a number of helpful guidelines that enable it to progress, but these can't be turned into rigid criteria. Doing so will only make "science" more ideological (a bias that overrides evidence and argument) and reductionistic (an arbitrary confinement of what counts for "science" or "knowledge").

What sets apart *science* from *nonscience*—or, some might say, *sense* from *nonsense*? Some have proposed *verification, falsification, testability, observability, repeatability, following natural laws,* and other "lines of demarcation." Sure, it's easy to sort out science from nonscience when we compare physics or chemistry with palm reading and astrology. But when we move away from the far ends of the spectrum of clear examples of science (at one end) and nonscience (at the other), things get a bit murky in the middle. We find there's really no litmus test (or set of tests) to help us do the job of demarcation between science and nonscience.[1] Many philosophers of science have recognized this problem, and it's just not accurate to say that there's a problem-free method that sets science apart from nonscience.[2]

For example, if we say that something needs to be *observable* as a condition for doing "real science," then what do we do about, say, the Big Bang? While astronomers can actually track much of the universe's history from the Big Bang to today (looking into remote galaxies is actually a look into the past), we still are making *inferences* about what took place. Now these inferences are often plausible, but a lot of what is believed about the universe's past isn't directly observable.

Or what about the smallest of subatomic particles? We *infer* their existence without observing them. In fact, Richard Swinburne makes an interesting point in his book *The Existence of God*. He claims that the "structure of the cumulative case for theism" is "the same as the structure of the cumulative case for any unobservable entity such as a quark or neutrino."[3] Sure, God can't be directly "observed," but neither can quarks and neutrinos, which many physicists take for granted.

Philosopher of science Robert Koons suggests that verification, falsifiability, and other proposed criteria are really just *useful guidelines to keep in mind.* As we noted, we could talk about the importance of falsification or testability when it comes to theological claims as well. Theologians have long spoken about theology as the "queen of the sciences." So there is something "scientific" about doing theology. The natural sciences utilize basic common sense and good instincts, trying to stay away from extreme rigidity of method and dogmatism that stifles creative research and openness to new lines of inquiry.

As helpful as they may be, guidelines shouldn't be made into rigid tests, since they have their limitations.[4] Otherwise, science can become *ideological* (bias overrides evidence or important philosophical concerns) and *reductionistic* (all knowledge becomes reduced to following certain guidelines that have turned into rigid criteria).

Second, the philosophical assumptions and biases made by certain scientists unfairly cordon off scientific inquiry to purely naturalistic explanations. However, if a God exists who created and designed the world, then these scientists are excluding a massively helpful source of explanation. Those who assume that science studies *reality* believe, therefore, that all science should operate *naturalistically* and be "provisionally atheistic." That is, scientific work should assume that miracles don't occur, that God doesn't exist, that the universe and the things in it have no *purpose*.

However, this "natural laws" criterion is simply wrongheaded prejudice. To say, for example, that "intelligent design"[5] is out-of-bounds for proper scientific discussion *wrongly assumes that a naturalistic explanation is always superior to a nonnaturalistic (or supernaturalistic) one.* But what if a supernaturalistic one *does a better job* of explaining the data?[6] After all, *what if God actually created and designed the universe and evidence is available to support this?* To say that we need to stick only to naturalistic explanations for the origin and fine-tuning of the universe is arbitrary and dogmatic; after all, doing so would ironically exclude the *nonnaturalistic and ultimate explanation for the natural world and for what purpose it exists.* It may actually *stifle* or *hinder* legitimate explanations rather than advance a true understanding of certain features of the universe.

The Christian faith *supports* the scientific enterprise. All truth is *God's* truth, Augustine said. In fact, we'll see that the advance of science in the West was due to the fertile ground the Jewish-Christian worldview provided. This perspective assumes that God's good and orderly creation is worthy of study by human beings made in his image. But there's the shrill voice of some who claim "science" as their yardstick for knowledge; they are committed to naturalism and wouldn't consider anything but naturalistic, nontheistic explanations—no matter how bad or counterintuitive they are. For example, the Harvard biologist (and Marxist) Richard Lewontin has proclaimed his unshakable faith in a materialistic philosophy of life:

> It is not that the methods and institutions of science somehow compel us to accept a material explanation of the phenomenal world, but, on the contrary, that we are forced by our *a priori* adherence to material causes to create an apparatus of investigation and a set of concepts that produce material explanations, no matter how counter-intuitive, no matter how mystifying to the uninitiated. Moreover, that materialism is absolute, for we cannot allow a Divine Foot in the door. The eminent Kant scholar Lewis Beck used to say that anyone who could believe in God could believe in anything. To appeal to an omnipotent deity is to allow that at any moment the regularities of nature may be ruptured, that miracles may happen.[7]

The late Sir Fred Hoyle propounded the steady state theory of the universe; that he had maintained that the universe is eternal is hardly startling. A temporally finite universe implies a Creator! We're not surprised to read that Hoyle openly confessed his antitheological biases: As a youth he came to believe that miracles and other supernatural phenomena were "contradictions." So he rejected them in favor of a naturalistic approach to life.[8]

Daniel Dennett of Tufts University is another example of this left-wing, dogmatic fundamentalism. As far as he's concerned, neo-Darwinism is essentially *atheistic*. With almost fanatical zeal, he says that those who hold intolerably threatening "religious" beliefs should be quarantined in "cultural zoos" since they threaten the well-being of our descendants:

> If you insist on teaching your children falsehoods—that the Earth is flat, that "Man" is not a product of evolution by natural selection—then you must expect, at the very least, that those of us who have freedom of speech will feel free to describe your teachings as the spreading of falsehoods, and will attempt to demonstrate this to your children at our earliest opportunity.[9]

And some people think that only the "religious" are dogmatic and narrow-minded! Ironically, leaving God out of the scientific picture will actually further remove us from important answers to key questions.

Take a parallel case: What if someone wants to study *political philosophy*, which involves discussing the nature of rights, equality, and justice? Now, if God exists and we human beings have been endowed by God with "certain unalienable rights" (as the Declaration of Independence notes), then it would be foolish to say, "We can't bring God into the discussion. That's out-of-bounds in political philosophy." Well, in this case (as with science), we'll be *leaving out* many important metaphysical and theological considerations that can actually give us greater clarity on key issues.

*Third, scientism commits the "fallacy of misplaced concreteness." This involves making what is actually a **false** opinion/belief into a concrete reality. In the case of scientism, it takes one legitimate area of study and (wrongly) reduces all reality to this one area **alone**.* British philosopher Roger Trigg correctly observes what scientism takes for granted: "Science is our only means of access to reality."[10] This, of course, raises questions: How can we use science to prove that *only* science gives us knowledge? Was this conclusion discovered through *scientific* observation? How can it be shown *scientifically* that there's no God, no objective moral obligation, no soul, or no design?

Now, no right-thinking person is going to deny that scientific research has yielded much good for humanity. And most people will freely admit that many scientific theories or studies in medicine, chemistry, and physics have shown themselves to be true with a high degree of probability. But we must beware of taking one legitimate area of study and reducing all of reality to that one area. Even if science gets a lot right, there's no reason at all to think that science *alone* speaks truth.[11]

*Fourth, the very operations of science assume a certain vision of reality before the scientist's work can even get under way. These assumptions aren't scientifically provable; they are simply **taken for granted** so that science can get off the ground.* What often goes unnoticed by many scientists who put on their lab coats to "do their work" is this: they make massive *philosophical*—and scientifically unprovable—assumptions before their work can even get going. And some of these assumptions themselves are debated among scientists.

What are these assumptions? Here's a start:

- *A physical, mind-independent world exists:* Most of us take for granted that a physical world exists that is not mind-dependent. However, in some schools of Eastern thought, the physical world is an illusion. Or some take a classical "idealist" approach to the physical world: Bishop George Berkeley and philosopher-theologian

Jonathan Edwards[12] denied the existence of a material world—even though they believed in the legitimacy of the scientific enterprise. Or consider the famous Cambridge physicist Stephen Hawking: because of certain philosophical commitments, he questions the existence of an objective reality (one which is independent of human minds): "I'm a positivist . . . I don't demand that a theory correspond to reality because I don't know what it is."[13]

- *The laws of logic are inescapable.* Scientists assume that if one hypothesis is true, then a radically opposing view must be false. Why is this? Science can't show that such logical laws must be used; rather, scientists assume them to get their hypotheses off the ground. As Dallas Willard writes, "Logical results have a universality and necessity to them which no inspection of facts can provide."[14]

- *The human mind can understand the natural world.* Why think that we should grasp anything intelligible about the natural world? Why think we can make sense of it? This assumption about the correlation between the world and human minds helps get science off the ground.

- *There are important criteria that make for a decent hypothesis.* We don't just move simplistically and without bias from particular observations to scientific conclusions. Francis Bacon (1561–1626) emphasized this methodology (which has come to be known as the "Baconian" method). However, Bacon's method is problematic in that the bits of data we collect—Bacon bits!—don't organize themselves. It takes a *mind* and a certain *theoretical framework* to determine what is relevant or irrelevant for a plausible hypothesis. The scientist begins with a hunch, insight, or key idea. Philosopher of science Ian Barbour remarks that "sense-data do not provide an indubitable starting point in science, for they are already conceptually organized and theory-laden."[15]

- *Nature is, generally speaking, uniform and therefore capable of being observed and studied.*

- *What we observe in nature can provide clues and indicators of unobservable processes and patterns (such as unobservable subatomic particles).* It's a philosophical assumption that we can make inferences (based on what we can observe) that certain unseen

entities and forces may exist. On the other hand, some philosophers of science such as Bas van Fraassen deny the existence of
"unobservables" such as unseeable subatomic particles.[16]

- *We can trust our reasoning and sensory abilities, believing that they
  do not regularly deceive us.* Again, we can't prove scientifically
  that our minds are working properly. We must *assume* this to do
  scientific work.

Take note that *none* of these things can be established by scientific observation or analysis. Each one is a philosophical assumption utilized
by the scientist from the outset.

*Fifth, it's erroneous and misguided to say that the only reality that ex-
ists can be studied or accessed by science alone. Some areas of knowledge
go beyond scientific study (which is perfectly appropriate). This fact,
however, doesn't stop some scientists from making pronouncements on
these beyond-science matters.* Nobel Prize–winning physicist Steven
Weinberg declares:

> It is very hard to realize that [life on earth] is just a tiny part of an over-
> whelmingly hostile universe. . . . The more the universe seems compre-
> hensible, the more it also seems pointless. But if there is no solace in the
> fruits of our research, there is at least some consolation in the research
> itself. Men and women are not content to comfort themselves with
> tales of gods and giants, or to confine their thoughts to the daily affairs
> of life. . . . The effort to understand the universe is one of the very few
> things that lifts human life a little above the level of farce, and gives it
> some of the grace of tragedy.[17]

But if "scientific knowledge" is all we have available to us, then how
can Weinberg make such a statement, since questions about meaning
are theological and philosophical? They are clearly *beyond* the bounds
of science. Why should Weinberg assume that science can offer any
comfort *at all*?[18]

Furthermore, there's a lot that we can know without needing science
to tell us. I know adultery and rape are wrong; science doesn't show
why this is so. Science can't tell me about what I *ought* or *ought not*
do—what my *moral obligations* are. Science can't tell me whether life

has *meaning* or not. Science can't prove or disprove the *soul's existence.* Nor can it show whether we have *free will* or not. We can truly *know* a number of moral truths or what our inner subjective states are, but these don't come under the scrutiny of scientific study.

William J. M. Rankine, a noted nineteenth-century physicist, wrote a poem, "The Mathematician in Love," that reveals the absurdity of reducing all knowledge to science and mathematical equations:

> A mathematician fell madly in love
>   With a lady, young, handsome, and charming;
> By angles and ratios harmonic he strove
> Her curves and proportions all faultless to prove,
>   As he scrawled hieroglyphics alarming.
>
> . . . .
>
> "Let x denote beauty,—y, manners well-bred,—
>   "z, Fortune,"—(this last is essential),—
> "Let L stand for love"—our philosopher said,—
> "Then L is a function of x, y, and z,
>   "Of the kind which is known as potential."
>
> "Now integrate L with respect to $d\,t$,
>   "(t Standing for time and persuasion);
> "Then, between proper limits, 'tis easy to see,
> "The definite integral *Marriage* must be:—
>   (A very concise demonstration)."
>
> Said he—"If the wandering course of the moon
>   "By Algebra can be predicted,
> "The female affections must yield to it soon"—
> —But the lady ran off with a dashing dragoon,
>   And left him amazed and afflicted.[19]

There's more to love than math and science.

Sixth, just as one scientific discipline can't rule out theism, stacking them all up together can't do so either. The naturalistic scientist E. O. Wilson speaks of the "consilience" of all things: "The Central Idea of the consilience worldview is that all tangible phenomena, from the birth of the stars to the workings of social institutions, are based on material processes that are ultimately reducible, however long and torturous the sequences, to the laws of physics."[20] People like Wilson are under the mistaken impression that the sum total of the sciences necessarily excludes theistic explanations. Let's take a look at this claim more closely.

What if someone attempts to put *all* the natural sciences together into a "grand unified theory" or "theory of everything"? Would theism then be considered false? First we should look at the *individual scientific disciplines* and ask if any one of them rules out God's existence. Does *biology* rule out God's existence? Certainly not. Even if, say, evolution could fully explain the diversity of species, this still wouldn't exclude God's existence. (Even if we don't agree with this view, there *are* theistic evolutionists who hold that the evolutionary process was guided by God.) In fact, if macroevolution were true, it would serve as an excellent argument for design!

What's more, it looks as though some naturalistic scientists are actually *suppressing* the truth of design. Richard Dawkins declares, "Biology is the study of complicated things that give the appearance of having been designed for a purpose."[21] Sir Francis Crick, the Nobel laureate, gives this naturalistic advice: "Biologists must constantly keep in mind that what they see was not designed, but rather evolved."[22] Of course, there's no way Dawkins and Crick can scientifically show whether God is involved in the evolutionary process or not. So if *God* is behind the evolutionary process, then organisms are *really* designed, not just *apparently* designed. There's just no obvious reason that biology by itself rules out God's existence and his involvement in the world.[23]

Let's throw in *chemistry*. As with biology, it's hard to see how chemistry would exclude God's existence. What about *astronomy* and *physics*? Well, the Big Bang and the intricate fine-tuning of the universe support God's existence. But even if the evidence *were* ambiguous, astronomy and physics wouldn't rule out God's existence. And what about *neurophysiology*? Surely we can't rule out the existence of God based on this study. We could go on and on.

The point is this: *No one natural science* rules out God's existence; so why think that when we stack them all *together* into one big theory ("Science"), *then* God will be ruled out? There's just no good reason—apart from pure philosophical prejudice—that God should be ruled out on the basis of the natural sciences.

*Seventh, science isn't an end in itself. There are potential areas of "scientific investigation" that just **shouldn't** be explored; doing so would bring about moral decline. Scientists need to be guided by wisdom and important moral considerations rather than simply assume that any kind of experimentation is legitimate "scientific progress."* The late quadriplegic actor Christopher Reeve once said in a CBS interview, "I still believe that the purpose of government is to do the greatest good for the greatest number of people. And that's a great concept."[24] So he called for embryonic stem-cell research, which involves the destruction of a human being, in order to "harvest" component cells that could be used to develop tissues and organs. He opposed government "inaction" for the sake of the "good" for the "greatest number." What's truly a sad irony is that Reeve invoked the *utilitarian* philosophy that humans have no value in and of themselves; they have value only insofar as they contribute to the society as a whole. That is, humans have *instrumental* value, not *intrinsic* value. This was precisely the environment in Nazi Germany, where the handicapped and disabled were often killed or experimented upon for "the greater good."

There's a profound arrogance involved in many scientific research projects—an assumption that scientific "progress" is good and justified in itself. To oppose any scientific research is "backwards" or "out of step with the times." But there are some things that science *shouldn't* pursue—say, researching the possibility of weapons of mass destruction or pursuing human cloning. Just because something is "science" doesn't mean it's good. Wisdom often calls for restraint in scientific research.

Here's another irony: Some scientists (or spokespersons for science) often appeal to some *moral standard* to justify, say, stem-cell research on fertilized human embryos. Christopher Reeve declared that the government has a "moral obligation" to pursue stem-cell research.[25] We're told that "we *ought* to do this because it will help so many lives." Yet the question surfaces: *Where does this moral standard itself come from?* What makes human beings morally significant creatures, and how can science justify their moral value? Here's the problem: Science can't justify a moral position. Scientists may be authorities in some areas of the natural sciences, but *that doesn't make them moral authorities or social authorities about what is best for the human community.*

Physician Leon Kass writes about the moral questions some medical technologies raise:

> In the absence of standards to guide and restrain the use of this awesome power, we can only dehumanize man as we have despoiled our planet. The knowledge of these standards requires a wisdom we do not possess, and what is worse, we do not even seek.
>
> But we have an alternative. In the absence of such wisdom, we can be wise enough to know that we are not wise enough. To repeat: When we lack sufficient wisdom to do, wisdom consists in not doing. Restraint, caution, abstention, delay are what this second-best (and maybe only) wisdom dictates with respect to baby manufacture, and with respect to other forms of human engineering made possible by other new biomedical technologies.[26]

Kass raises a very haunting question:

> Do we know what constitutes a deterioration or an improvement in the human gene pool? Might one not argue that, at least under present conditions, the crusaders against the deterioration of the species are worried about the wrong genes? After all, how many architects of the Vietnam War or the suppression of [Poland's] Solidarity [movement] suffered from Down's syndrome? Who uses up more of our irreplaceable natural resources and who produces more pollution: the inmates of an institution for the retarded or the graduates of Harvard College? . . . *It seems indisputable that the world suffers more from the morally and spiritually defective than from the genetically defective.*[27]

Scientists should therefore recognize their limits; science should *serve* humanity, not *enslave* it. C. S. Lewis reminds us of the danger when science goes beyond its limits:

> In reality of course, if any one age really attains, by eugenics and scientific education, the power to make its descendants what it pleases, all men who live after it are the patients of that power. They are weaker, not stronger; for though we may have put wonderful machines in their hands, we have pre-ordained how they are to use them. . . . Man's conquest of Nature, if the dreams of some scientific planners are realized, means the rule of a few hundreds of men over billions upon billions of

men. There neither is nor can be any simple increase of power on Man's side. Each new power won *by* man is a power *over* man as well. Each advance leaves him weaker as well as stronger. In every victory, besides being the general who triumphs, he is also the prisoner who follows the triumphal car.[28]

Eighth, scientists aren't necessarily more objective than another community of scholars; they—like the rest of us—must check themselves to make sure that their biases or philosophical outlooks don't override, distort, or close off relevant evidence and argument. Romans 1:18 speaks of the tendency of human beings to suppress the truth in unrighteousness. When it comes to the area of science, scientists may actually marshal their intellectual capacities to suppress the truth. God's gifts of reason and the study of his world are often turned against God in rebellion.

Yes, even academics and scientists are not immune from the quest of personal autonomy. God's existence would mean a serious rearrangement of one's priorities. This would dramatically alter how we "do life"—including how we approach science. Aldous Huxley, author of *Brave New World*, illustrates how studying the created order can be twisted to support rebellion against the Creator. He wrote:

> *I had motives for not wanting the world to have meaning,* consequently assumed that it had none, and was able without any difficulty to find satisfying reasons for this assumption. . . . For myself, as, no doubt, for most contemporaries, the philosophy of meaninglessness was essentially an instrument of liberation. The liberation we desired was simultaneously liberation from a certain political and economic system and liberation from a certain system of morality. *We objected to the morality because it interfered with our sexual freedom.*[29]

There are other factors as well that indicate that science isn't as objective as it's cracked up to be. *An individual scientist's perspective, skill, creativity, and "personal knowledge" may be remarkably different from all the others.* Michael Polanyi made this point in his book *Personal Knowledge: Towards a Post-critical Philosophy.* Two scientists can have an identical understanding of the universe and of scientific laws and the same level of education, yet one might end up working in a laboratory all his life and the other might develop into an Einstein or a Newton.

What's the difference? It's their individual creativity and imagination to see what others have failed to see.[30] Of course, this emphasis doesn't make "doing science" relative and just a matter of perspective. The scientist must still seek to *persuade* his colleagues about the soundness of his judgments.[31]

A further factor is the subtle but powerful influence of the community of scientists. Thomas Kuhn's book *The Structure of Scientific Revolutions*,[32] despite some of its flaws, pointed out that science isn't done in a vacuum. There are many subjective elements that enter into the scientific enterprise. Science isn't as "neutral" and "open to the evidence" as it's cracked up to be. The pressure of fellow scientists often shapes the assumptions and methodology of the individual scientist so that it's difficult—though obviously not impossible—to break away from the prevailing viewpoint or "paradigm."

Let me give a telling example of this kind of pressure. The distinguished biology professor Dean Kenyon of San Francisco State University and author of *Biological Predestination* began becoming increasingly skeptical that biogenesis (the origination of life) could occur through strictly natural chemical processes. As a result of an honest search, he came to embrace the belief that intelligent design had to be responsible for the emergence of first life. This shift in thinking brought him under intense pressure and criticism from the SFSU administration.[33] The community put pressure on him to conform to its naturalistic, materialistic philosophy, but Kenyon didn't back down. This incident illustrates that (1) metaphysical views *can* be changed in light of the evidence (such as rational consistency, factual adequacy, and having better explanatory power than another view),[34] and (2) it takes a strong person to stand up against this kind of pressure.

Ninth, from the outset, theism and science weren't enemies but allies. The alleged "warfare" between theistic belief and science is a relatively recent **invention** *that should be set straight. Christian theism has actually offered the necessary worldview context for the flourishing of modern science.* We're often told that science and God are opposed to each other. This, however, is a relatively recent fiction. The presumed animosity between God and science began to emerge in the late nineteenth century, when Thomas Huxley actively attempted to pit science against religion in hopes that naturalistic science would win out.[35] This effort was followed by that of two authors—Andrew Dickson White[36] and John William Draper[37]—who claimed that religion and science were antagonistic toward one another. This manufacturing of history has been shown to be a ridiculous distortion of the facts. After all, modern science was begun by theists such as Nicolaus Copernicus (astronomer), Galileo Galilei (astronomer), Johannes Kepler (astronomer), Isaac Newton (mathematician/physicist), Robert Boyle (chemist), John Ray (biologist), Carl Linnaeus (botanist), and Georges Cuvier (zoologist). We could also mention other believing, ground-laying scientists who preceded them—Jordanus de Nemore, Albert of Saxony, Jean Buridan, Nicole Oresme, and others.

The work of White and Draper—a work of *propaganda* rather than solid history—isn't defended by credible historians today. Many people have been taken in by their rhetoric, however. In fact, the truly remarkable thing about the explosive growth of modern science is that it happened in Christian Europe in the later medieval and early modern period, rather than at other times and places—within societies that were richer, more populous, and better organized (such as Rome, China, India, Central America, or the Islamic Empire). Many historians have concluded that the impetus of Christian theism provides the answer to this puzzle.[38]

What the writings of White and Draper fail to show is that the alleged clash between "religion" and "science," say, with Galileo, was really the *clashing of scientific (or philosophical) "paradigms"—ways of viewing the world*. Let's go back to the time surrounding the Galileo controversy. Interestingly, Copernicus and (later) Galileo actually had the strong support of many *churchmen*. However, they were opposed by the *scientists* and *philosophers* of the day who held to an Aristotelian view of things—a mathematically perfect, unchanging, earth-centered universe. In 1572, a new star was discovered by European observers, but according to Aristotelian thinking, the heavens were changeless. Some learned professors even called it an optical illusion! A comet sighted in 1577 was another blow to the Aristotelian worldview.[39]

As to Copernicus, his own disciples were religious Protestants or Catholics—and so were hardly antagonistic toward religion. The clash that he and Galileo provoked was more philosophical or ideological; it wasn't ultimately a religion versus science conflict. Copernicus and

Galileo were up against the staid Aristotelian and Neoplatonic philosophical ways of thinking.[40] Any churchly opposition to Galileo was
because Aristotelian scientists and university students put pressure
on church officials to oppose him.[41] In 1615, Galileo wrote a letter to
the Grand Duchess Christina of Tuscany, defending his commitment
to the truth of the Bible. He declared that *once the true meaning of the
Scriptures is grasped*, there's no conflict with science:

> It is most pious to say and most prudent to take for granted that *Holy
> Scripture can never lie, as long as its true meaning has been grasped*; but
> I do not think one can deny that this is frequently recondite [i.e., dif-
> ficult to grasp] and very different from what appears to be the literal
> meaning of the words . . . the Holy Scripture and nature derive equally
> from the godhead . . . so it seems that a natural phenomenon which is
> placed before our eyes by sensory experience or proved by necessary
> demonstrations should not be called into question, let alone condemned,
> on account of scriptural passages whose words appear to have a differ-
> ent meaning. However, by this I do not wish to imply that one should
> not have the highest regard for passages of Holy Scripture; indeed, after
> becoming certain of some physical conclusions, *we should use these as
> very appropriate aids to the correct interpretation of Scripture* and to the
> investigation of the truths they must contain, for *they are most true and
> agree with demonstrated truths*. . . . I do not think one has to believe
> that the same God who has given us senses, language, and intellect
> would want to set aside the use of these and give us by other means
> the information we can acquire with them, so that we would deny our
> senses and reason even in the case of those physical conclusions, which
> are placed before our eyes and intellect by our sensory experiences or
> by necessary demonstrations.[42]

Philosopher of science Ian Barbour states that Galileo's theories
"called into question the Aristotelian system which the church had
adopted in the Thomistic synthesis."[43]

Hungarian physicist and Benedictine priest Stanley Jaki and others have suggested that the Judeo-Christian worldview provided fertile
ground for the birth of modern science. Newton, Copernicus, Galileo,
and their ilk were Bible-believing theists who took for granted the rationality and orderliness of God's creation, the distinction between creature

and Creator, and the difference between rational humans and animals. Their conviction that miracles are possible if God exists did not detract from their studying the universe he had made. Chinese, Greek, Babylonian, and Egyptian civilizations had no such resources within their worldview to give birth to modern science.[44] Indeed, any conflict between Christianity and science—even if accurate—is a matter of *history* rather than *logic*, physicist-priest John Polkinghorne has argued. Whatever conflict there has been historically between theology and science, none of this "logically denied the validity of religious experience or the existence of God. Yet it marginalized such claims in the minds of men."[45]

For those who claim that religion (God) has nothing to do with science, the "damage" has already been done! Assumptions about human rationality as well the world's knowability and orderliness are the result of theism's profound influence on modern science. Physicist Paul Davies writes: "Science began as an outgrowth of theology, and all scientists, whether atheists or theists . . . accept an essentially theological worldview."[46]

The towering philosopher Immanuel Kant (1724–1804) himself said science can't get underway unless we make certain theistic assumptions such as the world's knowability and orderliness in an "artfully arranged structure." Of course, Kant maintained that the universe has a "determinative purpose, carried out with great wisdom"; the universe was created by a "sublime and wise cause."[47] But Kant believed that science couldn't be carried out without assuming design. Ironically, assumptions that naturalistic scientists take for granted have been handed down to them from their theistically-minded forebearers!

Often Christians can feel intimidated by the claims of "science." However, scientists have philosophical and theological assumptions like everyone else, and it's important that we be able to discuss some of the problems found within their naturalistic and materialistic worldview. The demand to "prove it scientifically" offers the thoughtful Christian much to explore with those who are scientistically minded.

SUMMARY

- There's no clear or obvious criterion that helps us differentiate between science and nonscience ("lines of demarcation"). Rather, science has a number of helpful guidelines that enable it to progress, but these can't be turned into rigid criteria. Doing so will only make "science" more ideological (a bias that overrides evidence and argument) and reductionistic (an arbitrary confinement of what counts for "science" or "knowledge").

- The philosophical assumptions and biases made by certain scientists unfairly cordon off scientific inquiry to purely naturalistic explanations. However, if a God exists who created and designed the world, then these scientists are excluding a massively helpful source of explanation.

- Many scientists and philosophers wrongly assume that a naturalistic explanation is always superior to a nonnaturalistic (or supernaturalistic) one. Excluding the nonnaturalistic (or supernaturalistic) and ultimate explanation for what exists and for what purpose it exists may actually *stifle* or *hinder* legitimate explanations rather than advance a true understanding of certain features of the universe.

- Scientism commits the "fallacy of misplaced concreteness." This involves making what is actually a *false* opinion/belief into a concrete reality. In the case of scientism, it takes one legitimate area of study and (wrongly) reduces all reality to this one area *alone*.

- The very operations of science assume a certain vision of reality before the scientist's work can even get under way (e.g., a physical, mind-independent universe exists; there's a regularity and predictability to nature; the human mind has the capacity to understand nature; our rational faculties are generally reliable). These assumptions aren't scientifically provable; they are simply *taken for granted* so that science can get off the ground.

- It's erroneous and misguided to say that the only reality that exists can be studied or accessed by science alone. Some areas of knowledge go beyond scientific study (which is perfectly appropriate). This fact, however, doesn't stop some scientists from making pronouncements on these beyond-science matters.

- Just as one scientific discipline can't rule out theism, stacking them all up together can't do so either.

- Science isn't an end in itself. There are potential areas of "scientific investigation" that just *shouldn't* be explored; doing so would bring about moral decline. Scientists need to be guided by wisdom and important moral considerations rather than simply assume that any kind of experimentation is legitimate "scientific progress."
- Scientists may be authorities in some areas of the natural sciences, but this doesn't make them moral authorities or social authorities about what is best for the human community.
- Scientists aren't necessarily more objective than another community of scholars; they—like the rest of us—must check themselves to make sure that their biases or philosophical outlooks don't override, distort, or close off relevant evidence and argument.
- From the outset, theism and science weren't enemies but allies. The alleged "warfare" between theistic belief and science is a relatively recent *invention* that should be set straight. Christian theism has actually offered the necessary worldview context for the flourishing of modern science.

FURTHER READING

Lewis, C. S. *The Abolition of Man*. New York: Macmillan, 1965.

Luley, Scott, Paul Copan, and Stan W. Wallace, eds. *Science: Christian Perspectives for the New Millennium*. Dallas/Atlanta: Christian Leadership Ministries/Ravi Zacharias International Ministries, 2003.

Pearcey, Nancy R., and Charles B. Thaxton. *The Soul of Science: Christian Faith and Natural Philosophy*. Wheaton: Crossway, 1994.

6

THE SOUL IS NOTHING MORE THAN THE BRAIN

Who *are* you? Children's writer Dr. Seuss gives some metaphysical points to ponder in his book *Happy Birthday to You*. If there weren't any birthdays, then "you wouldn't be you." If you hadn't been born, Dr. Seuss suggests, you might be a fish, a toad in a tree, a doorknob, three baked potatoes, or a bag filled with hard green tomatoes. But worse than this, perhaps you'd be "a WASN'T," which isn't any fun at all. After all, a "Wasn't just isn't"; he isn't present. But since you are you, that's very pleasant! If you hadn't been born, well, you'd possibly be "an ISN'T." He doesn't have any fun—no "he disn't." What's worse, he doesn't have birthdays, which isn't pleasant. Without being born, "you don't get a present."

What should the response be to such reflections? Dr. Seuss says that you should be grateful you're not a clam, a ham, or "a dusty old jar of sour gooseberry jam."[1] While metaphysics—the study of ultimate reality—wasn't a specialty of Dr. Seuss, he raises some important questions related to human identity.

Who am I? The Buddhist doctrine of impermanence declares that *all* things are changing. Nothing endures. Thus there's no everlasting Creator God. Today's most famous Buddhist, the Dalai Lama, declares: "Among spiritual faiths, there are many different philosophies, some just opposite to each other on certain points. Buddhists do not accept a creator; Christians base their philosophy on that theory."[2] Not only is there no enduring *God*—there is no enduring *self* over time (*anatman*—"no self"). Each human life is characterized by, literally, *self-lessness.* One's identity is simply a *stream of consciousness*; it's *constantly* changing throughout the cycle of rebirths. The self is like the old celluloid films: each frame is distinct and unconnected.

While we're on the subject of Buddhism, we could add a few comments suggesting the intuitive implausibility of this view.

- While Scripture affirms that there is a transience to creatureliness, this can serve as a reminder of God's permanence. But if we go along with the Buddhist, then we would believe that *impermanence is a permanent feature of reality.* However, in this case, to speak of a *permanent impermanence* ends up being incoherent. We simply can't rid ourselves of permanence by saying that everything is impermanent. In doing so, we affirm the inescapable permanence of impermanence in reality. (It's like saying, "There is no reality—only appearances." But in this case, at least the appearances would be real.) In fact, the very universal logical laws that enable the Buddhist to draw the conclusion that everything is impermanent are permanent.

- We can build on this point, noting that *change presupposes sameness.* How can we understand change without the more basic understanding of sameness? Some stable substance must exist that endures change from one state to another. Some*thing* is changed that has an absolute identity. As J. P. Moreland suggests, "In successive moments of experience, I not only have an awareness of those successive experiences, but I also am aware of an I which is identical in each moment and which is identical to my current self."[3]

- *There seems to be no strong reason to reject personal identity. This too is a fundamental feature of reality.* As philosopher Peter van

Inwagen notes, the Buddhist view of the self is a fiction; van Inwagen says he's "unable to take this proposal seriously" because "the idea of personal identity across time . . . is so central to a vast array of ways of thinking that have served us and our ancestors for millennia that we should abandon it only in the face of an unanswerable argument."[4]

Another worldview, philosophical naturalism, maintains that you *are* your body—or your mind depends on your body and cannot survive without it. Each of us is a material being. There's no soul or mind that's distinct from the body and therefore nothing that's capable of surviving death. Nobel laureate Francis Crick declared that "you" are merely "the behavior of a vast assembly of nerve cells and their associated molecules."[5] Philosopher Owen Flanagan bluntly asserts, "There are no such things as souls or nonphysical minds"—adding that if they did exist, then "science would be unable to explain them."[6] But there aren't minds and souls; so science can explain such things. He claims that "the mind is the brain in the sense that perceiving, thinking, deliberating, choosing, and feeling are brain processes."[7]

The naturalistic philosopher Jaegwon Kim of Brown University writes: "The idea of minds as souls or spirits, as *entities* or *objects* of a special kind, has never gained a foothold in a serious scientific study of the mind and has also gradually disappeared from philosophical discussions of mentality."[8] Kim gives two reasons for taking this position:

1. *Why think immaterial things exist?* There seems "no compelling reason" to think that there are wholly immaterial things in this world.

2. *How can material and immaterial things interact?* It is doubtful, Kim argues, that "an immaterial substance, with no material characteristics and totally outside physical space, could causally influence, and be influenced by, the motions of material bodies that are strictly governed by physical law."[9] How could an immaterial substance "affect the motion of even a single molecule?"[10]

Not surprisingly, the "scientific" view about humans is guided by the belief that (1) we are material beings and that (2) what we do is causally determined. It seems that when Christian philosophers and theologians want to take a more "scientific" view of the soul, they end up embracing some naturalistic assumptions. They tend to take a materialistic or physicalistic view of the Bible's references to "soul" or "spirit," and they also incline toward a view of causally determined choices (i.e., our genes, brains, environments, influences, and habits cause the decisions that we make). As a result, they end up denying a more robust sense of freedom. The consequences are not insignificant when it comes to moral responsibility.

We'll come back to the naturalistic aversion to a body-soul (or body-mind) distinction, but it might be helpful to discuss a few preliminaries to set a context. (Some readers may wish to skip these preliminaries and jump ahead to the defense of the soul—the immaterial aspect of human existence—in the next chapter.)

First, each human being is an ensouled body and an embodied soul; body and soul function as an organic whole; they are distinct, however, and even capable of temporary separation (e.g., during the intermediate state in heaven—between death and the final bodily resurrection). Philosopher René Descartes—after whom my wife and I named our first kitten, *René De Cat!*—claimed that the essence of a physical entity (such as a body) is that it is extended in space. On the other hand, the essence of the mind/soul is that it is a "thinking thing" and it is not extended in space.[11] Although Descartes was making an important point about the essential differences between these two substances, many philosophers have rightly criticized Descartes for rigidly compartmentalizing body and soul/mind. A more organic, integrated, and interactive understanding of body and soul is called for. After all, the body's workings affect the soul, and the soul's workings affect the body. When my soul (that is, *I*) happens to choose to raise my hand, the results appear in my body's activity: my hand is raised. When I am worried in my soul, this can set my stomach churning; when my head hurts, this can affect my soul.

Second, "substance dualism" rightly maintains that there are two distinct but interacting substances—a physical body and an immaterial soul; each has its own unique/distinct properties—although deeply integrated.[12] On the mind-body topic, there are three basic views to consider, the first two being inadequate, as we'll see:

View 1: The Mind-Equals-the-Brain View (Reductive Materialism): This view maintains that all mental operations (self-reflectings, intendings, beliefs) can be reduced to brain/neural functions. Just as temperature is identical to the motion of kinetically energized molecules, so mental activity is identical to (or nothing more than) brain/neural activity.

View 2: The Mind-Depends-on-the-Brain View (Property Dualism/ Nonreductive Materialism): Some philosophers claim that the human body has two properties or characteristics: (1) physical and (2) mental. This is known as *property dualism*. One approach of property dualism maintains that consciousness and other mental events *emerge from* ("supervene upon") the body because it has evolved into a sufficient complexity of brain and nervous system. The *mental* property, although it *can't* be reduced to the purely physical, can exist *only* because of the *physical* body. Without the human body, there would be no human mind. Once the body dies, the mind dies with it.

View 3: The Mind/Soul-Is-Essentially-Distinct-from-the-Brain View (Substance Dualism): This view maintains that there are two enduring substances—one physical (body) and the other immaterial (soul)—and they are distinct by their very nature—even if organically related.[13] When it comes to the human being, the soul is "present" at every point in the human body, directing the body to grow and develop from conception to adulthood and "informing" it to carry out actions determined by the soul. The soul itself has its own set of capacities—to be (self-)conscious, believe things, intend things, feel things, reason about things, learn languages, and know and relate to God (this last function involves what the New Testament refers to as the "spirit"—the spiritual or God-oriented capacity of the soul). Many of these thousands of capacities may not be realized, however. Perhaps this is the case because of a physical handicap (e.g., Alzheimer's disease, Down's syndrome) that *blocks* or *prevents* the soul from thinking clearly. Or maybe, say, my eyeballs work just fine, but *my soul is not paying attention*; then I'll fail to take note of what is in front of me.[14] And even in the midst of many bodily changes (and even death), my soul gives me my identity and enables me to continue being who I am.

J. P. Moreland summarizes for us what the soul is:

> The soul (which is the same thing as the self or the I) is that immaterial,
> invisible thing that makes me a conscious, living human being. . . . The
> soul is a substantial, unified reality that informs its body.[15]

*Third, the Scriptures strongly favor the view of a distinctive soul (sub-
stance dualism): there is an immaterial aspect to human beings—the
soul, mind, or spirit—which is potentially separable from the material
body—even though this is not the final state.* According to the traditional
Christian view of humans, we are not—to put it crudely—hulks of pro-
toplasmic guck, nor are we to be identified exclusively with our bodies.
Body and soul are distinct but interactive substances—one physical and
the other immaterial. I *am not* my body; rather, I *have* a body. I *am* my
soul, which organically belongs to a body suited to it.

The plain biblical teaching bears this out. Let's look at a number of
examples:

- Jesus tells the criminal on the cross: "*Today* you will be with me
  in paradise" (Luke 23:43 NIV, italics added). For the criminal
  to be with Jesus *immediately* after death and prior to the bodily
  resurrection implies a position incompatible with a materialistic
  view of the human person.[16]
- When Jesus speaks with Moses and Elijah at the transfiguration
  (Matt. 17:1–9; Mark 9:2–10; Luke 9:28–36), the implication is
  that Moses and Elijah are *alive in some manner* and are able to
  talk with Jesus. The presumption is that they survived physical
  death.
- Just after his friend Lazarus died, Jesus declares that "he who
  believes in Me will live even if he dies" (John 11:25; cf. John 8:51).
  Since Lazarus had died physically (but not for long!), surely Jesus
  means that *even though we may experience bodily death*, we can
  continually experience spiritual/eternal life. Again, the assumption is that a person can survive bodily death.
- In his dispute with the resurrection-denying Sadducees, Jesus,
  harking back to Yahweh's declaration to Moses in Exodus 3:6,

declares that "He is not the God of the dead but of the living; for all [Abraham, Isaac, and Jacob] live to Him" (Luke 20:38). Jesus is not saying that the patriarchs *will* live, but that they *still* live. That is, they are still alive even without physical bodies. As Joseph A. Fitzmyer notes, "The main point in the argument is that Yahweh identifies himself to Moses as the God of the patriarchs long after they have died. . . . Only living people can have a God, and therefore Yahweh's promise to the patriarchs that he is/will be their God requires that he maintain them in life."[17]

- Jesus distinguishes between body and soul as distinct entities in Matthew 10:28 (cf. Luke 12:4–5): "Do not fear those who kill the body but are unable to kill the soul; but rather fear Him who is able to destroy both soul and body in hell [Gehenna]." The thrust here is that the death of the body is not the end of the matter: "Something [else] remains thereafter as a candidate for inclusion in Gehenna."[18]

- Paul declares to the Philippians that *he desires to depart—at death—and be with Christ* (Phil. 1:23–24).

- In Revelation 6:9–10, we read of the *souls of martyred saints* in heaven (during the intermediate state, when they have not yet received their resurrection bodies) crying out for God's judgment upon those on the earth who have shed their blood.

- In his famous passage on the "intermediate state," Paul writes in 2 Corinthians 5:3–4: ". . . inasmuch as we, having put it [the resurrection body] on, will not be found naked. For indeed while we are in this tent [corruptible body], we groan, being burdened, because we do not want to be unclothed [i.e., souls without bodies], but to be clothed [with the resurrection body], so that what is mortal will be swallowed up by life."

- In 2 Corinthians 5:8, Paul declares that dying and immediately being with Christ in heaven—*absent* from the body but *present* with the Lord—involves a *temporary state of "nakedness"*—in which the soul is separated from the body. This is an unnatural concept to the Jewish mind, for whom the *fullest* kind of living is an *embodied living*.

Recently, some biblical scholars and theologians have resisted taking this last passage as supportive of an intermediate state of disembodiment;[19] but such a reading is a departure from the straightforward understanding of Scripture. As New Testament commentator Ben Witherington says, for Paul "the fullness of life was unthinkable without a body, and thus life in heaven [in a disembodied existence] was not for Paul the ultimate desideratum [or desirable state] by any means."[20] Another commentator, Colin Kruse, observes that

> the nakedness which Paul expects to avoid when he puts on the heavenly dwelling [of the resurrection body] is *the nakedness of a disembodied soul*. Paul, as a Jew, would regard existence as a disembodied soul as something to be eschewed [shunned]. The promised heavenly body will save him from that.[21]

While the soul is made for embodiment and is deeply intertwined with the body, the soul can temporarily survive without embodiment. That is, we can continue to live even if our bodies perish.[22]

This substance dualism is theologically significant, reminding us that, for example, (1) persons are capable of surviving bodily death and (2) the incarnation (God, who is spirit, becomes man) is possible, as the *person* of Jesus is *not identical* to his body (the person of Jesus didn't simply emerge because his organized bodily matter was sufficiently complex).[23] Also, belief in substance dualism was part of the worldview of Jew and Greek alike. Robert Gundry points out, "Despite much current opinion to the contrary, Jews as well as Greeks regarded physical death as separation of the soul from the body."[24]

Fourth, the human soul (and the potential for the soul's disembodiment at death) is crucial for understanding personal identity. That is, there must be an enduring soul experiencing an intermediate, disembodied state (between the time of bodily death and the receiving of a resurrection body at the end of the age). If the soul/mind depended upon the body's existence, then the same person could not exist if his body—that is, *he*—is blown to smithereens in an explosion and then receives a resurrection body afterward. We would have a completely different person since he has a different body.[25]

*Fifth, it is **not** biblically accurate to speak of the "immortality of the soul" since immortality in Scripture is connected with the resurrection of the body.* The soul's immortality was a view common among Greeks; it is *not* one rooted in the Scriptures.[26] The Jewish-Christian tradition views the resurrection body as immortal. The term *immortality* (along with *incorruptibility* and *imperishability*) is never used in conjunction with the word *soul* (*psychē*); it is associated with the physical resurrection body (*sōma*), which takes on *immortality*. All eight references to human immortality are found within 1 Corinthians 15 itself.[27] This body is called *spiritual* (i.e., animated by the Holy Spirit), as opposed to *not* the *physical* body but the *natural* body (i.e., a soul-animated body). This new physical body is called "spiritual" (1 Cor. 15:44, 46) because it is now equipped for communication with the heavenly world and is endowed with new capacities.[28] Now, Paul *isn't* contrasting the physical and spiritual; rather, he's distinguishing between two types of physical body—one *naturally* animated by the human *soul* and the other *supernaturally* animated by God's *Spirit*. This is supported by Paul's declaration that we long for "the redemption of our body" (Rom. 8:23).

Not only this, there's a *historical continuity between the soul-animated body and the spiritual/Spirit-animated body*. (Keep in mind that a resurrection without a physical body would have been extremely odd to the Jewish mind. A non-physical body just isn't a body! So it's simply false to consider the spiritual body of 1 Corinthians 15 as immaterial and invisible.)[29] The Bible never tells us that the soul is immortal. Since God "alone possesses immortality" (1 Tim. 6:16), immortality is derived. We aren't inherently immortal; this is, rather, a gift from God. Immortality is *the immunity from decay and death that results from having or sharing the eternal divine life*.[30] That is, when we are "raised imperishable" (1 Cor. 15:52), the transformation or change that results in immortality *coincides with* the resurrection event itself. This is a *transformed physicality*.

*Sixth, the believer's ultimate final state is **not** heaven, but it is the new heavens and new earth—complete with a resurrection body.* This point is very important. The common view of the afterlife in much evangelical theology, literature, and hymnody is heaven-after-death—end of story. The fundamental flaw in this way of thinking is that *death isn't swallowed up in victory!* Death does have the final word after all; it isn't defeated.

Without a robust view of a final resurrection of believers, death ends up having the victory rather than being conquered by Christ's death and resurrection, which revealed the rule/kingdom of God breaking into the world, the beginning of a new era foretold by the prophets. The bodily resurrection of Christ, which foreshadows our own, heralds the defeat of death. In the final state, heaven (including the New Jerusalem portrayed as a bride—the assembly of redeemed souls) breaks into history and comes to a renewed physical, earthly existence (see Revelation 21). As N. T. Wright urges, Christ will come again not to take us away from the earth but to establish us within the new earth. It's not an abandonment of creation but a renewal of it. This view affirms rather than denies the importance of God's working in history and the goodness of the physical realm.[31]

Seventh, we should probably be careful about overemphasizing the distinction between "soul" and "spirit"; the "spirit" appears to be the spiritual faculty of the "soul."[32] There has been an ongoing debate between Christians on how human beings are constituted: Is the human comprised of *body* and *soul* ("dichotomist" or "dipartite") or of *body, soul,* and *spirit* ("trichotomist" or "tripartite")? In recent history, some Christian thinkers have even maintained (incorrectly) that the person is material and the "soul" is not a separate substance but is rooted in the physical ("monistic").[33]

Now there is certainly *overlap* between *soul* (*psychē*) and *spirit* (*pneuma*) in Scripture. In the Magnificat, Mary uses *soul* and *spirit* interchangeably (Luke 1:46–47). The terms *spirit* and *soul* were used interchangeably during the intertestamental period also (e.g., Wisd. Sol. 1:4–5; 15:11; 16:14). At times the term *body and soul* was used to describe the whole person (2 Macc. 6:30; 7:37). In the New Testament, Paul is concerned about the "souls" of his converts: "I will most gladly spend and be expended for your souls" (2 Cor. 12:15; see also 1 Thess. 2:8, where Paul has expended his very "soul/life" for the Thessalonians).

If there is any difference at all, *spirit* may reflect the Godward side of humankind whereas *soul* may represent our human side. This is reflected in the fact that *God (as well as God's Spirit) is called "spirit" rather than "soul."* Also, the reason Paul uses *spirit* more frequently than *soul* is because of his own experience as a believer with the Spirit of God and his indwelling presence and his communicating and connecting with our *spirit* (Rom. 8:15–16). Incidentally, this emphasis is a departure from intertestamental and rabbinic literature, which stressed *soul* (Hebrew: *nephesh*; Greek: *psychē*) rather than *spirit*. For instance, Paul speaks of his *spirit* praying (1 Cor. 14:14) when he prays in tongues. This reflects the language of communion between God's *Spirit* and our *spirit* (cf. Rom. 8:16).

So when we speak of the soul, we speak of *our essential core*. This core ultimately makes us persons, since we would *still* be persons after death in a (temporarily) disembodied state. In light of the death and decay of our physical bodies, there must be some immaterial aspect of our humanity—our souls—to provide the *continuity* of our existence and memories—and our own individual *identity*. Philosopher Stephen Evans nicely summarizes things:

> Christians are very clear that we are meant to be embodied. In this life, and in our ultimate intended state after death, personhood is expressed in bodily form; it is incarnated. But our personhood can survive the death of our present bodies. The power of God, which gives us life now, can continue our conscious, personal history in a new body.[34]

SUMMARY

- Some problems with the Buddhist understanding of the soul (a kind of stream-of-consciousness view) are: (a) In denying any permanence, Buddhists make impermanence a permanent feature of reality; at least this reality and the "impermanence principle" endure! (b) Change presupposes sameness; if something is changed from one state into another, then there must be some actual thing that endures the change; (c) There seems to be no strong reason to reject personal identity. This too is a fundamental feature of reality. We should deny it only in the face of an unanswerable argument.

- Naturalists reject an immaterial soul for two major reasons: (a) Why think immaterial things exist? (b) How can material and immaterial things interact? The "scientific" view about humans (one taken by even some Christian thinkers) is guided by the belief that we are material beings and that what we do is causally determined. A more robust sense of freedom is denied.

- Each human being is an ensouled body and an embodied soul; body and soul function as an organic whole; they are, however, distinct and even capable of temporary separation (e.g., during the intermediate state in heaven—between death and the final bodily resurrection).

- *Reductive materialism* (the Mind-Equals-the-Brain View) reduces all mental activity to the operations of the brain/nervous system. *Property dualism/nonreductive materialism* (the Mind-Depends-on-the-Brain View) maintains that the body has two distinct properties—physical and mental. But when the body dies, mental life ceases as well. *Substance dualism* (the Mind/Soul-Is-Essentially-Distinct-from-the-Brain View) correctly maintains that there are two distinct but interacting substances—a physical body and an immaterial soul; each has its own unique/distinct properties—although deeply integrated. (René Descartes, unfortunately, held a more compartmentalized view.)

- The Scriptures strongly favor the view of a distinctive soul (substance dualism): there is an immaterial aspect to human beings—the soul, mind, or spirit—which is potentially separable from the material body—even though this is not the final state.

- The human soul (and the potential for the soul's disembodiment at death) is crucial for understanding personal identity.

- It is *not* biblically accurate to speak of the "immortality of the soul" (though the Greeks typically believed this) since immortality in Scripture is connected with the resurrection of the body.

- The believer's ultimate final state is *not* heaven, but it is the new heavens and new earth—complete with a resurrection body. Without God's restoration of the heavens and earth and without his furnishing us with an imperishable resurrection body, this would prove death to be victorious in the end.

- We should probably be careful about overemphasizing the distinction between "soul" and "spirit"; the "spirit" appears to be the spiritual faculty of the "soul."

FURTHER READING

Cooper, John W. *Body, Soul, and Life Everlasting: Biblical Anthropology and the Monism-Dualism Debate.* Grand Rapids: Eerdmans, 1989.

Moreland, J. P. *What Is the Soul?* Atlanta: Ravi Zacharias International Ministries, 2001.

Moreland, J. P., and Scott Rae. *Body and Soul: Human Nature and the Crisis in Ethics.* Downers Grove, IL: InterVarsity, 2000.

7

WHY THINK IMMATERIAL THINGS LIKE SOULS EXIST?

Having made some introductory comments in the previous chapter, we can look at some reasons for why belief in the soul makes not only good *theological* sense but good *philosophical* sense. Substance dualism has greater explanatory power than a view that reduces the soul to the physical—or one that makes the existence of the soul dependent upon the physical. In this chapter, we want to tackle one of Jaegwon Kim's questions: *Why think immaterial things exist?* In the next chapter we'll look at the "interaction problem" Kim raises.

First, the existence of a personal, self-aware Supreme Being affords a very plausible explanatory context for the existence of consciousness; this serves as an argument for theism and against naturalism. For naturalists, the existence of consciousness (whether in humans or animals) raises huge problems: How could consciousness emerge from the context of nonconscious matter? Can matter really think? The naturalist philosopher of mind Colin McGinn asks: "How did evolution convert the water of biological tissue into the wine of consciousness?" His answer is that "we know of no comparable force [as with the force of gravity's accounting for the Big Bang's leading to the creation of galaxies] that might explain how ever-expanding lumps of matter might have developed an inner conscious life."[1] Another naturalist philosopher, Ned Block, declares that researchers are "stumped" regarding the emergence of consciousness (or subjective experience) from matter; there is "nothing—zilch—worthy of being called a research programme" to explain this phenomenon.[2] Thus, as Charles Taliaferro argues, theists *do not have the problem of explaining the origin of consciousness as naturalists do*.[3] The context of a supremely self-aware Being, in whose image self-aware humans have been made, provides an explanatory context for consciousness; the naturalist, on the other hand, claims that consciousness somehow emerged from nonconscious matter. But there is no reason we should expect such metaphysical rabbits to appear out of naturalistic hats.

Second, matter, by definition, doesn't include the concept of consciousness or other mental features. Because consciousness or mental activity clearly belongs in the "nonmatter" category, we have very good reason for thinking that body and soul are distinct substances. We have no good reason for thinking that consciousness could emerge from nonconscious matter. "What is matter? Never mind. What is mind? No matter!" So the joke goes. But it contains a nugget of truth. Matter and mind are radically distinct—so distinct that we can speak of them being two entirely different substances—even if they are organically related and deeply interconnected.

As we've observed, some naturalists claim that human beings *are* their brains and nervous systems (*the Mind-Equals-the-Brain View*). Others claim that the mental *emerges* ("supervenes" upon the physical) once the nervous system is sufficiently complex—just as wetness emerges once we put two atoms of hydrogen and one atom of oxygen together (H_2O). As wetness *supervenes* upon the H_2O molecule, so the mind/mental activity emerges upon a complex, highly evolved brain and nervous system. In this scenario, psychological properties and events are *not identical with* physical properties and events but are dependent upon physical conditions. So a person's body is physical but possesses some nonphysical properties. The mental or psychological is just another property of the physical body (*the Mind-Depends-on-the-Brain View—or Non-Reductive Materialism*).[4]

Here's the problem, though: When we consult physics textbooks to understand what matter is, *there's nothing psychological, subjective, or mental about matter*. Matter might be described as having the properties of spatial location, spatial extension, weight, texture, color, shape, size, density, mass, or atomic or chemical composition. But what will always be missing in these textbooks describing matter is *consciousness* as a characteristic or property of matter. The assumption is that matter is different from mind.[5] We're left wondering: How could *matter* produce mind? How could nonconscious material produce consciousness?

I can think of myself as myself. By the very nature of the case, I have my own inner life that no one else can have; I have *my own* experiences, not someone else's. In fact, not even God—who knows each of us intimately, better than we know ourselves—can have *my* experiences. (If he had *my* inner experiences, then he wouldn't be God but Paul Copan!) But what accounts for the existence of this inner life? How does that lumpy gray matter of the brain produce subjective, technicolor experience? It just doesn't seem possible that every characteristic of the *brain* (matter) can be a property of the *mind* (and vice versa).[6] Consider:

- Does the mind—or events within it—*weigh* anything? How many grams does a mental event weigh?
- While we can dye the brain red or blue, the *mind*—or particular thoughts—cannot be dyed. I may imagine a color (say, brown), but that does not mean that my brain is therefore the color of brown.
- I can *think about* pain without *feeling* pain. My thoughts about pain don't necessarily bring me pain. *Or* I can think of some given pain experience *without* entertaining any idea of the accompanying material or physical activity. So clearly there is a lack of identity between these psychological and physical properties.[7]
- Thoughts can't be located in space. Is my thought about eating Ben & Jerry's New York Super Fudge Chunk ice cream[8] nearer to my left ear than my right?
- While *beliefs* can be true or false, *matter* cannot be. Matter just *is*; it's not true or false.[9] As C. S. Lewis observed, "To talk about one

bit of matter being true of another seems to me to be nonsense."[10] So belief can't just be a brain state and nothing more.

The fact that we can't locate, weigh, or dye thoughts—as we can physical objects—reveals the inadequacy of a view identifying the physical with the mental/soulish—or reducing the mind/soul to the physical.[11] Brains just don't have the same properties that minds (or souls) have, and minds don't have the same properties brains do. Therefore, *the mental can't be identical with the brain—or even produced by the physical brain*.[12] So if I have properties that no physical object can have, then it follows that I am not a physical object.[13]

No wonder naturalist Colin McGinn writes, "We know that brains are the *de facto* causal basis of consciousness, but we have, it seems, no understanding of how this can be so. It strikes us as miraculous, eerie, even faintly comic."[14] Naturalist philosopher of mind Jerry Fodor is similarly baffled: "Nobody has the slightest idea how anything material could be conscious. Nobody even knows what it would be like to have the slightest idea of how anything material could be conscious."[15] Earlier we noted Ned Block's declaration that naturalist philosophers of mind have "zilch" to go on for giving a materialistic account of consciousness.

The atheist Michael Martin declares that, while atheism is not necessarily "committed to materialism," there is no reason to think that moral values could not be made up of matter.[16] This is odd too—those physics textbooks don't list moral value as being part of the definition of matter either!

Remember the Soviet cosmonaut Yuri Gagarin? He declared that because he couldn't see God in space, God must not exist! Similarly, however much we study the brain and the nervous system, our studies can't tell us whether a soul exists or not. *Science can't settle the mind-body problem.* It can't tell us whether or not the soul exists—any more than it can tell us whether or not freedom of the will and objective moral values exist. I would suggest that, as helpful as neuroscience is, *philosophy* and *theology* offer us the more fundamental tools in addressing this problem.

Third, many people throughout history and across civilizations have held that the soul can be separated from the body; so we should be careful about dismissing a body-soul (substance) dualism as counterintuitive.[17]

The ancient Egyptians were known for their expertise in mummification of their pharaohs, nobles, and officials. At death, pieces of their brains would be extracted with a hook placed through the nostrils; the internal organs would be removed and preserved in canopic jars; the body would be drained of fluids and thoroughly dried with a salty substance called *natron*. It was the heart—not the brain—that was believed to be the seat of intelligence; so it remained in the body. The body itself housed the soul/spirit. To the Egyptian way of thinking, there were three "parts" to the immaterial side of human beings. The "double" of a person (*ka*) would remain in the tomb and enjoy the offerings and objects left near the corpse. The soul (*ba*) could "fly" out of the tomb and return to it. The spirit (*akh*) would travel to the Underworld and enter into the afterlife.[18]

These sorts of beliefs about the afterlife and possible disembodiment have been commonly held across the ages and nations. Does this demonstrate that the soul is distinct from the body, that substance dualism is true? Not necessarily; but it offers some evidence that the notion of disembodiment is intelligible and not incoherent or counterintuitive.[19] Philosopher of religion Charles Taliaferro declares that given the vast preponderance of persons who have found talk of disembodied agents intelligible, it seems that the burden of proof would be on those who contend that such an idea is nonsensical.[20]

Fourth, there is the "possibility argument" (or "modal argument") for substance dualism: If a soul's disembodied existence is even logically possible (which, whether consciously or not, we tend to assume), then it cannot be dismissed as irrational. Without logical contradiction, we can conceive of being disembodied. Also, we can without contradiction mentally put ourselves in the bodies of others: we can imagine being in another's body, living at another time, living in another culture, having another's skin pigmentation, and so on. C. S. Lewis writes about how literature can lead us

> to newer and fresher enjoyments, flavours, atmospheres, nowhere accessible but by a mental journey into the real past. I have lived nearly sixty years with myself and my own century and am not so enamoured of either as to desire no glimpse of a world beyond them. As the mere tourist's kind of holiday abroad seems to me rather a waste of Europe—there is more to be got out of it than he gets—so it would seem to me to

be a waste of the past if we were content to see in the literature of every
bygone age only the reflexion of our own faces.[21]

Notice that in these thought-experiments my identity doesn't change
by taking on another body. Rather, by imagining, my soul experiences
new things in bodies different from my own—and in cultures and time
periods different from my own. We intuitively tend to accept as plausible
the metaphysical possibility of such scenarios. And, therefore, so long
as such metaphysically plausible scenarios are logically possible and
hardly counterintuitive, then we can't rule out the possibility of body-
soul dualism as part of the fabric of reality.[22]

*Fifth, the very strong evidence for near-death experiences (NDEs) or
out-of-body experiences (OBEs) taking place suggests that body and soul
are different substances.* During a four-minute time period of being
clinically dead, the late atheist philosopher A. J. Ayer was aware of an
"exceedingly bright and also very painful" red light. Ayer concluded
that "death does not put an end to consciousness."[23]

A little girl named Katie almost drowned before being rushed to the
hospital. She remained in a coma (with a swollen brain) and on a respira-
tor for several days. After she recovered consciousness and was able to
speak about her experience, Katie not only gave verifiable, documented
details about what was going on in the hospital, but she also had knowledge of what was happening *outside* the hospital—including the particular details of what her family ate at the evening meal at home and even
the toys with which her brother played. All the facts checked out.[24]

In November 1977, a fifty-two-year-old man from northern Florida
("Mr. P.") experienced a massive heart attack, followed by cardiac arrest while in the hospital—a first-time experience for him. During
this cardiac arrest, he had no pulse or respiration. Though having
only a "layman's knowledge of medicine," he described in detail what
happened after this as though he was watching the medical experts
attending to his body while he watched from "outside" his body: he
was lifted and strapped onto a stretcher, a doctor administered a blow
to his chest (CPR) followed by manual chest compression, a plastic
airway was placed into his mouth, and a defibrillator (electric shock
paddles) applied to his chest—after which he came to consciousness. Mr. P. was aware of medical procedural details that make good

sense in the context of an out-of-body experience—and the existence of a soul.[25]

Another Floridian ("Mr. S."), a retired pilot, experienced a massive heart attack in 1973. Without medical knowledge, he described in amazing detail ("like a dream . . . watching it as a bystander") the defibrillation procedures (three shocks interspersed with the doctor "pounding" on the chest) and the machinery used on him, how the meters registered (with two needles—one fixed and one that moved to about one-third and then to one-half and then to three-quarters), and so on. The doctor interviewing him commented: "The movement of these two needles is not something he could have observed unless he had actually seen this instrument in use."[26]

Another scenario: While lying unconscious in a hospital after a cardiac arrest, Brent heard the "Code Blue"—a call for medical help in immediate life-threatening situations. It dawned on Brent that the Code Blue was for him! He saw medical personnel pulling off his clothes, and he was yelling, "Stop! What are you doing?" The doctors couldn't hear him since there was a period of disembodiment. Another patient who experienced a near-death experience was Pam Reynolds, at age thirty-five, who was able to describe in significant detail the instrument (like an "electric toothbrush") used on her during surgery for an aneurysm at the base of her brain.[27]

These types of dramatic stories are legion, and they support the point that bodily functions may shut down without the soul's shutting down. Now these sorts of examples don't *demonstrably prove* that substance dualism is indeed true. But they do offer some further supportive evidence that the notion of disembodiment is intelligible and that materialism is inadequate to explain them.[28] Indeed, the apostle Paul, in 2 Corinthians 12:1–6, suggests the possibility of disembodiment in his own personal experience.

Sixth, if human beings have libertarian freedom, then this would strongly support substance dualism and undermine physicalism/materialism. It has been observed that if human beings are genuinely or robustly free, then this would be a strong argument for substance dualism. It's interesting that naturalists tend to reject a robust (libertarian) view of human freedom—even though many admit it's intuitively plausible—because this suggests substance dualism.[29] Let's look a bit more closely at this in the following points:

1. *Freedom isn't simply doing what we want.* A drug addict or an alcoholic may do what he wants, but he has become enslaved over time through a series of choices he has made. A brainwashed or hypnotized person may do what he wants, but this doesn't really strike us as free.[30]

2. *True (libertarian) freedom isn't the result of previous conditions, inner states, habits, or motives. For me to be morally responsible, my choices must truly be up to me or under my control.* A more robust—and to my mind, intuitively obvious—view of freedom holds that I am a self-mover, unmoved mover, or agent; by my choosing, I have the capacity to bring about certain potentialities rather than others.[31] The buck stops with the human agent. Our choices are simply basic, or primitive—they are up to us. They don't need to be explained by Cause A, which is explained by Cause B, which is then explained by Cause C—leading to an infinite regress of causes. This infinite regress of causes removes a proper sense of full individual responsibility, since my choices are nothing more than the result of previous conditions. We must reach a point beyond which no further explanation is needed. I decide between options—many of them very significant—and these aren't determined simply by my genes, my environment, my motives, my habits, or my character.[32]

3. *While our choices are **influenced** by habits, motives, and previous conditions, they don't **necessitate** or **cause** our choices. We have the divinely endowed capacity to make a difference through our choices.* Of course, genes, motives, habits, or character will certainly *influence* the choices I make, but they don't determine them. They are *sufficient* to account for my choices, but they don't *necessitate* that I will choose in a particular way. (I would suggest that *our character is shaped by our choices* rather than our choices by our character. In fact, without the capacity to choose freely, how could we *develop our character* if our character determines how we act?) We cause certain events to happen, and "nothing—or no one—causes us to cause those events to happen."[33]

4. *Every human being is a self-mover who can make future-oriented and truth-directed decisions.* Ultimately, the buck stops with the agent. There's no reason to look further for the cause of human

decisions.[34] In fact, rather than thinking of choices as being determined by the past, our character, or our motives, the choices
we make can be *future-oriented*.[35] What motivates us is not necessarily the past; it can be *for a reason or purpose or goal ("in order
to")*. Choosing can be *future*-oriented rather than determined by
the past.[36] Choosing can be *truth*-oriented because we recognize
falsehood and choose to live by what's true. For those claiming
that we are determined to choose because of our past, isn't *their*
belief determined because of *their* past? For those claiming that
our motive dictates what we do, what about *their* motives in
asserting this? Even if they were right in their assertions, it's
because their past and/or their motives *coincidentally* dictated
these conclusions to their minds—not because they freely opted
for truth over falsehood.

Why this discussion of free will? Again, if we're free in this robust
sense and not determined by a string of causes and effects going back to
the Big Bang (including the physical processes going on in my brain and
nervous system), then this would be an argument against physicalism
(materialism) and naturalism. The atheist philosopher Thomas Nagel
admits, "There is no room for agency in a world of neural impulses,
chemical reactions, and bone and muscle movements."[37] Nagel suggests
that human actions are best explained as utterly unique—"basic" and
not reducible to something physical.[38]

The philosopher John Searle admits to having a common intuition—
we know "we could have done something else" and that human freedom
is "just a fact of experience."[39] However, because of his commitment to
the "scientific" approach to reality, he rejects libertarian freedom since
we'd have to believe a self exists that could potentially interfere with
"the causal order of nature."[40] So Searle claims that we intuitively think
we have free will, but if the will is truly free, then this allegedly throws
science into upheaval.

But if this intuition is so common, *maybe there is something to it!*
According to the commonsense *principle of credulity*, we should accept
the basic reliability of our everyday intuitions—whether about our
freedom, the general trustworthiness of our rational faculties and sense
perceptions, or our moral intuitions about the wrongness of murder,

rape, and theft. The burden of proof is upon the one who would deny these obvious features of our daily lives.

The standard naturalistic claim that our choices are the result of a cause-and-effect string of events beginning from the Big Bang to the present, Nagel claims, *is not plausible compared to libertarian accounts of freedom.* And given naturalism, he admits it's hard not to conclude that we are "helpless" and "not responsible" for our actions.[41] So if we're merely physical beings, then libertarian free will can't be accounted for. Moral obligations and moral responsibility for our actions—and thus free will—suggest that a nonphysical soul exists.[42] The basic capacity to act as responsible agents—rather than as mere bundles of instincts or genetically determined organisms—is taken for granted in society, as is evidenced by a constitution, laws, courts, and prisons. Naturalism doesn't provide us with sufficient "elbow room"[43] for free will—even though we take it for granted in everyday life. Rather, as naturalist philosopher Derk Pereboom argues, "our best scientific theories indeed have the consequence that we are not morally responsible for our actions."[44] Despite feeling that we are free beings who are the source of our moral actions, we human beings are "more like machines than we ordinarily suppose."[45] We are part of nature and therefore governed by natural laws. Naturalism undermines moral responsibility.

Seventh, why think that mechanistic cause-and-effect explanations are always to be preferred above personal, goal-directed ones? If we really do make choices that aren't mechanistically determined, then it's plausible to affirm the soul's existence. If the naturalist believes that our choices and beliefs are mechanistically determined, then this belief is itself mechanistically determined. We noted earlier that a materialist view of personhood will often result in a mechanistic (cause-and-effect) view of human choices. Naturalist philosopher Keith Parsons claims that appealing to "souls" to explain our actions is to appeal to "inscrutable acts" and "incomprehensible powers" of an "occult being" (such as souls or God), which only deepens the mystery. "The soul" isn't an explanation. So what does Parsons propose? What we should look for, he says, is (a) some universal or general law that predicts an expected outcome, (b) what caused something, and/or (c) why this state of affairs should be preferred over a different one.[46]

Let's think about this by way of an example. Being a die-hard Cleveland Browns football fan, I—and those who know me—can speak with confidence that it's very likely that I'll be happy about a Browns victory and disappointed if they lose. In fact, if Cleveland beats up on the (rival) Pittsburgh Steelers, then one can predict that the victory will be especially sweet to me. *If someone were to provide a neurophysiological account of why I'm celebrating a Browns triumph, this would provide far* **less** *understanding of my behavior than a commonsense, goal-oriented (intentional) explanation.* In fact, if physicalism is true, then there *must* be some further mechanistic (physical) explanation for my celebrating. But a goal-oriented explanation is commonsensical and much more basic—and it seems silly and unnecessary to resort to a physical explanation. This would just muddy the explanatory waters. My jubilant response to the Cleveland Browns' win is *highly probable* (there happens to be a certain predictability to it). The fact that my response can't be predicted *deterministically* doesn't negate a goal-oriented (nonmechanistic) explanation.[47] Besides, if a mental event occurs simply because certain initial conditions and natural laws dictate how the brain will behave, then Parsons' own beliefs are merely *accidentally* true since there's no soul to act upon what's true.

Eighth, if the atoms/cells of my body are constantly being renewed (every seven years my cells are almost entirely replaced), it suggests that a nonphysical soul gives me my identity over time. It's commonly known that the body's cells are completely replaced every seven years or so—including brain cells. This raises some interesting questions. Am I literally the same person as that interesting-looking infant represented in pictures in my photo album? If I am nothing more than my body, then how do I maintain my identity or continuity when my cells are constantly being overhauled? I have memories of events beyond seven years. In fact, I'm periodically reminded of events in my life that I haven't thought about in decades. But if my cells were overhauled and replenished, how did that happen? For the substance dualist, there's a very ready answer. The soul that animates the body continues to exist when the body undergoes changes. As Stephen Evans argues: "Even in this life I am not simply a physical object; the atoms which compose my body are constantly changing, yet my 'person' remains."[48] While this point isn't a knock-down argument for substance dualism, my continued identity—despite massive physical changes—better supports substance dualism than physicalism.

Ninth, the enduring soul helps us to make better sense than naturalism of (1) the unity of past personal experience and memory (not to mention personal moral responsibility) and (2) the unity of logical reflection and of experiencing the present moment. Let's take a look at each of these subpoints.

1. *The unity of past experience and memory (and personal responsibility):* In light of the fact that our bodies' cells change completely every seven years or so, consider this scenario: A Nazi officer (who ordered the murder of thousands of Jews in World War II) escapes to Argentina and is found out and tracked down some forty or fifty years later. When he's caught, he tells the authorities, "You're too late. You see, the cells of this body have completely changed about six or seven times since the Second World War. So you've actually caught the wrong person!" We intuitively know that such a statement is wrongheaded; we know that he *is* the same person—although with decades of guilt-suppression under his belt!

   However, if I'm constantly changing because (a) the cells of my body are constantly being replaced or (b) my life events and experiences are just a "stream of consciousness" existence, then why think that who I am now is the same person I was as an infant or will be as a senior citizen? But if I claim that I'm a completely different person, then why should I fear the future, since my identity will be completely changed? Why should I fear death that may be decades down the road? After all, I won't exist then. As Dr. Seuss wrote, I'll be an *Isn't.* Or if I look at pictures of myself taken in my childhood or adolescence, why should I enjoy reminiscing about the past (or perhaps cringing about it), since *a completely different set of bodily cells existed back then* (several times over)? Why be ashamed or gratified at what "I" have done many years ago?

   If a criminal is justly imprisoned for years, couldn't he say after twenty or thirty years, "I'm not the same person I used to be. The authorities should let me go since *I* didn't commit the crime. *Another* person did it." To reject that there's an underlying *I* to unify a lifetime of experiences in an ever-changing body leads to counterintuitive results. It ultimately undermines *personal responsibility* for acts committed.

And forget the *distant* past or future for the moment. Consider the very recent past. *As I'm thinking through a logical syllogism or singing along with a Bach cantata, what holds together these experiences that are extended over time?* Am I the *same* person before the syllogism or cantata as after? Of course! Why is this? Because there is some underlying self to make these events coherent.

2. *The unity of logical reflection and of various experiences within the present moment:* Consider something we can routinely relate to—*having several distinct experiences at a given time.* While I'm working on this chapter, I'm at a Honda dealership where my car is being worked on. What am I presently experiencing? I am (a) typing on the computer, (b) feeling a slight pain in my knee from an eleven-mile hike in the North Georgia mountains that I took last weekend with my friend Jim, (c) hearing the TV playing in the background, (d) noticing that a song by the singer Enya is playing over the public address system, (e) seeing a person walking in front of me, (f) hearing a person talking on a cell phone nearby. Different physical parts of my body may be involved in these experiences, but what holds these experiences together? Well, if we look to the brain, capacities such as memory, decision, thought, and pain are located in different places in the brain. If we went on the basis of this information, "we would conclude that one part of the brain remembers, another decides, yet another philosophizes, and still another experiences pain."[49]

A more coherent, simpler explanation is available: I—my soul or self—am having each of these experiences simultaneously; I am aware of them at the same time. There aren't four, five, or six different selves having one of these experiences each. A better explanation is the existence of an enduring soul that holds all of these experiences together. This unified awareness presents another support for the existence of the soul that cannot be reduced to the physical.

*Tenth, while there is a **correlation** between brain/body function and soulish capacities such as emotional and mental functioning, this is insuf-*

*ficient to show that the mind/soul is nothing more than the brain/body. Correlation is not enough to establish physicalism; the physicalist must show that all mental functions can be **reduced** to the material.* Persons suffering from bipolar disorder (characterized by mood swings) or depression may be given various drugs that bring them out of their emotional instability so that they can function reasonably well without being debilitated. Drugs are being developed to overcome the effects of diseases such as Alzheimer's and other types of dementia. The materialist will say, "These kinds of drugs act on the *body*; our 'souls' or 'minds' are nothing more than bodily functions. There is no soul."

But this doesn't follow at all. No substance dualist will—or at least he shouldn't!—claim that there isn't a deep, organic interaction between body and soul. (One of the problems with Descartes' view is that he gave the impression that body and soul/mind are compartmentalized entities rather than deeply united substances.)[50] The substance dualist can simply assert that the *correlation* of brain/body functions and soulish/mental activities are closely and intimately linked, but the soul (or mind) can't be *reduced* to these functions. *Correlation* doesn't equal *reduction*. This is why Christian philosopher Stewart Goetz claims that substance dualism is "no worse off" than naturalistic attempts to explain the relationship between the psychological and the physical.[51]

Eleventh, we have good reason to think that physicalism is false because there are good reasons to believe that nonphysical things (such as God, moral values, and rationality) really exist. As we saw earlier, naturalist Jaegwon Kim asks the question: Why think immaterial things exist? Well, here are some reasons for thinking immaterial entities exist. And if these are realities, then physicalism and naturalism are false.

- *Very good reasons can be given for God's existence, and if God (an immaterial Being) does exist, then physicalism is false.*
- Objective moral values exist, *but these cannot be reduced to something physical. Physical objects in and of themselves don't have value.*
- Reasoning toward the truth is undermined by physicalism. *Physicalism must ultimately deny the possibility of rationality since it allegedly can tell us how we do think, but not how we ought to think (that is, we should embrace as many true beliefs and reject*

as many false beliefs as possible). This problem with physicalism should prompt us to look seriously at the possibility of immaterial minds (which can rise above physical influences) to help account for rationality.

- *If consciousness is unlike anything physical and "stumps" naturalistic philosophers of mind, then maybe we should look elsewhere (such as to the idea of the soul) to resolve such problems.*

- *Intentionality (which is the mind's of-ness or about-ness) is a mark of the mental—not the physical. The mind has the ability to transcend itself (unlike a computer).* I can *think about* another person, *dread* a final exam, *wish* for a sunny day. *No physical state is about or of another physical state.* This is characteristic of the mental (nonphysical).[52]

- Even naturalists admit that we have a basic intuition that we have freedom to make a difference through our decisions or choices. We generally act as though we're not causally determined to act by physical forces affecting our helpless consciousness. *The existence of human freedom suggests that something nonphysical is acting as an agent.*

So one of the two chief objections to the soul—the "'Why think immaterial entities exist?' problem"—doesn't really have as much punch as the naturalist supposes. In the next chapter, we'll look at the "interaction problem." The naturalist has to deal with enough problems of his own—suppressing the intuition of free will, accounting for the existence of consciousness, and so on. The soul's existence goes a long way in dealing with immense problems that naturalism simply can't escape.

SUMMARY

- The existence of a personal, self-aware Supreme Being affords a very plausible explanatory context for the existence of consciousness; this serves as an argument for theism and against naturalism.

- Matter, by definition, doesn't include the concept of consciousness or other mental features. Because consciousness or mental activity clearly belongs in the "nonmatter" category, we have very good reason for thinking that body and soul are distinct substances. We have no good reason for thinking that consciousness could emerge from nonconscious matter.

- Many people throughout history and across civilizations have held that the soul can be separated from the body; so we should be careful about dismissing a body-soul (substance) dualism as counterintuitive.

- There's the "possibility argument" (or "modal argument") for substance dualism: If a soul's disembodied existence is even logically possible (which, whether consciously or not, we tend to assume), then it can't be dismissed as irrational.

- The very strong evidence for near-death experiences (NDEs) or out-of-body experiences (OBEs) taking place suggests that body and soul are different substances.

- If human beings have libertarian freedom (and many naturalists admit we have an intuition of freedom), then this would strongly support substance dualism and undermine physicalism/materialism. (a) Freedom isn't simply doing what we want (a drug addict might do what he wants, but this isn't truly free). (b) True (libertarian) freedom isn't the result of previous conditions, inner states, habits, or motives. For me to be morally responsible, my choices must truly be up to me or under my control. (c) While our choices are *influenced* by habits, motives, and previous conditions, they don't *necessitate* or *cause* our choices. We have the divinely endowed capacity to make a difference through our choices. (d) Every human being is a self-mover who can make future-oriented and truth-directed decisions.

- Why think that mechanistic cause-and-effect explanations are always to be preferred above personal, goal-directed ones? If we really do make choices that aren't mechanistically determined, then it's plausible to affirm the soul's existence. If the naturalist believes that our choices and beliefs are mechanistically determined, then this belief is itself mechanistically determined.

- If the atoms/cells of my body are constantly being renewed (every seven years my cells are almost entirely replaced), it suggests that a nonphysical soul gives me my identity over time.

- The enduring soul helps us to make better sense than natural- ism of the following: (a) the unity of past personal experience and memory, including personal moral responsibility (Why be punished for deeds done long ago if the perpetrator is "a differ- ent person now"?); and (b) the unity of logical reflection and of various experiences within the present moment (one self or soul—rather than several of them—holds together/unifies diverse inputs, sensations, and experiences at one moment).

- While there's a *correlation* between brain/body function and soul- ish capacities such as emotional and mental functioning, this is insufficient to show that the mind/soul is nothing more than the brain/body. Correlation is not enough to establish physicalism; the physicalist must show that all mental functions can be *reduced* to the material.

- We have good reason to think that physicalism is false because there are good reasons to believe that nonphysical things (e.g., God, moral values, rationality, and free will) really exist.

FURTHER READING

Cooper, John W. *Body, Soul, and Life Everlasting: Biblical Anthropology and the Monism-Dualism Debate*. Grand Rapids: Eerdmans, 1989.

Moreland, J. P., and Gary Habermas. *Beyond Death: Exploring the Case for Immortality*. Eugene, OR: Wipf and Stock, 2004.

Moreland, J. P., and Scott B. Rae. *Body and Soul: Human Nature and the Crisis in Ethics*. Downers Grove, IL: InterVarsity, 2000.

Reppert, Victor. *C. S. Lewis's Dangerous Idea: In Defense of the Argument from Reason*. Downers Grove, IL: InterVarsity, 2003.

Taliaferro, Charles. *Consciousness and the Mind of God*. Cambridge: Cambridge University Press, 1994.

8

How Can an Immaterial Soul Influence a Material Body?

We've addressed the first key question that Jacgwon Kim raises in objection to the existence of a soul: Why think that immaterial things exist? Here we address his second major objection: How could even one molecule be affected by an immaterial entity?[1] How do we respond? In all of this, we should keep in mind that *just because we don't know exactly how two unlike things (an immaterial soul and a material body) can interact, this isn't necessarily a strong or forceful argument against the existence of the soul.*

*First, it's a big jump from saying that we don't know **how** two unlike things can act upon each other to saying that no such activity is **possible**.* The philosopher C. D. Broad pointed out that although we know there's a causal connection between two unlike things such as *windy drafts* and *head colds*, we're warranted in making a causal connection.[2] Even though we *know* that one thing causes another in numerous instances, we still don't know *how* this takes place. A magnetic field can move a nail; gravity can act on a planet millions of miles away; protons can exert a repulsive force on one another.

Second, there are far more bizarre interactions within the realm of physics than the body-soul interaction, but this doesn't prevent scientists from reasonably believing them. Science itself has some amazing puzzles and conundrums of its own to try to untangle. The noted philosopher of science Bas van Fraassen points out a few items in scientific discussion that he finds quite bewildering:

> Do concepts of the soul . . . baffle you? They pale beside the unimaginable otherness of closed space-times, event-horizons, EPR correlations,[3] and bootstrap models.[4] . . . How could anyone who does not say [quoting St. Anselm, "*I believe that I may understand*"] be baffled by a desire to limit belief to what can at least in principle be disclosed in experience? Or, more to the point, by the idea that acceptance in science does not require belief in truth beyond those limits?[5]

Why should the concept of the soul baffle Jaegwon Kim and others? Is the "interaction problem" a greater difficulty than many of the puzzles found in science today?

Third, the theist can offer a ready example of a disembodied entity interacting with the physical world—namely, God. The atheist might make the claim: "Whenever we see agents acting in the world, they are *bodily* agents—not *immaterial* ones. We don't have any examples of disembodied agents acting on the physical. We just witness one physical thing acting on another." But at this point, the theist would disagree. Theists would argue that the *material* universe, for instance, has been created by a *spiritual* being ("God is spirit," Jesus states in John 4:24). This idea involves more than God not having a body (which is true). It involves God's ability to *encompass both spirit and matter*. God as Creator can cross metaphysical boundaries to interact and engage freely with what he is not (the *created*). We could add that we created human beings have, by God's grace, the spiritual capacity to approach the presence of God, our *Creator*.[6]

In fact, there is strong reason to think that this spirit Being, who is distinct from our universe, brought the space-time world into existence (through the Big Bang). Theists would also argue that this Being *continues to sustain* the material universe by his power. If it is possible that God, who has no body, can act on physical entities, then this could serve as a model for how human beings (who are ensouled bodies and embodied souls) could act.

So it seems rather odd that even Christian physicalists (e.g., Peter van Inwagen) deny the possibility of a disembodied soul based on the "interaction argument," since this appears to conflict with a number of traditional Christian beliefs:

- God—an immaterial being—created the physical universe out of nothing.[7]
- God continues providentially to sustain that physical universe.
- God miraculously acts in history, affecting physical objects (e.g., making water pour from a rock, causing Jericho's walls to fall, making an axhead float, raising Jesus from the dead).
- The incarnation—God becoming man—involves the "enfleshment" of an immaterial person (God the Son).
- Immaterial demonic beings are able to act upon human beings/bodies through demonization.

Fourth, there is nothing logically impossible about the interaction between physical and immaterial entities. We've observed earlier that there's nothing self-contradictory about the soul's possible disembodiment; similarly, there seems to be nothing logically impossible about the soul's interaction with the body (and vice versa). The philosopher Stephen Davis suggests as a possible example the phenomenon of *psychokinesis*—that is, the phenomenon of moving a physical object purely by mental effort or "willing" and without any physical contact (direct or indirect) with that object. Such a scenario certainly seems logically *conceivable* and not metaphysically or actually impossible:

> I have no idea (nor even any firm opinion) whether psychokinesis actually occurs, but I am quite sure that it is conceivable—that the notion of psychokinesis is coherent. And if it is conceivable, it seems a short step to hold similarly that an immaterial thing can conceivably cause physical events to occur—to act as an agent.[8]

Fifth, even some physicalists who are property dualists believe in some interaction between the physical and the mental. Why don't they take seriously their own interaction problem? As we've seen, a number of naturalists acknowledge that it's difficult to move from physical materials produced in the Big Bang to conscious awareness, from the brain's gray cells to subjective, technicolor experience. In other words, it's not *in principle* a problem for the two to interact. So why is *substance dualism*, and not *physicalism* (in the form of property dualism), rejected as problematic? It can correctly be said that the interaction problem is a problem for *both* views. At least the substance dualist who believes in God has a context for explaining how a soul can interact with the body and vice versa. An immaterial Being created and sustains the material universe.[9]

Sixth, many physicalists (property dualists) who reject the existence of the soul because of an "interaction problem" can look right into their own backyard for their own interaction problem: they themselves acknowledge they don't know how the physical and mental interact (or how consciousness could emerge from nonconsciousness). We've seen that naturalistic philosophers like Jaegwon Kim have problems with the soul: How could an immaterial substance "affect the motion of even a single molecule?" From his glass house, Kim is throwing stones at those who believe in the soul. But if we follow Kim's advice, then we can toss some philosophical stones right back at him. If physical-mental interaction is a problem for one view, then it is a problem for the other. What is humorous about all this is that Kim *himself* declares his own befuddlement about his particular views:

> It is not an exaggeration to say that the mystery of the mind is by and large the mystery of consciousness, and this mystery consists in our seeming inability to understand the phenomenon of consciousness as part of a world that is essentially physical, and, what is worse, not knowing just what it is that we need to know if we are to achieve such an understanding.[10]

So it just won't do for Kim to reject substance dualism, saying, "We don't know how the body and soul can interact." Yes, he believes that the mental exists, but he himself can't explain how the mental fits into a strictly physical world. Based on his critique of substance dualism, we should reject his naturalistic view as well.

Seventh, despite the claims of various atheists, having a physical body **isn't** *required to be a just, kind, loving, or forgiving person. In fact, we could fool people by performing* **outward** *(bodily) acts that conflict with what goes on* **within** *our souls/minds. This suggests the existence of a soul that can act on the body without being reduced to that body.* Atheist philosopher William Rowe claims that God (and, by extension, human beings) must be bodily in order to be able to forgive or pardon:

> One major difficulty with the view that terms which seem to designate mental activities (forgiving or loving) can be applied to God in their primary or literal sense is that the ways in which we tell whether an individual is forgiving or just do include bodily behavior—what she or he says and how she or he behaves. How then does one determine that a purely immaterial being has performed an act of forgiveness?[11]

Atheist Paul Edwards puts it similarly: Words like "divine justice" or "divine mercy" would "lose their meaning if we were told that God does not possess a body." That is, to be just, "a person has to *act* justly—he has to behave in certain ways. . . . But how is it possible to perform these acts, to behave in required ways without a body?"[12]

This isn't really much of an objection, however. If a person is angry or in pain, how do we *really* know it? Merely from bodily actions? This is commonly how we discover what is going on in a person's mind. But there are limits. A person may be *pretending* to be angry or in pain by expressing this through bodily behavior. In such pretend scenarios, a person's bodily actions tell me *nothing* about her mental state. Or a person could use *body language* to give every impression of showing forgiveness. She could speak in a sincere-sounding manner and with apparent gentleness, expressing a kind and understanding look in her face. *But* this person may still yet harbor an unforgiving *spirit*. In other words, if a person's mental states *do* exist, we *still* don't have direct access to them merely through bodily actions. We can say that the *normal* means of detecting love, justice, or compassion is through bodily actions, but bodily actions *aren't necessary* for love, justice, or compassion to be present.[13]

The atheist Michael Martin claims he doesn't know what personhood without a body means:

> If one interprets God as a nonspatial, nontemporal being without a body, what sense can one make of God's performing a speech act? Such a being would seem incapable of an act that assumes, if not a body, at least some spatial and temporal point of origin. The only sense one can make of a divine command is to understand God in a nontranscendent way as a being operating within space and time. But even this concession may not be enough, for it is unclear how a being within time and space could fail to have a body or how such a being could issue commands. The existence of a voice issuing commands seems to presume some physical vocal apparatus; golden letters written in the sky would seem to presume some physical writing appendage.[14]

Thus Martin believes the idea of God speaking is incoherent. We just can't make sense of a spiritual being performing *speech acts*. We simply have no category of *immaterial agent* to make sense of such a notion. Without a body, acting in the world is allegedly impossible.

In response to this criticism, one can argue that if the soul exists, then *this would give us some kind of analogy or picture of how God could act on the material world*. Although many people won't grant this point, we've seen that there are many good reasons for the existence of the soul.[15] *If* the soul exists, then certain *physical* events (e.g., my moving board game pieces while playing with my children) are caused by certain *mental* events (e.g., *deciding* to play a game with my children and *deciding* to move *this* piece rather than *that* piece). And certain *mental* events (e.g., my being in a state of fear) are caused by certain *physical* events (e.g., a king cobra or a black mamba appearing under my hammock while I'm relaxing).

So we should ask the question of the materialist: *Why think that having a body is required for understanding agency?* Why is it impossible to conceive of action without a body? Can't there be *mental* activity? In other words, the meaning of "agent words" like *love, justice, kindness,* or *cruelty* isn't lost in the absence of a body—even if a body is the *normal* means of detecting their presence.[16]

In this chapter we've seen that the naturalist has his own "interaction problem" to deal with. Furthermore, the theist has an example of a spiritual entity interacting with a physical entity—namely, God's creation and sustenance of the universe. Furthermore, we seem to have clear indications that bodily actions aren't enough to account for justice, love, and compassion. These qualities can be *faked* through bodily actions. It seems there's an underlying soul closely connected with the body that enables the soul to genuinely express its own inner qualities through bodily actions—just as the soul is able to deceive others through actions expressed in the body. (All we need to do is think of very persuasive Hollywood actors: their bodily actions on the set *don't* reflect their inner states!)

SUMMARY

- The claim that we don't know exactly how two unlike things (an immaterial soul and a material body) can interact isn't necessarily a strong or forceful argument against the existence of the soul.
- It's a big jump from saying that we don't know how two unlike things can act upon each other to saying that no such activity is possible.
- There are far more bizarre interactions within the realm of physics than the body-soul interaction, but this doesn't prevent scientists from reasonably believing them.
- The theist can offer a ready example of a disembodied entity interacting with the physical world (e.g., God's creating and sustaining the physical universe; the incarnation; demonic beings).
- There's nothing logically impossible about the interaction between physical and immaterial entities.
- Even some physicalists who are property dualists believe in some interaction between the physical and the mental. Why should they assume that this interaction can take place if there's no soul but that it can't if there is a soul?
- Many physicalists (property dualists) who reject the existence of the soul because of an "interaction problem" can look right into their own backyard for their own interaction problem: they themselves acknowledge they don't know how the physical and

mental interact (or how consciousness could emerge from non-consciousness).

- Having a physical body isn't required to be a just, kind, loving, or forgiving person, as some atheists suggest; we could fool people by performing outward (bodily) acts that conflict with what goes on in our souls/minds. (Consider actors when they are on the set.) This suggests the existence of a soul that can act on the body without being reduced to that body.

FURTHER READING

Cooper, John W. *Body, Soul, and Life Everlasting: Biblical Anthropology and the Monism-Dualism Debate.* Grand Rapids: Eerdmans, 1989.

Moreland, J. P., and Scott B. Rae. *Body and Soul: Human Nature and the Crisis in Ethics.* Downers Grove, IL: InterVarsity, 2000.

Reppert, Victor. *C. S. Lewis's Dangerous Idea: In Defense of the Argument from Reason.* Downers Grove, IL: InterVarsity, 2003.

Taliaferro, Charles. *Consciousness and the Mind of God.* Cambridge: Cambridge University Press, 1994.

9

You're a *Speciesist* If You Think Humans Are Superior to Nonhuman Animals

In June 2002, the upper house of the German parliament voted by a two-thirds majority to add "and animals" to the constitutional clause declaring the German government's obligation to respect the rights and dignity of humans.[1] Earlier in 1992, Switzerland passed a similar amendment, declaring that animals should be referred to as "beings" rather than "things."

Animal rights activists or animal "liberationists" certainly aren't in short supply. One such group is PETA (People for the Ethical Treatment of Animals).[2] There are bumper stickers telling us "Meat Stinks," "Respect Your Fellow Earthlings; Don't Eat 'Em," and "Thou Shalt Not Kill; Go Vegetarian!" Of course, there are people who think that such organizations are just silly and misguided. So there's another "PETA" website—*People Eating Tasty Animals*! It claims to be a resource "for those who enjoy eating meat, wearing fur and leather, hunting, and the fruits of scientific research."[3]

How do we respond to the "animal liberationist" who asserts that (certain) "nonhuman animals" have "just as much of a right" to protection under the law as human beings do? What should we think of Tom Regan's assertion—admittedly a minority view among animal liberationists—that nonhuman animals have "inherent value"?[4] What of Peter Singer? Though he denies that any "rights" exist, Singer declares that those who believe humans to be inherently superior to nonhuman animals are guilty of "speciesism," which is *arbitrarily favoring one species over another.* He claims that suffering caused by "the tyranny of human over nonhuman animals" today can be compared to that of "centuries of tyranny by white humans over black humans."[5] Ingrid Newkirk, the cofounder of PETA, is known for her famous statement, "A rat is a pig is a dog is a boy." *Should* we reject the idea that humans are superior (which some charge as being "anthropocentric") to other life forms and call other animals "persons"? Are we obligated to become "vegans" (vegetarians) and eat veggie burgers and tofu? Should we consume animal meat only under the direst of circumstances? Should animals be given *rights* to ensure their proper treatment?

We'll look at the specific question of animal rights in the next chapter. But the charge of *speciesism* and the assumption of the basic moral equality of humans and animals by many animal liberationists must be addressed *theologically* and *philosophically* first. We should do this because *animal liberationists often hold to a number of shaky and inconsistent philosophical and metaphysical assumptions. Their positions are often merely asserted, not defended.* As we'll see, one's *worldview* makes a huge difference in how one approaches the question of animal rights and our responsibilities toward animals. What one believes about *reality* will affect how one thinks about *ethics* and *rights.* For example, *why think that animals or human beings have rights or value if we are the products of valueless, mindless processes?* We'll explore some of these issues in the next chapter. But let's look at some biblical and philosophical preliminaries here.

First, to give perspective, keep in mind that God originally created the food chain as part of his "very good" creation, which involved animal death. The fall introduced human—not animal—death (in addition to human vulnerability to dangers from the animal kingdom). However, there will be no fear of predatory animals in the new heavens and earth.[6]

Although Genesis 1 emphasizes the order, goodness, and beauty of the natural world that God created, we see in other Scriptures that God created the "food chain" and the preying of one species upon another. Indeed, this is exactly what we see from the fossil record: carnivorous activity was present long before human beings appeared on the scene. We can't escape the fact of an animal food chain and, consequently, animal death in the nonhuman world before the fall.[7]

While Genesis 1 exclusively mentions the beauty of creation, other passages describe its bloodiness—a "Nature, red in tooth and claw," as Alfred Lord Tennyson put it.[8] For example, in Psalm 104, a creation psalm, we read that the "lions roar for their prey and seek their food from God" (v. 21 NIV). These animals also die: "When you [God] hide your face, they [man and animals] are terrified; when you take away their breath, they die and return to the dust" (v. 29 NIV). In the book of Job, God talks about his creation, which involves predatory activity. We read of the hawk (or eagle/vulture) spying out prey from the rocky crags (Job 39:26–29); its nestlings suck the blood of it, and "where the slain are, there is he" (v. 30 NIV). Job 41 speaks of God creating the fierce Leviathan (crocodile) with "fearsome teeth" (v. 14 NIV). Note that there is not even a hint of this being a post-fall situation. It seems built in to creation from the outset. Also, Job 38:39–40 speaks of the prey of the lion and of lions crouching in wait in a thicket.

Animal death and the food chain are presupposed as part of God's creation—without apology or qualification. The fall introduced human death (Rom. 5:12), not animal death.[9] Carnivorosity existed before the fall in the animal kingdom. Just check out the teeth of the Tyrannosaurus rex—not your average herbivore!

Furthermore, while God gave humans every kind of tree and plant for consumption (Gen. 1:29), this doesn't mean humans were originally vegetarians—nor does it mean that meat-eating reflects human fallenness or hardness of heart! Although it's not uncommon to hear that both humans and all animals were originally vegetarians, there are some important points that would suggest another scenario. While Genesis 9:3 affirms that "every moving thing that is alive shall be food for you," Gordon Wenham points out that this merely *ratifies* or *confirms* the legitimacy of meat-eating.[10] After all, God repeats the command to Noah, "Be fruitful and multiply" (9:1) and that all creatures are given into Noah's hands (9:2)—just as with Adam. The difference is the fear factor (9:2). Genesis, however, isn't interested in whether people were originally vegetarian or not, but that God supplied them with food.[11] Henri Blocher suggests that Genesis doesn't move from the *prohibition* of meat-eating (in Genesis 1) to *permission* (Genesis 9). This shift in emphasis is more likely *stylistic*: *Genesis 1 omits this feature—though the food chain is not an evil—to suggest the perfection of harmony in the creation. Genesis 9 adds this aspect of permissibility to convey the feeling that the peace has been broken.*[12] This fits what 1 Timothy 4:3–4 points out: that meat-denying ascetics were rejecting what God *created good* (echoing Genesis 1, where God declared his creation "very good"). These gifts were to be received with thanksgiving.

Furthermore, God tells human beings to "rule over the fish of the sea" (Gen. 1:28 NIV); one wonders what this could mean apart from permission to eat them. Abel kept sheep, presumably to eat (4:2–4). Noah himself distinguished between "clean" and "unclean" animals (7:2), which clearly assumes the edibility of meat prior to the flood. Old Testament scholar John Goldingay writes that death is in the background of Genesis 1:

> Genesis's readers know that the animal world does not live in harmony but lives on the basis of dog eat dog. Genesis 1 implies that this is not God's [final] intention, but neither is it simply the result of a human "fall." Animal inclination to kill and eat other animals is built into their nature as animals and is part of the "goodness" of creation.[13]

Not only does the Old Testament endorse the goodness of eating (kosher) meat—ox, sheep, goat, deer, gazelle, and the like (Deut. 14:3–6)—but the New Testament declares all foods clean (Mark 7:19). In fact, because "the earth is the Lord's, and all it contains" (1 Cor. 10:26), even meat which had been sacrificed to an idol could be bought from a meat market and freely eaten, Paul declares.

PETA engaged in a (false) advertising campaign claiming that "Jesus was a vegetarian." He wasn't. Besides eating lamb every year at Passover, he, being a good Galilean, certainly ate fish on a regular basis (e.g., Luke 24:42–43). Jesus also helped some of his fishermen-disciples catch fish (Luke 5:1–9; John 21:1–12)—a legitimate livelihood. He also would provide fish for his disciples to eat (John 21:9, 13). He miraculously fed fish to over five thousand people on one occasion (Mark 6:33–44) and to over four thousand people on another occasion (Mark 8:1–9). The celebration at the return of the prodigal son in Luke 15 calls for a feast—a killing of the fattened calf—a portrayal of the fact that Jesus "receives sinners and eats with them" (v. 2) and rejoices at the repentance of the lost.[14]

So the food chain *isn't* abnormal or "anticreational," and humans can freely eat meat as a good gift from God (although this doesn't mean consuming animals to the point of their extinction—something that would negate the "cultural mandate" in Genesis 1–2 to care for the earth as God's co-regents). If the food chain is built into creation, what was the difference *after* the fall? The fall meant that humans could be threatened by and become fearful of many animals. The *safety* and *invulnerability* of our first ancestors was removed. They became vulnerable to thorns, earthquakes from shifting tectonic plates, and other natural phenomena God built into the created order.

For the new heavens and new earth, however, God has promised to make a "covenant" for redeemed humans with the "beasts of the field, the birds of the sky, and the creeping things of the ground" (Hosea 2:18). There will be no more fear of predatory animals. Rather, the wolf will dwell with the lamb, and the cow and the bear will feed together (Isa. 11:6–9; 65:25). Wild animals will be *domesticated*.[15] One caution is in order: we have to be careful about overliteralizing these texts that refer to the new heavens and new earth (cf. Isa. 65:1). For instance, Isaiah 65:20 says that "the youth will die at the age of one hundred." But surely this is a picture of *living a long and full life* since there's no more death in this final state! British New Testament scholar C. F. D. Moule comments on Isaiah 11:6–9 (which mentions the bear grazing and the lion eating straw): "No one with a grain of sense believes that the passage . . . is intended literally, as though the digestive system of a carnivore were going to be transformed into that of [an] herbivore. What blasphemous injury would be done to great poetry . . . by laying such solemnly prosaic hands upon it!"[16] Even though the food chain was built into the animal kingdom at the first creation, there will be no danger in the renewed creation of the new heavens and earth.

Second, animal liberationists take philosophical naturalism for granted, but this worldview has deep philosophical problems. If God exists, then naturalism (and therefore the charge of speciesism) is false. As we've seen in an earlier chapter, naturalism doesn't have the kind of explanatory power that theism does. Naturalism faces immense intellectual challenges regarding its inability to explain, say, the origin of the universe, of first life, and of consciousness. Beyond this, there are many resources within theism that undercut and negate naturalism as the more viable worldview.[17] So why should a naturalistic worldview just be *assumed*?

There are excellent reasons for belief in God and for his creating us in his image. This should make one very cautious about undermining human uniqueness and our intuitions about it in the name of naturalism.

Third, animal liberationists claim that evolution justifies their position about nonhuman animals, but why think this is the case? Even if evolution were true, this by no means excludes God from consideration. For the sake of argument, what if God guided and utilized the evolutionary process to bring about his purposes, eventually endowing extraordinarily and complexly developed beings with dignity, moral responsibility, spiritual capabilities, culture-making gifts, and freedom? Some animal liberationists give the impression that if evolution is true, then objective moral values and human rights rooted in God are ruled out—or that humans are no different from nonhuman animals.

However, let's just say that large-scale evolution from a common ancestor took place. Even if biological evolution could explain how the diversity of species emerged, *this still wouldn't show God doesn't exist and that he couldn't have providentially directed the evolutionary process to accomplish his purposes.* Humans could *still* be considered unique and endowed with divine capacities—intrinsically superior to all animals—even if evolution could fully explain the diversity of species.[18] The bottom-line issue is not *creation versus evolution* but *naturalism versus supernaturalism.*

Fourth, evolution itself can't adequately explain (a) how the universe came into existence, (b) its amazing suitability to allow for biological life on earth, (c) the actual emergence of first life, and (d) the remarkably complex functions of an organism's very cells. These are all supportive of theism, not naturalism. Oxford zoologist Richard Dawkins has declared that Darwin made it possible to be an "intellectually fulfilled atheist."[19] Well, not so fast. To appeal simply to evolution as the blanket explanation for (and substitute for God's creation of) the existence of various animal (and plant) species makes some huge assumptions.

What's needed for evolution to have any chance of success? Let's look at some major factors that naturalistic evolutionists tend to bypass:

- The universe's *beginning*: The most widely accepted cosmological theory today—and one that fits very nicely with Genesis 1:1—is the Big Bang hypothesis. As Cambridge physicist Stephen Hawking points out: "Almost everyone now believes that the universe, and *time itself*, had a beginning at the Big Bang."[20]

- The amazing *fine-tuning* of the universe for biological life: The universe is "just right" for human existence (what has been called "the Goldilocks effect"). This earth is "tailor-made for life"—that is, it is uniquely inhabited and situated in the universe.[21]

- The emergence of *first life*: Five hundred to six hundred million years ago during "the Cambrian explosion," both simple and fairly complex life forms (e.g., trilobites) burst on the scene. To date, there has been no good naturalistic explanation for how life could emerge from nonlife.[22] (Incidentally, even if scientists *were* able to produce life from nonlife, it would be an indication of the need for much intelligent planning to pull this off!) The late evolutionist Stephen Jay Gould called this gap from nonlife to life "the enigma of paleontological enigmas."[23]

- *Irreducible complexity*: Biological evolution presupposes the existence of irreducibly complex cells of organisms; the various interworking parts of a cell are required all at once for a cell to function. This strongly suggests intelligent design and should not be taken for granted by the naturalist.[24]

So, clearly we have to go beyond the "evolution explains it all" argument since naturalistic evolution takes a lot for granted. The Big Bang, the universe's fine-tuning, the emergence of first life, and the irreducible complexity of cells are necessary for the journey of reproduction and survival even to get off the ground. Given naturalism, we should expect, if a universe could exist at all, a *lifeless* and *chaotic* one—hardly conducive to evolutionary development.

Fifth, animal liberation often involves making certain arbitrary assumptions regarding personhood. But why deny a fixed human nature, and why accept certain arbitrary criteria regarding personhood and what makes for a worthwhile life? In opposing "speciesism," some animal liberationists are often simply another brand of speciesists. Peter Singer, the chair of bioethics at Princeton University's Center for Human Values, is perhaps the most prominent spokesperson today for the animal liberationist position. Because of his commitment to atheism and biological evolution, he denies inherent human rights and the existence of a human nature. For Singer, to affirm human uniqueness is to be guilty of speciesism—the arbitrary favoring of one's own species over against others.

There's more to Singer's radical views. He goes so far as to say that *bestiality* is morally permissible. The reason for the "taboo" against bestiality has been the Judeo-Christian tradition: "Humans alone are made in the image of God. . . . In Genesis, God gives humans dominion over the animals." But in Singer's view, humans are just "great apes." Recognizing our alleged evolutionary connection to apes implies that bestiality will cease to be "an offence to our status and dignity as human beings."[25]

Given Singer's assumptions, he arbitrarily sets up his own list of criteria for personhood—self-consciousness, rationality, quality of life—by which an animal (human or nonhuman) can be judged fit to live. As in George Orwell's *Animal Farm*, Singer believes that "some animals are more equal than others." Certain *functions*—not your *nature*—make your life worth living. So Singer thinks that infants with Down's syndrome, hemophilia, spina bifida, or other "defects"—as well as elderly Alzheimer's patients—can justifiably be killed. In fact, Singer pronounces pigs or chimpanzees to be worthier of life than these *humans*, who are not *persons*.

We can ask: *Isn't Singer's position itself a kind of speciesism?* Ironically, Princeton University itself has a policy of no abusive or harassing behavior that "threatens" or "injures" another person—including the category of "handicap."[26] But hasn't Singer singled out certain humans for abuse and injury—namely, the young and the old? Isn't this a form of speciesism? In fact, philosopher Jenny Teichman calls Singer "cowardly." After all, the "bioethics lobby never targets anybody who might be able to hit back."[27]

Singer arbitrarily asks us to deny our fundamental instincts and accept his definition of personhood—based on measuring pleasure versus pain. He has arbitrarily assigned his own definitions of what a person is. Once he gets rid of human nature (which makes humans what they are and sets them apart from animals), then we are left with how organisms *function*. In light of his new functional definitions, he pronounces his blessing upon parents who kill their unwanted children. Singer and his ilk[28] assume a lot of suspicious metaphysical baggage, and these assumptions can be rightly questioned.

Sixth, animal liberationists like Singer who deny objective moral values exist demand that we suppress our deepest moral intuitions—the "Yuck factor"—and accept some Singerian assumptions (e.g., that individual humans don't have intrinsic worth). However, there's no good reason to deny what seems so obvious to us in favor of some animal liberationists' dubious denials. (Singer himself appears to have had difficulty denying them when it came to caring for his own mother.) I was speaking at a university in upstate New York, and during the Q&A time a female student stood up and charged me with being "ethnocentric." (At least she believed that ethnocentrism was wrong for all people everywhere!) When I asked why, she replied, "You believe that your morality should be imposed on other people."

I asked her, "If you're walking down a dark alley and you're about to be raped and there's a bystander who could help you, would you want that bystander to impose his morality on your attacker?"

She literally started trembling and said, "You're distorting what I'm saying."

I replied, "I'm not distorting what you're saying. It's easy to claim morality is relative when it's 'out there' and doesn't immediately affect me, but when someone violates my rights, deeply humiliates me, or steals my property, then I immediately recognize it as evil."

You see, we have certain intuitions in which we are *immediately or directly aware of something*. Why deny the intuition—in this case, an innate repulsion—toward rape, torturing babies for fun, or murder? We instinctively recognize that kindness and trustworthiness are virtues.

Romans 2:14–15 reminds us of this fact. Even pagans without the benefit of special revelation ("Gentiles") "who do not have the Law [of Moses] do instinctively the things of the Law," so that their conscience testifies to the rightness or wrongness of their actions ("alternately accusing or else defending them"). In Amos 1–2, God warns various Gentile nations of judgment because *they should have known better*. The Syrians acted ruthlessly ("they threshed Gilead with implements of sharp iron" [1:3]). The nation of Tyre would be judged because they broke the "covenant of brotherhood" with Israel and "delivered up an entire [Jewish] population" to Israel's enemy Edom (1:9; cf. 1:6). The Edomites (the descendents of Esau) as well shouldn't have "stifled . . . compassion" by pursuing and killing their Israelite blood brothers (1:11). The Ammonites suppressed their God-given conscience when they "ripped open the pregnant women of Gilead" to expand their territory (1:13).

These moral intuitions are a reflection of the image of God, and they should be taken seriously—particularly when there are no overriding reasons to reject them. Even though we don't *perceive* things perfectly, we don't stop trusting our senses. Similarly, just because our moral instincts aren't infallible, this doesn't mean we shouldn't take them seriously. These intuitions—our immediate grasp of the morally obvious—aren't simply hardwired into us for our survival; we don't "simply inherit" them, as skeptic Michael Shermer alleges.[29] If so, then morality simply is the way it is, but there's no reason to think we *ought* to follow it. After all, we are just acting according to predictable "scientific analysis"—what our DNA, evolution, and culture pass on to us.

Our instinctive revulsion toward rape, bestiality, or child abuse has been called the "Yuck factor." Now, rather than seeing this as evidence that objective moral values exist, Singer asks us to reject them in favor of his own utilitarian position, in which humans (or animals) have no value in themselves; they have *instrumental* worth: *results* determine the goodness of the action. (So it doesn't really matter what your *motives* are. All that counts is the *consequence* of your actions. But, of course, we *instinctively* know that wrong motives can undermine the goodness of an act—even if the consequences don't reveal it.)

Singer advises that instead of spending huge sums of money on care for the disabled or on cancer research, we spend money on the poor. Instead of waiting until severely brain-damaged human beings die, we should kill them and harvest their organs for healthier human specimens whose futures look "brighter."

Although we can disagree with Tom Regan's claim that animals have inherent worth and, therefore, rights, he's correct about the problem with utilitarianism. According to utilitarianism, humans are like liquid-holding *vessels*. What's important or valuable isn't the *vessel*, but the *liquids* themselves (i.e., the experience of pleasure):

> Here is an analogy to help make the philosophical point clearer: a cup contains different liquids—sometimes sweet, sometimes bitter, sometimes a mix of the two. What has value are the liquids: the sweeter the better; the bitterer the worse. The cup—the container—has no value. It's what goes into it, not what they go into, that has value. For the utilitarian, you and I are like the cup; we have no value as individuals and thus no equal value. What has value is what goes into us, what we serve as receptacles for; our feelings of satisfaction have positive value, our feelings of frustration have negative value.[30]

Furthermore, *Singer himself can't escape his own sense of moral obligation when it comes to his own mother.* When Singer's mother, Cora, became stricken with Alzheimer's and couldn't even recognize her own son or other relatives, did Peter Singer insist on having her put to death? No. Even though his mother had said, "When I can't tie my shoes and I can't read, I don't want to be here," Singer and his sister hired a group of home health aides to care for her—despite her inability to reason "as a person."[31] When he was asked how he could justify spending tens of thousands of dollars each year on his mother's care (instead of killing her and giving his money to the poor), he rationalized: "[It is] probably not the best use you could make of my money. That is true. But it does provide employment for a number of people who find something worthwhile in what they're doing."[32] It's easy for Singer to theorize about *another* person's seriously ill mother, but when it's Singer's own mom, he changes his tune. *Singer was borrowing from the Judeo-Christian ethic he so despises.* He couldn't deny the Yuck factor.

Seventh, we have basic moral instincts or intuitions that reflect an objective moral order. This is part of God's general revelation; people don't need the Bible to discover that murder, rape, or child abuse is wrong. Those who deny them need psychological or spiritual help. The burden of proof is on those who would deny what is so obvious to so many. It's this kind of moral recognition (and the moral responsibility that goes with it) that sets humans apart from animals.[33] In *The Abolition of Man,* C. S. Lewis has documented that the same sorts of moral standards—don't murder, don't take another's property, don't defraud, don't commit adultery, and so on—continually surface across civilizations/cultures and throughout history (Egyptian, Babylonian, Greek, Native American, etc.).[34] We don't need to look far to find commonalities. Such moral principles are *discovered,* not *invented.* This is part of God's *general revelation.* Without such principles, the idea of moral reform makes no sense. If one can't see that rape or murder is wrong, then something's definitely malfunctioning! Perhaps this is due to self-deception or hard-heartedness. But rightly thinking, morally sensitive people across the board readily recognize rape and murder as wrong. As part of God's general self-revelation, all people—unless they ignore or suppress their consciences—can and should have basic moral insight, knowing truths generally available to any morally sensitive person. We *just know* the rightness of virtues (kindness, trustworthiness, unselfishness, etc.). *The burden of proof falls on those who deny this.*

Atheist philosopher Kai Nielsen comments on the vileness of child abuse and wife-beating:

> It is more reasonable to believe such elemental things to be evil than to believe any skeptical theory that tells us we cannot know or reasonably believe any of these things to be evil. . . . I firmly believe that this is bedrock and right and that anyone who does not believe it cannot have probed deeply enough into the grounds of his moral beliefs.[35]

As we'll see in the next chapter, this basic moral awareness and the capacity to freely live in accordance with it (or resist it) are what set human beings apart from animals.

*Eighth, the very charge of "Speciesist!" presupposes an objective moral standard and makes a value judgment. Where did **this** come from in a naturalistic world? Why think that value should emerge from valueless processes? Why ought I assume all animals—human and nonhuman—are morally equal and ought to be treated as equals? It's easier to believe that value would come from value (e.g., God) rather than from valueless* *physical processes.* In an engaging debate book on God's existence, the agnostic philosopher Paul Draper says that our bias toward human beings over animals is really unjustified *prejudice.* Animals "have full moral standing" and shouldn't be harmed.[36]

Christian philosopher William Craig writes in response: While animals shouldn't be abused or treated cruelly in the Jewish-Christian view, why think that *any*thing has moral worth if we are just the products of evolutionary development? We should *expect* nature to be "red in tooth and claw," and it seems that one animal's preying upon another is simply *neutral.* In going through the metaphysical supermarket, Draper has actually helped himself to typically theistic features of the universe by applying moral values to humans and animals. Draper seems to take for granted the existence of objective moral values that are already in place and aren't dependent upon evolutionary development of moral awareness.[37] Again, why think moral *value* should emerge from *valueless* processes? It makes better sense to say *value comes from value*—which fits theism very nicely.

Naturalist philosopher Simon Blackburn admits that he can't adequately answer the relativist's challenge: "Nature has no concern for good or bad, right or wrong. . . . We cannot get behind ethics." And questions of moral knowledge and moral progress can only be answered "from within our own moral perspective." And while he admits that "dignity" is better than "humiliation,"[38] it is reasonable to ask: *Why can't this desire for affirming rights and dignity actually support God's existence—especially since naturalism doesn't have the resources to account for such values?*

Ninth, because there are basic moral values, we must be careful not to confuse matters by making moral judgments starting with gray areas. When making moral judgments, we must begin with the clear and move to the unclear; we begin with the obvious and move to the less obvious. We've all heard the question, "Who are *you* to impose your morality on others?" Of course, the person raising this question believes it's *morally wrong* to impose morality on another! The question presupposes a moral standard. But where did *that* standard come from?

After "Who are *you* to impose your morality on others?" the question that generally follows is: "Okay, then *whose* morality should we follow? The Hindu's, the Buddhist's, the atheist's?" At this point we can raise the question: "Do you really have any problem with saying that rape, murder, child abuse, or torturing people for fun is wrong?" This is an excellent and nonarbitrary place to start. Such moral norms are available to all morally sensitive people (through God's general revelation). As C. S. Lewis observed in *The Abolition of Man*, these sorts of moral principles are obvious to properly functioning human beings. Objective moral values do exist, and we can recognize them.

However, some people think that if moral gray areas exist, then this somehow calls into question the existence of objective moral values. Once when I spoke to a philosophy class at a college in Indiana, some of the students wondered how there could be objective moral values if moral dilemmas and challenges exist. However, the existence of gray areas doesn't mean that we can't readily recognize general moral principles. In making moral judgments, we must begin with the clear and move to the unclear, not vice versa. Just because moral uncertainty or ambiguity exists, this doesn't eclipse the morally obvious. As the lexicographer Samuel Johnson put it, "The fact that there is such a thing as twilight does not mean that we cannot distinguish between day and night."

We intuitively and immediately recognize human moral worth, dignity, and rights. What's far less obvious—or not obvious at all—is that "nonhuman animals" have these qualities. But we'll look at this topic in more detail in the next chapter.

Tenth, since ideas have consequences, we should take seriously the dreadful consequences that flow from naturalistic assumptions. Perhaps it's instructive to illustrate the implications of a bold naturalism that diminishes human dignity, claiming that humans are merely animals. We've already seen this with Peter Singer, but let's take a look at Jeffrey Dahmer.

Despite being brought up to believe in God and that human beings are intrinsically valuable, Jeffrey Dahmer was exposed to naturalistic evolution. The result was devastating. This sexual predator and cannibal "placed the blame for [his] murders on his atheistic beliefs and the theory of evolution." Given naturalism, he found no basis for affirming intrinsic human dignity. His father, Lionel Dahmer, expressed Jeffrey's rationale: "If it all happens naturalistically, what's the need for a God? Can't I set my own rules? Who owns me? I own myself."[39]

In the absence of God, human dignity, objective moral values, and a sensitive conscience, such a move isn't surprising. On one hand, we can be grateful that there are many "moral atheists" who experience God's common grace through conscience, communal cooperation, and cultural development. On the other hand, it's not surprising that the rejection of God by some brings with it a removal of any solid foundation for objective moral values and human dignity. This can obviously diminish moral motivation and lead to the suppression of conscience, even to Dahmer-like behavior.

Let's summarize where we've been. When comparing naturalism and theism, we've seen some very good reasons to believe that God's existence helps us make better sense of the available data than do competing hypotheses.[40] Also, the naturalistic appeal "evolution explains it all" is inadequate because (a) it is theoretically possible that God could have guided the evolutionary process to accomplish his purposes, and (b) evolution presupposes the origin and fine-tuning of the universe as well as the origin of first life and the functioning of amazingly complex cells—all nicely explained by theism and without which biological evolution couldn't get going. Thus animal liberationists who assume that evolution "explains everything" are mistaken; they must go beyond this pseudo-explanation to account for the origin and fine-tuning of the universe—and the most basic (cellular) structures of organisms. Furthermore, we saw that hardcore animal liberationists like Peter Singer can't consistently deny the Yuck factor, which stands as yet another support for God's existence. Furthermore, the claim of "speciesism" assumes a moral standard—that it's always wrong to be speciesist—and that value emerged from valueless processes.

So some of these philosophical questions related to the animal-liberation question should be considered and defended before simply declaring that animals have rights, that primates and humans are pretty much alike, or that not believing this is "speciesist."

SUMMARY

- Animal liberationists often hold to a number of shaky and inconsistent philosophical and metaphysical assumptions. Their positions are often merely asserted, not defended.

- God originally created the food chain as part of his "very good" creation, which involved animal death. The fall introduced *human*—not animal—death (in addition to human vulnerability to dangers from the animal kingdom). However, there will be no fear of predatory animals in the new heavens and earth.

- Animal liberationists take philosophical naturalism for granted, but this worldview has deep philosophical problems. If God exists, then naturalism (and therefore the charge of speciesism) is false.

- Animal liberationists claim that evolution justifies their position about nonhuman animals, but why think this is the case? For the sake of argument, what if God guided and utilized the evolutionary process to bring about his purposes, eventually endowing extraordinarily and complexly developed beings with dignity, moral responsibility, spiritual capabilities, culture-making gifts, and freedom?

- Evolution itself can't adequately explain (a) how the universe came into existence, (b) its amazing suitability to allow for biological life on earth, (c) the actual emergence of first life, and (d) the remarkably complex functions of an organism's very cells. These are all supportive of theism, not naturalism.

- Animal liberation often involves making certain arbitrary assumptions regarding personhood. But why deny a fixed human nature, and why accept certain arbitrary criteria regarding personhood and what makes for a worthwhile life (e.g., level of rationality, self-consciousness)? In opposing "speciesism," some animal liberationists are simply another brand of speciesists.

- Animal liberationists like Singer who deny that objective moral values exist demand that we suppress our deepest moral intuitions—the "Yuck factor"—and accept some Singerian assumptions. However, there is no good reason to deny what seems so obvious to us in favor of some animal liberationists' dubious denials. (Singer himself appears to have had difficulty denying moral obligation when it came to caring for his own mother.)

- We have basic moral instincts or intuitions that reflect an objective moral order. This is part of God's general revelation; people don't need the Bible to discover that murder, rape, or child abuse is wrong. Those who deny basic moral instincts need psychological or spiritual help. The burden of proof is on those who would deny what is so obvious to so many. It is this kind of moral recognition (and the moral responsibility that goes with it) that sets humans apart from animals.

- The very charge of "Speciesist!" presupposes an objective moral standard and makes a value judgment. Where did *this* come from in a naturalistic world? But why think that value should emerge from valueless processes? Why ought I assume all animals—human and nonhuman—are morally equal and ought to be treated as equals? It's easier to believe that value would come from value (e.g., God) rather than from valueless physical processes.

- Because there are basic moral values, we must be careful not to confuse matters by making moral judgments starting with gray areas. When making moral judgments, we must begin with the clear and move to the unclear; we must begin with the obvious and move to the less obvious.

- Since ideas have consequences, we should take seriously the dreadful consequences that flow from naturalistic assumptions.

FURTHER READING

Budziszewski, J. *What We Can't Not Know*. Dallas: Spence, 2004.

Hare, John. *Can We Be Good without God?* Downers Grove, IL: Inter-Varsity, 2002.

Wiker, Benjamin. *Moral Darwinism: How We Became Hedonists*. Downers Grove, IL: InterVarsity, 2003.

10

ANIMALS HAVE RIGHTS JUST LIKE HUMANS DO

What makes humans different from chimps? Just slightly different DNA? Or are the differences deeply significant? In this chapter, we build on the previous one. Here we want to look beyond important worldview considerations to the animal-rights or animal-liberation question specifically. There *are* good reasons for thinking human beings have intrinsic dignity and rights and that animals—though important and part of God's good creation—do not have such rights. Rights come with having been made in the image of God. In fact, because humans have been made in God's image, they (as co-regents with God) are to care for creation, not despoil it. The solution *is not* to ascribe rights to animals, but rather to recognize what our God-given responsibilities are as human beings to the rest of creation for the glory of God.

*First, why, given naturalism, should **any** animals—human or non-human—have any rights or value at all? Why think that **anything** has value if all organisms have emerged from valueless processes? How could we justify moving from the "is" (the way things are) to the "ought" (the way things should be), from mere descriptive, scientific facts to moral values and rights?* Tom Regan claims that while *humans* are "moral agents," *animals* are "moral patients." He says that a mammal (though not fish, birds, or other nonmammals) is a "subject-of-a-life." Because of its consciousness, memories, and feelings of pleasure and pain, it has "inherent value."[1]

However, it's hard to see how we should logically move from these psychological features to conclude that they confer rights upon animals. This, philosopher David Oderberg remarks, "is not something Regan is able to tell us."[2] Again, an animal-rights activist like Regan can't just *assert* the value of animals; he must show *why* they have it. Along these lines, I think of the United Nations Universal Declaration of Human Rights (1948), which announces—without foundation—that human beings have rights:

> All human beings are born free and equal in dignity and rights. They are endowed with reason and conscience and should act towards one another in a spirit of brotherhood.[3]

Unless we have value given from the outset, it's hard to see how value could emerge from nonvalue. However, the existence of a supremely valuable Being, who made humans in his image, would furnish us with just such a basis.

Second, if human beings are thought to have greater value than (non-human) animals, then this would suggest a theistic worldview (in which humans are made in God's image) rather than a naturalistic worldview (in which humans are merely more complex animals). According to Darwin and Darwinists, humans are *not* different from animals in *kind*, only in *degree*. Darwin claimed that the "mental powers of the higher animals" are the same kind found in humans, differing only in degree. Humans have no elevated status. However, Darwin did slip up when he considered some civilizations superior to others. He spoke of "the inferior and less favoured race," the "civilized" *versus* the "savage" and "lower" races. Without any trace of political correctness, Darwin proclaimed that the "western nations of Europe . . . now so immeasurably surpass their former savage progenitors, and stand at the summit of civilization."[4]

But if naturalistic evolution is true, why think there's an ideal civilization at all? Why think one civilization is *better* than another? Wouldn't this suggest some kind of standard toward which humans should strive? If Darwinists suggest there's some standard ("organisms or civilizations are *better* this way than that way"), then an assumed design-plan that is *beyond* nature has been slipped in.

Animal liberationists hold a "continuist" view: there's an evolutionary connection—and thus a continuity—between humans and "nonhuman animals." British philosopher Mary Midgley has said that there's no "progress" or evolutionary "ladder." Consistent Darwinists reject the idea of "higher" or "lower" life-forms, which would suggest improvement and thus an ideal. Nor is there any "human nature" to set us apart from nonhuman animals. Humans are just advanced animals. This "continuist" view assumes our "kinship" with nonhuman animals because we both have *sentience*—the capacity to feel pleasure or pain—which our nervous system makes possible. Midgley writes that there's no "progress" in evolution, as this would imply a *purpose* or *design-plan*. Animals "either survive, or they don't."[5] That's all.

We've seen that animal liberationist Peter Singer rejects the Judeo-Christian worldview. This philosophy of life (in which humans are made in God's image) is in competition with his naturalistic views. But if evolutionists slip into the belief that humans have rights or dignity or that some forms of life are "higher" than others, such a view better reflects theism, not naturalism.

Third, some animal liberationists charge that the belief that humans— and not "nonhuman animals"—have intrinsic dignity is "speciesist"—comparable to racism or sexism. However, racism denies that those from other races are **equal in their essence or nature,** *and sexism denies that those of the opposite sex are equal in their essence or nature as well.* It's not unusual to hear some animal liberationists claim that belief in the unique status of human beings is *speciesism*, which is comparable to *racism* or *sexism*. But this is a false accusation. Comparing *speciesism* to *racism* or *sexism* mixes up certain categories. On the one hand, racism and sexism *deny the equality of nature*, which is morally wrong. All human beings—regardless of race or gender—have intrinsic dignity. On the other hand, those crying, "Speciesist!" *claim equality where there is none.* Naturalistic evolution denies—without adequate justification—that there's any such thing as a nature or essence (which makes each thing what it is and not something else).[6] Speciesism reintroduces *nature* or *essence*, which runs contrary to naturalistic evolutionary thinking. (Ironically, the same persons who argue for animal rights and desperately try to preserve the eggs of endangered turtle species don't bat an eye at the abortion of unborn humans. They're speciesists toward the unborn.)

Fourth, rights are linked to personhood. Because humans are made in the likeness of a personal God, they are intrinsically (essentially) valuable. Our essence or nature—not our function—is more basic and defining. Some people assume that if humans have rights because they have the capacity to be rational, self-conscious, or morally responsible, then they must have this capacity *right now.*[7] And since, say, human infants don't act rationally or with moral responsibility, they must not have intrinsic rights. However, rights come by virtue of *who we are by nature* (or essence), not simply because of *how we function in the present.* If our worth is determined by whether we are presently self-aware or able to reason with some sophistication (unlike infants or Alzheimer's patients), then *wouldn't we all lose our rights while we are sleeping?* What if we're temporarily comatose (because of a brain injury) but then recover? Did we *lose* our personhood and rights while we were "out of it"—only to regain them shortly thereafter? This seems absurd. It's because of our *nature* that we have certain capacities that can be realized.

So we must be careful about defining ourselves simply by how we function—although functions (self-consciousness, moral awareness, language) can serve as important indicators of human uniqueness. We have intrinsic rights because of our *nature*, which makes us what we are—humans—and not some other creature. So even the tiniest of human beings has rights, not because she *presently thinks rationally and freely chooses and is self-conscious*, but because of her *nature*. It is our common human nature that actually enables us as human beings to have these capacities.

Fifth, animal liberationists often draw comparisons between humans and animals on the basis of language, but this is flawed. Chimps/apes are quite incapable of the profound language-use that human beings possess. Some animal rights activists will say that animals—like humans—have the capacity to learn language. However, in study after study, "the attempt to teach apes language can only be viewed objectively as a failure."[8]

Usually the language trainers tend to be wishful thinkers, and skeptical observers who are allowed to see "language learning" tend to be just as skeptical (or more so) than they were before. Indeed, "language-trained" apes don't approach total strangers and initiate conversation.[9] Naturalist Steven Pinker of Harvard declares that the "chimp's abilities at anything one would want to call grammar [are] next to nil."[10]

Sixth, animals, by their nature, don't have free will (the power of self-determination), and they don't act with any awareness of moral responsibility. Without such a capacity, animals don't have rights. Because humans have such a capacity by nature (through God's gracious gift of the divine image), this confers upon them a certain moral shield or moral protection which animals don't have.

Jane Goodall tells of her study of the chimpanzees ("our closest relatives") of Gombe National Park in Tanzania. It's not a pretty picture. She observed that these chimps would hunt the smaller colobus monkeys for meat (sometimes eating them alive), and female chimps would kill the young of other females in their own troop to maintain their dominance.[11] She was shocked when adult males attacked females and killed babies that got in their way.

On one notable occasion, she was horrified to see a particular chimp, Satan, drinking the blood of another. And the usually "benign" Rodolf was standing to throw a four-pound rock at another prostrate chimp. Jomeo was tearing the skin off De's thigh. Passion was gorging on the flesh of Gilka's baby. However, Goodall states that there are notable differences between such animals and humans: "Only humans, I believe, are capable of *deliberate* cruelty—acting with the intention of causing pain and suffering."[12] She admits that humans "have developed intellectual abilities which dwarf those of even the most gifted chimpanzees."[13]

While animals may be *conscious* or *aware*, they lack an important aspect of moral responsibility—namely, *self-awareness*. This capacity enables us to be aware of what we're doing. Unlike animals, *we're aware that we're aware; we can think about our own thoughts—as well as our actions*. Oderberg writes:

> Nor is there evidence that chimpanzees or other animals have self-consciousness in the sense of being able to think *about their own*

thoughts, reflect on their own reasoning processes, to make judgements about their own judgements. Apes can learn, like many other kinds of animal, but there is no credible evidence that they learn *from their mistakes,* as opposed to learning from their trainers or their environment. To learn from your mistakes you need first to know *that you have made a mistake,* that is, that your original thought about something was in some way wrong. No animal behavior suggests this to be the case.[14]

Without this capacity for self-awareness, animals inherently lack what is required for acting morally. Acting morally involves *being aware of what we are doing* and *that we are doing it freely.* Without this awareness of what our action involves and that we are acting *freely,* we can't make sense of moral actions. *Humans* can act with this awareness; animals can't. Animals simply act *according* to their nature, and no one thinks that animals are morally blameworthy for their actions. The male mallard duck commits acts that look like "rape" (forcing himself on any available female), but we don't suggest that this is immoral. If lion parents happen to kill their offspring, we don't consider this wrong or evil—something like cannibalism. We don't lock up or punish cheetahs for killing zebras. We don't force veggie burgers on carnivorous animals, throwing the food chain off balance. Why is it fine for animals to eat meat but not for humans to do so?

We intuitively or immediately recognize that animals are distinct from human beings. While there's some overlap (e.g., both possess a biological existence that involves eating, sleeping, reproducing, etc.), we still don't hold animals responsible for their actions. Of all earthly creatures, *only* human beings are able to act in a manner that is *contrary* to their nature—the human nature God created to be good. That is, humans are able to act in a manner to enhance and develop themselves or to destroy themselves.[15]

Seventh, animals operate according to instinct and react to their environmental constraints in order to survive and reproduce. Human beings have the capacity to pursue the truth and to live by it—even if doing so doesn't provide any biological advantages. In an earlier chapter, we saw that an increasing number of naturalists are separating truth from knowledge, and knowledge is becoming increasingly linked to survival-

and reproduction-enhancement. Truth takes a backseat to survival. The pragmatist Richard Rorty goes so far as to say that truth is simply un-Darwinian:

> The idea that one species of organism is, unlike all the others, oriented not just toward its own increated prosperity but toward Truth, is as un-Darwinian as the idea that every human being has a built-in moral compass—a conscience that swings free of both social history and individual luck.[16]

If we're concerned about the truth, perhaps there's more to us than mere biological function.

Eighth, unlike animals, humans have many capacities that animals don't have—the capacity to grasp the meaningfulness and depth of their relationships, actions, and abilities; to be self-conscious; to rise above instinct and environment; to create culture; and to relate to God. In the movie *Turner and Hooch*,[17] police detective Scott Turner (played by Tom Hanks) takes in a French Mastiff, Hooch, after realizing that his owner (an acquaintance of Turner's) has been killed. In addition to his remarkable capacity for bringing disorder out of order, Hooch's ability to slobber and drool is simply astonishing. The first night in Turner's home, Hooch the Pooch single-pawedly trashes it, knocking over food containers, destroying furniture, and—for a brief moment—even locking Turner out of his own home!

At one point in the movie, Turner leaves Hooch in his car while he stops by his office. When he returns, he sees that his adorable French Mastiff has just torn the car's interior to shreds. Horrified, Turner yells at the dog—with no visible impact. Realizing the fruitlessness of screaming, he asks in exasperation, "What am I yelling at you for? You're a dog." Indeed.

Animal rights proponent Tom Regan claims that some animals are "moral patients" while humans are "moral agents." Why should we consider animals to be "moral patients"? Because, it's argued, they can feel pain and pleasure (*sentience*) because of their complex nervous systems. But is sentience enough to confer rights upon them? It's hard to see how. Animals lack the necessary capacities for a morally and spiritually significant life:

- Animals can *sense*, but humans can *understand*.
- Animals act *instinctively*, whereas humans act *freely*.
- Animals *react to* their environment, but humans can *rise above* it and *reflect upon* it.
- Animals are *aware*, while humans are *self-aware*. Animals have *consciousness*, but humans are *self-conscious*—they can think about their own thinking.
- Animals can *act*, but humans can *knowingly, responsibly act* as agents.
- Animals operate by instincts and react to their environment in an *attempt to survive and reproduce*. Humans can *seek and live by truth apart from any survival value it may have*.
- Unlike animals, humans can *recognize that their lives have a deep moral significance*.
- Unlike animals, humans can *grasp the profundity of death*.
- Unlike animals, humans can *recognize the pain or pleasure that moral choices can bring*.
- Unlike animals, humans can *recognize the depths of evil and suffering*.
- Unlike animals, humans can *comprehend the depth of human relationships* and *meaningfully express these relationships through language*.
- Unlike animals, humans can *create culture*—that is, create order, appreciate beauty, enhance human flourishing, care for the earth, and so on.
- Unlike animals, humans (because they are made in God's image) can *relate to him and pursue/promote his kingdom* (i.e., rule or reign). Ultimately, the primary and most basic right human beings have is to participate (by God's gracious initiative) in the kingdom of God.

These monumental differences between animals and humans are striking. While animals should not be treated cruelly or with disregard, this doesn't mean that they have intrinsic rights. Animals don't possess within themselves key capacities—particularly the capacity to deliberate, freely choose, and rise above instinct and environment.

Ninth, the elevation of animals to the status of rights-bearers actually diminishes the significance of human beings. We've seen that animal liberationists, who are typically evolutionists, try to minimize differences between humans and nonhuman animals. PETA cofounder Ingrid Newkirk's mantra, "A rat is a pig is a dog is a boy," is rather frightening. But if humans are just animals, then why don't we just get rid of the word *person* from our vocabulary? To call animals "persons" (as Peter Singer does) is just playing word games since *person* adds nothing that isn't already contained in the term *animal*.[18]

Of course, we may actually be undermining medical advancement and progress in disease research if all medical experimentation on animals is prohibited by pressure groups like PETA or the Animal Liberation Front (ALF). And if humans are equal to rats and dogs *and* aren't "useful to society," why not do medical research on them? Believe it or not, this Nazi-like idea is exactly what Peter Singer proposes: "I'm not comfortable with any invasive research on chimps. I would ask, Is there no other way? And I think there are other ways. I would say, What about getting the consent of relatives of people in vegetative states?"[19] *These* are the depths we sink to when we reduce humans to animals.

Tenth, to treat animals humanely, we do not need to bestow rights upon them. Rather, we must treat them according to the creation mandate given us by God to be stewards of the earth and to care for it (Genesis 1–2; Psalm 8). The animal rights movement in the West has degenerated from the common humane treatment of animals (rooted in the Jewish-Christian worldview of humans as caretakers of animals) to a hard-line ideology.[20] It's ironic that animals in the West have generally gotten increasingly better treatment—often initiated by Christians concerned about being stewards/caring for the earth—and not by endowing them with rights.

Why shouldn't we purposelessly raze redwood or sequoia forests? Is it because trees have rights? Not at all. It would be an abuse of our human stewardship. It would ruin something beautiful and majestic and worth preserving. Why make the effort to preserve endangered animal species? Because they have rights? No, but because this is part of our stewardship. We must be careful about a particular danger: *By elevating the status of animals, the animal rights movement actually diminishes the significance of human beings.*

Eleventh, if the suffering of nonhuman animals is evil, then don't we have an obligation to prevent nonhuman animal predation? Shouldn't we stop lions from preying upon zebras and gazelles? However, doing so would mean massive interference with the natural habits and habitats of these animals. As we saw in the previous chapter, the "food chain" is just built into the way things are in the natural world.[21]

Furthermore, we must understand that human stewardship over the animal kingdom is not a reflection of a *human-centered* universe;[22] rather, it reflects a *God-centered* universe, in which humans are co-regents with God over creation. This responsibility should result in care for the earth (rather than spoliation of the earth), a concern about endangered species, and forethought for future generations of human beings and vital ecosystems. *Such concern, however, can produce proper care for animals without ascribing rights to them.*

Twelfth, while animals do not have rights, as humans do, they're a valuable part of the created order and should not be treated cruelly or mistreated. One doesn't have to advocate animal rights (or treat them as persons) in order to ensure proper care for animals; rather, one must uphold human responsibility to care for creation. We can be grateful for animal liberationists exposing legitimate abuses of animals. Animals shouldn't be mindlessly slaughtered, and we as stewards of God's creation should guard against the extinction of animals (although I think we could do with a lot fewer mosquitoes!). Bullfights and cockfights are examples of pointless harming of animals. If animals are under our care as pets, we shouldn't deny them proper food, water, and protection.[23] That said, we shouldn't infer that animals have rights.

Despite what animal liberationists like Peter Singer charge, the Christian Scriptures promote concern for and care of animals—even if they aren't rights-bearing creatures:

- *Exodus 20:10; 23:12; Deuteronomy 5:14:* God commanded Israel to allow rest on the Sabbath day—not only for the entire household, but for "your ox," "your donkey," and "your cattle" as well.

- *Exodus 23:4–5:* An ox or donkey that wanders away from its master is to be returned.
- *Leviticus 25:7:* Along with the needy poor, "your cattle and the animals that are in your land" can eat from fields left fallow during the Sabbath year.
- *Proverbs 12:10:* "A righteous man has regard for the life of his animal," whereas "even the compassion of the wicked is cruel."
- *Luke 14:5:* If an ox (or a child!) falls into a well on the Sabbath, any right-thinking person would help it out.

Humans have certain responsibilities toward animals, and when these are attended to, it becomes readily more apparent that there's no reason to pursue rights-status for them. The reason we don't abuse animals isn't because they have rights[24] but because we have responsibilities as stewards or caretakers of the earth.

Thirteenth, animals, though not possessing rights, do have value as part of God's creation; humans have a responsibility to care for and enjoy the benefits of God's creation without reckless destruction (say, to near-extinction) or cruelty. In the movie *As Good as It Gets,*[25] the writer Melvin Udall (Jack Nicholson) is a psychologically disordered, offensive bigot who is as bad as they get. To one woman who admires his writings and asks for the source of his insights about women ("How do you write [about] women so well?"), he sneeringly responds, "I think of men, and I take away reason and accountability." He is cruel to gays; he insults Jews; and he pushes his neighbor's dog, Virdell, down the garbage chute in his apartment complex. Carol Connelly (Helen Hunt) is the only waitress he likes at "his diner" (and the only waitress who can tolerate him). At one point she asks him, "Do you have any control over how creepy you allow yourself to get?"

After Melvin's neighbor Simon is attacked and hospitalized, Melvin is forced to take care of Virdell. Melvin finds himself softening toward the dog and actually caring for it, daily bringing home for him a treat of bacon strips from his breakfast at the diner. This is one of the many breakthroughs in Melvin's life that contribute to his learning about compassion and his becoming more human.

When young children take delight in destroying or harming animals, this should be a warning sign to parents: such lack of concern can spill over into other areas. Children should be taught to treat animals kindly, not cruelly. This can be good training ground for cultivating an attitude of compassion and for learning lessons in not taking advantage of the less powerful.

Fourteenth, even though animals do not have rights, they are part of God's good creation and can bring much benefit and blessing to human beings in a world created not for the glory of **humans** *but for* **God's** *glory: the creation should be viewed theocentrically rather than anthropocentrically.* Here we build on the previous point: Even if they don't have intrinsic rights, animals (like humans) have a certain role in the created order, and they can bring much benefit and delight to human beings. Humans, as those who were given a caretaking stewardship over creation, have a different *role* than animals do. One of the roles of animals may be to serve as food for human beings as part of God's gracious gift to human beings.[26] (Think of whole countries that depend heavily upon fish for protein in their diet; the obligation to be strictly vegetarian would simply be impractical.)

Besides this, animals have other roles to play that bring benefit to human beings:[27]

- Animals can *entertain* us. Having attended the famous Moscow Circus in 2002, I well remember the dancing bears that had been trained to do remarkable (and hilarious) feats.
- Animals can *teach us valuable lessons.* (Think of the references Scripture makes to animals and the lessons sparrows, ants, or oxen can teach us.) The avid bird-watcher and theologian John Stott has written a delightful book on birds in Scripture and how they can instruct us spiritually—an exercise in *orni-theology!*[28]
- Animals can *help us advance in areas of science and human health care.* As part of human stewardship of the animal kingdom, human health and well-being can be enhanced, thanks to animals.
- People (like Melvin Udall) can *learn to care* for pets or work animals, which can be instructive for caring within human relationships as well.
- Pets can *bring comfort.* Think of the lonely elderly who love and appreciate their dogs or cats, which bring cheer and a sense of companionship.

- Animals can *open our eyes to the beauty and joy of God's creation and prompt greater concern in us to preserve this beauty and the species that inhabit God's good earth.* The first time I went snorkeling (in the Bahamas) with friends of mine, a new world of delight was opened up to me. It gave me a greater appreciation for God's world and renewed gratitude for people who work hard to preserve delicate and endangered coral reefs.

On the other hand, animals shouldn't be so *sentimentalized* that they are somehow elevated to the level of human beings in our minds. Animated movies such as Disney's *Brother Bear* are particularly good at doing this. *Real* bears can maim and kill! In addition, there are times, for example, when deer or coyotes need to be weeded out to preserve human livelihoods or to prevent them from being hazards in other ways.

David Oderberg suggests that human beings be guided by the principle of modesty: "aversion to luxurious living, attention to necessities such as food, clothing and shelter, and respect for nature."[29] I would add that in all of our considerations we must be *God*-centered rather than *human*-centered. God made all things—including animals—ultimately for *his* pleasure. (Just think of the delight God must get from porpoises frolicking in the open sea, blue or sperm whales rising up and crashing back down into the ocean, otters sliding into the water and playing about, or the oddly configured platypus shoveling around for food on river bottoms!) While humans can enjoy what God has created, we must also remember for whom all things have been made. Animals are not "there" purely for humans to enjoy. We live in a God-centered world, not a human-centered one. This has ramifications regarding how we treat animals.

I should add that there's certainly nothing wrong with a strictly vegetarian diet. Paul says that someone might eat only vegetables, while another has meat in his diet (Rom. 14:2–3). Either is fine, although "nothing is unclean in itself" (Rom. 14:14). Whether one eats meat or refrains (and erring on the side of vegetables is a pretty good idea for one's health!), this shouldn't be made a measuring rod of one's spirituality (or lack thereof).

In the end we can *both* (a) deny that animals have rights *and* (b) show concern and respect for sentient creatures.[30] Affirming the intrinsic rights of human beings (as they have been made in God's image) doesn't mean animals will inevitably be abused. *That* is the result of ignoring our responsibility to care for the creation as divinely appointed stewards for *God's* glory—not our own.

SUMMARY

- Why, given naturalism, should *any* animals—human or nonhuman—have any rights or value at all? Why think that *anything* has value if all organisms have emerged from valueless processes? How could we justify moving from the "is" (the way things are) to the "ought" (the way things should be), from mere descriptive, scientific facts to moral values and rights?
- *If* human beings are thought to have greater value than (nonhuman) animals, then this would suggest a theistic worldview (in which humans are made in God's image) rather than a naturalistic worldview (in which humans are merely more complex animals).
- Some animal liberationists charge that the belief that humans—and not "nonhuman animals"—have intrinsic dignity is "speciesist"—comparable to racism or sexism. However, racism denies that those from other races are *equal in their essence or nature*, and sexism denies that those of the opposite sex are equal in their essence or nature as well.
- Rights are linked to personhood. Because humans are made in the likeness of a personal God, they are intrinsically (essentially) valuable. Our essence or nature—not our function— is more basic and defining.
- Animal liberationists often draw comparisons between humans and animals on the basis of language, but this is flawed. Chimps/apes are quite incapable of the profound language use that human beings possess.
- Animals, by their nature, don't have free will (the power of self-determination), and they don't act with any awareness of moral responsibility. Without such a capacity, animals don't have rights.

Because humans have such a capacity by nature (through God's gracious gift of the divine image), this confers upon them a certain moral shield or moral protection which animals don't have.

- Animals operate according to instinct and react to their environmental constraints in order to survive and reproduce. Human beings have the capacity to pursue the truth and to live by it—even if doing so doesn't provide any biological advantages.

- Unlike animals, humans have many capacities that animals don't have—the capacity to grasp the meaningfulness and depth of their relationships, actions, and abilities; to be self-conscious; to rise above instinct and environment; to create culture; and to relate to God.

- The elevation of animals to the status of rights-bearers actually diminishes the significance of human beings (e.g., inhibiting medical advancement by prohibiting all experimentation on animals).

- To treat animals humanely, we do not need to bestow rights upon them. Rather, we must treat them according to the creation mandate given us by God to be stewards of the earth and to care for it (Genesis 1–2; Psalm 8).

- If the suffering of nonhuman animals is evil, then don't we have an obligation to prevent nonhuman animal predation?

- While animals do not have rights, as humans do, they are a valuable part of the created order and should not be treated cruelly or mistreated. One doesn't have to advocate animal rights (or treat them as persons) in order to ensure proper care for animals; rather, one must uphold human responsibility to care for creation.

- Animals, though not possessing rights, do have value as part of God's creation; humans have a responsibility to care for and enjoy the benefits of God's creation without reckless destruction (say, to near-extinction) or cruelty.

- Even though animals do not have rights, they are part of God's good creation and can bring much benefit and blessing to human beings in a world created not for the glory of *humans* but for *God's* glory: the creation should be viewed theocentrically rather than anthropocentrically.

FURTHER READING

Oderberg, David S. "Animals." Chap. 3 in *Applied Ethics*. Malden, MA:
    Blackwell, 2000.

Preece, Gordon, ed. *Rethinking Peter Singer: A Christian Critique*. Down-
    ers Grove, IL: InterVarsity, 2002.

Reichmann, James B. *Evolution, Animal "Rights," and the Environment*.
    Washington: Catholic University of America Press, 2000.

Stott, John. *The Birds Our Teachers: Biblical Lessons from a Lifelong Bird
    Watcher*. Grand Rapids: Baker Books, 2001.

PART III

SLOGANS RELATED TO CHRISTIANITY

11

How Could God Command Abraham to Sacrifice Isaac?

Now it came about . . . that God tested Abraham, and said to him, "Abraham!" And he said, "Here I am." He said, "Take now your son, your only son, whom you love, Isaac, and go to the land of Moriah, and offer him there as a burnt offering on one of the mountains of which I will tell you." So Abraham rose early in the morning and saddled his donkey, and took two of his young men with him and Isaac his son; and he split wood for the burnt offering, and arose and went to the place of which God had told him. On the third day Abraham raised his eyes and saw the place from a distance. Abraham said to his young men, "Stay here with the donkey, and I and the lad will go over there; and we will worship and return to you." Abraham took the wood of the burnt offering and laid it on Isaac his son, and he took in his hand the fire and the knife. So the two of them walked on together. Isaac spoke to Abraham his father and said, "My father!" And he said, "Here I am, my son." And he said, "Behold, the fire and the wood, but where is the lamb for the burnt offering?" Abraham said, "God will provide for Himself the lamb for the burnt offering, my son." So the two of them walked on together.

Then they came to the place of which God had told him; and Abraham built the altar there and arranged the wood, and bound his son Isaac and laid him on the altar, on top of the wood. Abraham stretched out his hand and took the knife to slay his son. But the angel of the LORD called to him from heaven and said, "Abraham, Abraham!" And he said, "Here I am." He said, "Do not stretch out your hand against the lad, and do nothing to him; for now I know that you fear God, since you have not withheld your son, your only son, from Me." Then Abraham raised his eyes and looked, and behold, behind him a ram caught in the thicket by his horns; and Abraham went and took the ram and offered him up for a burnt offering in the place of his son. Abraham called the name of that place The LORD Will Provide.

Genesis 22:1–14a

Now and then we might read in the newspaper or hear on the evening news about a deluded person who has murdered someone, claiming, "God told me to do it!" Another individual might use this line to justify divorcing a spouse (in order to marry a co-worker, perhaps). God's name is often dragged into circumstances or actions that are wholly alien to his good character and for which he wouldn't want any credit. But what do we do when we're confronted with *God's* command to Abraham, "Take now your son, your only son, whom you love . . . and offer him . . . as a burnt offering"? Jews and Christians have wrestled with this perplexing command. Not a few critics have seen in this narrative a God whose commands are arbitrary and even immoral. Is it okay to kill one's own innocent child in the name of God? Jephthah apparently thought so (Judg. 11:29–40).

The Danish Christian philosopher Søren Kierkegaard, who has wrongly been portrayed as viewing the Christian faith as the foe of reason,[1] notes this possible objection someone might raise: Abraham had a "right" to be a great man and thus to do what he did, but "when another does the same, it is sin, a heinous sin."[2] Kierkegaard said that God's command to Abraham *suspended* typical ethical obligations. God appears to use his authority to violate basic moral standards.

Perhaps the following thoughts might help us make better sense of this command.

First, the command to Abraham must be taken in the broader context of the biblical narrative—that is, God's direct dealing with Abraham and his overarching plan for Israel. Otherwise, we'll distort God's command to Abraham in Genesis 22. One Old Testament scholar, commenting on Genesis 22, properly observes that "an event must be judged by its wholeness and not just by its introductory command."[3] The first time Abraham was told by Yahweh to "go" was when he left his home in Ur of the Chaldeans (Babylonians) to a place God would show him—a remarkable act of trust based on this promise—where God would make through him and his descendants a great nation (Gen. 12:1–3). But in Genesis 22:2, God commands Abraham once again to "go," and it is Isaac, the son of the promise—the covenant son—who is now involved. In chapter 12, God had *promised* that he would make Abraham into a great nation. After Abraham's obedience here, God *confirms* his promise that he would make this patriarch's offspring as numerous as the stars and the sand on the seashore (22:17; cf. 15:5).

There's a connection between the call (Genesis 12) and the obedience (Genesis 22) of Abraham. The firmness of the faith of Abraham, the father of Israel, was being tested, and this moment would shape the thinking and identity of subsequent generations of Israelites.[4] In the words of Roland de Vaux, "Any Israelite who heard this story would take it to mean that his race owed its existence to the mercy of God and its prosperity to the obedience of their ancestor."[5]

Abraham, who had left his home in Ur and given up his *past* for the sake of God's promise, was now being asked if he would trust God by apparently surrendering his *future* as well. Everything Abraham ever hoped for was tied up in this son of promise.[6]

Second, the message of the Pentateuch (the five books of Moses—Genesis through Deuteronomy) is faith. The positive example of trusting God is **Abraham** *(who trusted in God before the Law was given), and the negative example is* **Moses** *(who, though having the Law, failed to trust God and couldn't enter the Promised Land). The New Testament, particularly Paul's writings, emphasizes the priority of faith over the Mosaic law.*[7] The amazing faith of Abraham is actually a chief theme of the Pentateuch. It offers a contrast between Abraham and Moses. *Abraham has faith prior to the law of Moses;* because of his faith, he is declared righteous by God (Gen. 15:6)—though he still fulfills God's requirements, commands, and precepts (Gen. 26:5). On the other hand, despite Moses's crucial role in Israel's history, *Moses actually fails in his faith—even though he lived under the law given at Mount Sinai.*

It's no coincidence that when *having faith/believing* is mentioned in the Pentateuch, it's used positively *before* the giving of the Law at Sinai in Exodus 20 (Gen. 15:6; Exod. 4:5; 14:31; 19:9) but is used negatively (e.g., "you have not believed") *after* Sinai (Num. 14:11; 20:12; cf. Deut. 1:32; 9:23). The Pentateuch presents a contrast between Abraham and Moses, according to some Old Testament scholars. Though Abraham's faith wavered at times, it continued to grow. (Consider David who was called a "man after God's own heart" despite his failings.) It's significant that Abraham trusted God—and was declared righteous—before the law of Moses came. Even without the law, Abraham kept the intention or purport of the law. Genesis makes clear that he *kept the Law* even before it was given because he lived *by faith*: "Abraham obeyed Me and kept My charge, My commandments, My statutes and My laws" (Gen. 26:5). What's remarkable here—and hardly accidental—is *the post-Sinai language from Deuteronomy (the "second law") incorporated here ("obeyed," "charge," "commandments," "statutes," "laws") **before** the law at Sinai was given*. The point? To show that Abraham pleased God and kept the purport of the law because he lived by faith (Gen. 15:6). On the other hand, Moses, who had the law, failed in his faith, which prohibited him from entering the land across the Jordan.

In the New Testament, Romans 4 and Galatians 3 remind us of this fact. Abraham is a model of faith before the law was given—and he is seen as one who obeys the law because of his faith. The negative contrast to this is Moses: Even though he had the law, he died in the wilderness because of his *and Aaron's* lack of faith at Kadesh (Num. 20). Moses wasn't barred from the Promised Land just because he struck the rock (he had struck rocks before!). The Hebrew text makes clear that *both Moses and Aaron* displayed unbelief in their exasperation. They weren't trusting in God. Moses (along with Aaron, apparently) cries out in frustration, "Listen, you rebels, must we bring you water out of this rock?" (Num. 20:10 NIV). Moses and Aaron did not believe but "rebelled" against God (Num. 20:12, 24). Moses "broke faith" with God (Deut. 32:51). Psalm 106:32–33 reinforces the theme of Moses' *unbelief*; the rebellion of the people prompted Moses to *speak rashly* (not *act* rashly): "Rash words came from Moses' lips" (Ps. 106:33 NIV).

So because of the unbelief of *both* Moses and Aaron, God rebuked *both of them*: "Because you [Moses *and Aaron*; the pronoun is *plural*] have not believed Me, to treat me as holy in the sight of the sons of Israel, therefore you shall not bring this assembly into the land which I have given them" (Num. 20:12). Indeed, God continued to address *both* men in the narrative.

God used Abraham as a picture of trust—without the benefit of the law—as an illustration through the ages of how God's people should live. Moses also serves as an important example—that having the law and living by it are inadequate for relating to God. We are to approach him trustingly for his sufficiency rather than putting confidence in our own efforts. (See Romans 7:7–25, which portrays corporate Israel's failure at the receiving of the law at Sinai and while living under it.)[8]

Third, we can't make proper sense of God's command unless we correctly understand the more immediate narrative context—namely, what has just happened to Abraham's first son, Ishmael, and his mother, Hagar. This would be the preliminary testing ground for what Abraham would later experience.[9] Let's not forget Ishmael, who was conceived through Hagar the maidservant because Sarah assumed that her having a *biological* son of promise in her old age wasn't an option. In many ways, this turned out to be a huge mis-conception! Sarah, figuring that surrogate motherhood must be the way God wanted to fulfill his promise, told Abraham to take Hagar as her substitute. But when Hagar conceived and began to despise her mistress, Sarah, this caused much tension and Sarah drove her away. God met Hagar in her desperation in the wilderness and told her to go back to live with Sarah and Abraham. There Hagar gave birth to Abraham's first son. As Ishmael grew up, no doubt Abraham grew quite attached to him.

God, however, had different plans. He assured Abraham and Sarah that he wanted the son of promise to come from *both* their bodies, not just Abraham's. Through God's miraculous fulfillment of his promise, Isaac was born. But at the feast held when Isaac was weaned, Ishmael, now a teenager, mocked Isaac (Gen. 21:9). Now it had been painful enough for Sarah to have a handmaiden—rather than herself—give birth to Abraham's first son and then to be scorned by her. But Ishmael's mocking Sarah's own biological child was too much to take. She sent away not only Ishmael, but also his mother, Hagar, and this created a problem for Abraham (Gen. 21:11). Sending them off into the wilderness would mean they would face many challenges—perhaps even death. But God assured Abraham that Ishmael wouldn't die (21:12–13). In fact, Yahweh had already told him, "I will make him a great nation" (17:20), and Hagar had been told that God would "greatly multiply" her descendants (16:10). So Abraham, knowing this promise, could confidently send Ishmael away with Hagar and entrust them to God's care.

Then later when Abraham was commanded to sacrifice Isaac, *he had in mind the promise of God regarding Ishmael*: Abraham knew that even though he had sent his older son, Ishmael, away into the desert, God promised that he would live and become a great nation. *Without God's promise, Abraham would have been wrong to send Hagar and Ishmael away to an almost certain death*. So despite Sarah's anger with Hagar, God assured Abraham that he would provide for Ishmael and that Abraham need not worry that he was doing wrong. God would care for his life and fulfill his promises about him.

In the case of Ishmael, Abraham obviously didn't want conflict between his wife and her handmaiden (and son). Though it was hard to send Ishmael away into the desert, he was assured that God would care for him. Ishmael would become a great nation. But God had said that the son who came from Sarah's own body—"your [Abraham's] *only* son" (Gen. 22:2), the son of promise—would *also* become a great nation. *Ishmael was a preliminary test; Isaac was an even greater test.* Abraham knew that God would fulfill his promise regarding Isaac, but he couldn't figure out what God would do. All he could do was trust God's promises and obey. Somehow, someway God had to come through. We see that Abraham's obedience was carried out in the context of his awareness of God's *goodness* and God's *earlier deliverance* of Ishmael. We'll explore this more below.

Fourth, because Abraham already knew God's faithful—and even tender—character and his promises, he was confident that God would somehow fulfill his promise to him even if it meant raising Isaac from the dead. We see this faithfulness exhibited in three ways. (a) Even in the command to Abraham, God says something unusual. God's words in Genesis 22:2 can be rendered, "*Please* take your son." *There's a remarkable gentleness cushioning this harsh command.* It should not go unnoticed that this type of divine command (as a plea) is rare. Old Testament commentator Gordon Wenham sees here a "hint that the LORD appreciates the costliness of what he is asking."[10]

Another hint of God's faithful character is (b) *his covenant-acknowledgment that the promised son, Isaac—without whom the promise could not be fulfilled—was "your son, your only son, whom you love"* (Gen. 22:2). Abraham's deep love for Isaac is good and right. So in his instructing, God acknowledges not only his covenant promise to Abraham, but also that this is the most fearful and dreadful thing Abraham would ever have to do.

A third reminder of God's faithful character is that (c) *God is sending Abraham to a mountain in the region of Moriah* (Gen. 22:2, derived from the Hebrew word "provide, see" [cf. 22:14: "In the mount of the LORD it will be provided"]). Note the linking back to God's initial call to Abraham, who is to leave for a land "which I will show you" (Gen. 12:1). In the very word *Moriah*—"provision"—we have a hint of salvation and deliverance. Commentator Gordon Wenham writes, "Salvation is thus promised in the very decree that sounds like annihilation."[11]

In all of these points, we see that *God's faithful tenderness cushions the startling harshness of God's command.* It's as though God is saying to Abraham, "I'm testing your obedience and allegiance. You don't understand, but in light of all I've done and said to you, trust me. Not even *death* can nullify the promise that I've made." God himself told Abraham that it wasn't Hagar who would bear the child of promise—even though Abraham (going along with Sarah) thought it would be a good idea. He said to God: "Oh that Ishmael might live before You!" (Gen. 17:18). God replied, "No, but Sarah your wife will bear you a son . . . and I will establish My covenant with him for an everlasting covenant for his descendants after him" (v. 19). God assures Abraham that Isaac, not Ishmael, is the promised son.

So we can't separate God's *promise* in Genesis 12 and 17 from God's *command* in Genesis 22. Abraham had confidence that *even if the child of promise died, God would somehow accomplish his purposes through that very child.* Abraham believed *God could even raise Isaac from the dead.* This is why Abraham told his servants before he headed to Mount Moriah with Isaac, "*We* will worship and [*we* will] return to you" (Gen. 22:5). No wonder the author of Hebrews observes that since Abraham "had received the promises," he "considered that God is able to raise people even from the dead" (Heb. 11:17–19). In some way, God would fulfill his promises, and Abraham was confident of this—and commended for it.

Fifth, given the historical context of God's self-revelation and promises to Abraham, the command to sacrifice Isaac should not be confused with the infant sacrifice which God condemns—nor should this unique command be universalized to justify murder. In the ancient Near East during Abraham's time, human sacrifice and sacrificing children to foreign gods were commonly practiced, and Scripture condemns such practices (Lev. 18:21; 20:2; Jer. 19:5; Ezek. 20:30–31; 23:36–39). What is remarkable is that Abraham *isn't surprised* by God's demand.[12] Whereas the *regular* practice of infant sacrifice was offered to the local false god Molech, Yahweh (who had made himself known to Abraham and proven himself good and trustworthy) was now commanding Abraham in this *unique* event to offer Isaac to the sovereign Lord and the one who can thus make these demands. *So we must be careful about making unique historical narratives into universal norms for all believers.* We've seen that the command to Abraham presupposes God's previous interactions with him and promises to him. God's command can be understood in light of these particular historical realities.

Sixth, since God is the giver and sustainer of life, he's under no obligation to allow us a certain number of years on earth. The testing of Abraham serves as a reminder that God—in his good and sovereign purposes—may give and take away and even make demands we can't fully understand. God is the author of all life and thus has a right to demand it as he wills: "The LORD gave and the LORD has taken away. Blessed be the name of the LORD" (Job 1:21; cf. Deut. 32:39). Philosopher Charles Taliaferro observes:

> If there is a robust sense in which the cosmos belongs to God, then God's moral standing from the outset is radically unequal to ours. . . . Arguably our rights [to, say, property or privacy] are at least hedged if the ownership of God is taken seriously. Being thus beholden to God would not seem to entitle God to create beings solely to torment them, but if life is indeed a gift from God which no creature deserves . . . then certain complaints about the created order may be checked.[13]

During World War II, the Allied powers were united in their effort to stop a serious and evil threat. It wasn't immoral for these governments to call upon their citizens to sacrifice—even to the point of death—in a cause that was just and had sweeping implications for the future of humanity. How much more does God have a right to demand sacrifice—even to the point of death—since life itself is a gift from God![14]

*Finally, God, in his sovereignty, has used Abraham's faith in freely giving of his son as a picture of God's **providing** for our salvation by sacrificing his "beloved" and "one and only Son."* Abraham's unquestioned obedience to the covenant God not only helped shape and confirm Israel's identity in Abraham; it also provided a context for God's immense love for us in the giving of his Son. After Abraham's amazing obedience, God said: "Now I know that you fear God, since you did not spare your son, your only son, from Me" (Gen. 22:12; cf. v. 16).[15] In Romans 8:32, Paul had in mind Abraham's sacrifice of Isaac: "He who did not spare His own Son, but delivered Him over for us all, how will He not also with Him freely give us all things?" Abraham's giving up of Isaac serves as a foreshadowing (or type) of God's sacrifice of Christ. Abraham demonstrated his faithfulness to God, and God's sacrifice demonstrates his faithfulness to us.[16] We're reminded that the kind of demand God made of Abraham was one the Triune God was willing to carry out himself. However, rather than pitting Father against Son, Scripture presents Jesus freely and graciously coming to lay down his life, living moment by moment in the power of the Spirit— within the Father's love. John 10:17–18 indicates both that the Father loves him and that he lays down his life on his own initiative. So great is God's love for us (Rom. 8:31–32) that Scottish theologian Thomas Torrance is willing to go so far as to say that "God loves us more than he loves himself."[17]

Abraham provides us an illustration of faith in the context of God's particular dealings with and momentous promises to Abraham. And Abraham's trust in God—that he would fulfill his promises even if it meant raising from the dead the long-awaited child of promise—by being willing to offer Isaac serves as a picture for us regarding the lengths to which God will go for our salvation.

SUMMARY

- The command to Abraham must be taken in the broader context of the biblical narrative—that is, God's direct dealing with Abraham and his overarching plan for Israel. Otherwise, we'll distort God's command to Abraham in Genesis 22.

- The message of the Pentateuch (the five books of Moses—Genesis through Deuteronomy) is faith. The positive example of trusting God is *Abraham* (who trusted in God before the law was given), and the negative example is *Moses* (who, though having the law, failed to trust God and couldn't enter the Promised Land). The New Testament, particularly in Paul's writings, emphasizes the priority of faith over the Mosaic law.

- We can't make proper sense of God's command unless we correctly understand the more immediate narrative context—namely, what has just happened to Abraham's first son, Ishmael, and his mother, Hagar. This would be the preliminary testing ground for what Abraham would later experience. When Abraham was commanded to sacrifice Isaac, he had in mind the promise of God regarding Ishmael, who would not die in the wilderness but would live and become a great nation. (Without God's promise, Abraham would have been wrong to send Hagar and Ishmael away to an almost certain death.)

- Because Abraham already knew God's faithful—and even tender—character and his promises, he was confident that God would somehow fulfill his promise to him even if it meant raising Isaac from the dead: (a) Even in the command to Abraham, God says something unusual. God's words in Genesis 22:2 can be rendered, "*Please* take your son." There is a remarkable gentleness cushioning this harsh command. (b) God acknowledges that Abraham's promised son, Isaac—without whom the promise could not be fulfilled—was "your son, your only son, whom you love" (Gen. 22:2). (c) God's sending Abraham to a mountain in the region of *Moriah* (Gen. 22:2, derived from "provide, see," cf. 22:14) harks back to God's initial call to Abraham; he was to leave for a land "which I will show you" (Gen. 12:1). In the very word

Moriah—"provision"—we have a hint of salvation and deliverance.

- We can't separate God's promise in Genesis 12 and 17 from God's command in Genesis 22. Abraham knew that even if the child of promise died, God would somehow accomplish his purposes— even by raising Isaac from the dead. "*We* will worship and [*we* will] return to you" (Gen. 22:5; cf. Heb. 11:17–19).

- Given the historical context of God's self-revelation and promises to Abraham, the command to sacrifice Isaac should not be confused with the infant sacrifice which God condemns—nor should this unique command be universalized to justify murder. We shouldn't think that God's interaction with Abraham in these unique historical narratives should be universalized for all believers. We've seen that the command to Abraham presupposes God's *previous interactions* with him and *promises* to him. God's command can be understood in light of these particular historical realities.

- Since God is the giver and sustainer of life, he's under no obligation to allow us a certain number of years on earth. The testing of Abraham serves as a reminder that God—in his good and sovereign purposes—may give and take away and even make demands we can't fully understand.

- God, in his sovereignty, has used Abraham's faith in freely giving of his son as a picture of God's *providing* for our salvation by sacrificing his "beloved" and "one and only Son."

FURTHER READING

Sailhamer, John. "The Mosaic Law and the Theology of the Pentateuch." *Westminster Theological Journal* 53 (1991): 24–61.

———. *The Pentateuch as Narrative: A Biblical-Theological Commentary*. Grand Rapids: Zondervan, 1992.

Stump, Eleonore. "Evil and the Nature of Faith." In *Wandering in Darkness*. Oxford: Oxford University Press, forthcoming.

Wenham, Gordon. *Genesis 16–20*. Word Biblical Commentary, vol. 2. Dallas: Word, 1994.

12

MANY OLD TESTAMENT LAWS ARE STRANGE AND ARBITRARY

One day someone sent me an email containing "An Open Letter to Dr. Laura."[1] Dr. Laura Schlessinger, of course, is the Jewish radio talk show host who offers practical advice about relationships, parenting, and ethical dilemmas based on Old Testament principles. Here's part of that "open letter" saturated with sarcasm:

Dear Dr. Laura:

Thank you for doing so much to educate people regarding God's Law. I have learned a great deal from your show, and I try to share that knowledge with as many people as I can. When someone tries to defend the homosexual lifestyle, for example, I simply remind them that Leviticus 18:22 clearly states it to be an abomination. End of debate.

I do need some advice from you, however, regarding some of the specific laws and how to follow them:

- I would like to sell my daughter into slavery, as sanctioned in Exodus 21:7. In this day and age, what do you think would be a fair price for her?
- I have a neighbor who insists on working on the Sabbath. Exodus 35:2 clearly states he should be put to death. Am I morally obligated to kill him myself?
- A friend of mine feels that even though eating shellfish is an abomination (Lev. 11:10), it is a lesser abomination than homosexuality. I don't agree. Can you settle this?
- Leviticus 21:20 states that I may not approach the altar of God if I have a defect in my sight. I have to admit that I wear reading glasses. Does my vision have to be 20/20, or is there some wiggle room here?
- Most of my male friends get their hair trimmed, including the hair around their temples, even though this is expressly forbidden by Leviticus 19:27. How should they die?
- I know from Leviticus 11:6–8 that touching the skin of a dead pig makes me unclean, but may I still play football if I wear gloves?
- My uncle has a farm. He violates Leviticus 19:19 by planting two different crops in the same field, as does his wife by wearing garments made of two different kinds of thread (cotton/polyester blend)....

I know you have studied these things extensively; so I am confident you can help Thank you again for reminding us that God's word is eternal and unchanging.

Your devoted disciple and adoring fan.

When we read biblical commands given at Mount Sinai regarding food laws and skin diseases or various prohibitions against cutting the edges of one's beard, wearing tattoos, or cooking a kid goat in its mother's milk, we twenty-first-century Westerners are perplexed and bewildered about what appear to be odd, arbitrary, and even severe standards for theocratic (divinely ruled) Israel. The twelfth-century rabbi Moses ben Maimon (Maimonides) counted 613 distinct laws (365 prohibitions, 248 positive commands) in the books of Moses ("Pentateuch"). How can we begin to make sense of them and respond to the kinds of questions raised in this "open letter"? And what's the benefit of the law of Moses for the Christian, who isn't "under law but under grace" (Rom. 6:14)?[2] In this chapter we'll look at some of the Levitical (ritual, "cultic") commands that seem strange and arbitrary. In the next chapter, we'll look at commands for Israel that seem harsh and oppressive to modern ears.

First, Israel owed its very existence to the saving activity of God in history, and Israel's status as a theocracy was a privilege—and responsibility—rooted in the grace of God. It's inaccurate to think that the sum total of Israel's obligations under the law of Moses was just eating clean/kosher foods, remaining ritually clean (staying away from corpses and carcasses), and going to the health inspector-priest to have skin diseases and scabs examined. God's *actions* in history shaped the *identity* of his people, which in turn was to shape their *internal motivation*.[3] So being God's chosen people meant that Israel should live wisely before the nations (Deut. 4:5–6)—a heavy responsibility (Acts 15:10)—but this responsibility was seen as a privilege by godly Israelites (cf. Ps. 119; Rom. 3:1–2).

Because God graciously delivered his people from Egypt, he reminds them that, in response to God's grace, they should treat the strangers and less fortunate in their midst with compassion. His people shouldn't forget that they themselves were once slaves in a foreign land (Lev. 25:38, 42, 55; Deut. 15:15).[4] The Old Testament never presumes an "Israel can do no wrong" attitude; the Israelites would—and *did*—receive the *same* judgments that God brought upon morally corrupt nations surrounding them (Deut. 28:15–68; Josh. 23:14–16). God regularly reminded Israel that it *wasn't* their righteousness but God's grace that gave them their chosen status to be a blessing to the nations around them. God's gracious dealings with Israel were to be the basis for how Israelites were to treat their neighbors. Throughout the Old Testament, we repeatedly see the following *grace-gratitude* ideal expressed: "This is what God has done *for you*. Therefore, out of *gratitude* you should *do the same* for others."[5]

In fact, there's good reason to think that *the very animals that are forbidden and permitted in Israel's diet symbolically reminded Israel of what kind of community God requires or prohibits.* So let's be careful about being "chronological snobs"—thinking that if we moderns find something inconvenient or strange, it should automatically be rejected.[6]

Second, under the authority of Mosaic law, Old Testament Israel uniquely existed as a theocracy (i.e., governed or led by God) in preparation for the coming Messiah. A cultural and theological context needed to be established first to make sense of what Jesus as God's Messiah would do. Because of Israel's unique situation—as the nation through which the Savior of the world would come—we shouldn't conclude (and the New Testament confirms this) that the Old Testament prescribes the ideal model for all governments subsequent to the Ten Commandments being given. Although the media are quick to speak of attempts by Muslim clerics in this or that Muslim country to "set up a theocratic government," such language is misapplied. *Ancient Israel was the one and only genuine theocracy ever to exist.* Furthermore, God *temporarily* established it to set the religious, cultural, and historical context for the saving work of Jesus the Messiah later in history—when the fullness of the time came (Gal. 4:4).

The person writing Dr. Laura wrongly assumed *the* biblical position was that Mosaic law wasn't just for theocratic Israel in the past but for *all* countries and cultures in *all* ages. In fact, critics of the Old Testament and even filmmakers (e.g., *The Handmaiden's Tale*) will sometimes depict an allegedly "biblically ideal society" as a rigid, solemn, joyless, and oppressive community where horrible things are done in the name of God. They suppose that God wanted Israel to have—in satirist H. L. Mencken's words—"the dreaded fear that someone, somewhere, somehow is enjoying himself"![7] Such critics mistakenly assume that the Bible claims that an Israel-like theocracy is the ideal for *all* earthly governments at every period of history. Not so. God's rule over earthly Israel was unique (unrepeatable and preparatory in the unfolding plan of salvation history):

- God chose Israel, not all nations, but God's desire for Israel was that it be a light and a blessing to all the nations (Gen. 12:3).
- This theocracy was temporary: These laws were suited to a particular people in the ancient Near East at a particular time in history. Later, Jesus would declare that the kingdom would be taken

from national Israel and its leaders and given to an inter-ethnic community of believers who would produce the kind of moral and spiritual fruit that God desired (Matt. 8:11–12; 21:43). God brought judgment upon national, political Israel in AD 70, when Jerusalem was destroyed by the Romans.

• Israel's laws and culture set the theological context for the ministry and teachings of Jesus—the holiness, separateness, and purity of God; the connection between substitutionary sacrifice and cleansing; the need for a priestly mediator between God and us; and the way God's people are to "practice the presence of God" in every area of life. The book of Hebrews makes these connections clear.

So Old Testament Israel's theocracy was *provisional,* and it *anticipated future fulfillment.* The old order was fulfilled in the coming of Christ—the completer of the incomplete, the "substance" to which the Mosaic "shadows" pointed. While the Old Testament informs Christians of their very Jewish historical roots and how God's plan of redemption has unfolded through national Israel, this doesn't mean that all of the Old Testament laws are binding upon believers (more on this below).

Third, it's helpful to think of many Old Testament laws in terms of a redemptive-movement interpretation within Scripture; we must look beyond the isolated verses in question and observe the underlying spirit and the movement of Scripture. William Webb, in his excellent book, *Slaves, Women, and Homosexuals,*[8] compares a "static" method of Scripture interpretation with a "redemptive-movement" understanding of it. That is, as we move from the Old to the New Testament, there's a certain *redemptive spirit* that continues to unfold and progress. For example, we see a kind of progression from Deuteronomy 24 (which deals with a certificate of divorce *permitted* under Moses) to Jesus' discussion of this in Matthew 19. There Jesus acknowledges the limits in Deuteronomy 24 of permitting divorce due to human hard-heartedness. Jesus's approach reminds us that there's a multilevel ethic that cautions against a monolithic, single-level ethic that simply "parks" at Deuteronomy 24 and doesn't consider the *redemptive component* of this legislation. The certificate of divorce was to protect the wife, who would, by necessity, have to remarry to come under the shelter of a husband to escape poverty and shame. This law *took into consideration the well-being of the wife.* So when Jesus spoke to the Pharisees, their *wooden interpretation* made it difficult to see that Moses's words didn't represent an absolute ethic. (Keep in mind that God's commands involving divorce—and even slavery—are given not as ideals, but because of the hardness of human hearts [Matt. 19:8].) These Pharisees approached Scripture in a way that made it virtually impossible for them to see any further, as Jesus pointed out—to see that there was an even greater good of sacrificially serving in the kingdom by forgoing the joys and benefits of marriage (Matt. 19:10–12).[9] *Another* example is a progression from the *death penalty* in the Old Testament for sexually promiscuous acts within Old Testament *Israel* to the parallel of *excommunication* from the *church* in the New (1 Cor. 5:1–3).[10]

So as we look at many of these Levitical laws, we must appreciate them in their historical context, as God's temporary provision, but also *look at the underlying spirit and movement across the sweep of salvation history.* As we do so, we see that the movement of Scripture *consistently prohibits* homosexual activity (for example), on the one hand. However, the movement of Scripture *consistently affirms* the full humanity of slaves (e.g., Job 31:13–15), eventually encouraging slaves to pursue their freedom (1 Cor. 7:21). As we noted earlier, slavery wasn't *commanded* but *permitted* (as was divorce) because of the hardness of human hearts. Homosexuality is a different matter. New Testament scholar R. T. France writes that direct references to homosexual activity in Scripture are "uniformly hostile"; homosexual behavior—so common in surrounding cultures (ancient Near Eastern/Greco-Roman)—was "simply alien to the Jewish and Christian ethos."[11] Note too that *acts*—rather than mere *inclinations/tendencies* (whether homosexual or heterosexual)—are judged to be immoral and worthy of censure in Scripture.

So it's wrongheaded to claim that homosexual acts were "just cultural" or simply "on the same level" as the kosher or clothing laws that God gave to help set Israel apart from its pagan neighbors. *Levitical law also prohibits adultery, bestiality, murder, and theft, and surely these go far beyond the temporary prohibitions of eating shrimp or pork!*

Fourth, the God of holiness wanted his people to be reminded constantly that they were to be holy in every dimension of life. Because God is holy or set apart, his people are to be as well (Lev. 11:44). Holiness wasn't simply a priestly preoccupation; it was for *everyone* in Israel.[12] All God's people were to be "set apart" or "marked off" (cf. Gen. 2:3, where the Sabbath day is "marked off" or "made holy" [NIV] to the Lord).[13] Biblical scholar Richard Bauckham remarks that this motto ("be holy . . .") could be rephrased: "You shall be my people and mine alone, for I am your God and yours alone."[14] In other words, to be God's covenant people involves *a calling to be lived out in a life dedicated to God in every dimension.*[15]

Even though God's laws for Israel—whether food laws, clothing laws, planting laws, civil laws, or laws regarding marriage and sexual relations—weren't exhaustive, they were to be viewed first as *visible reminders to live as God's holy people in every area of life.* There wasn't any division between the sacred and the secular, between the holy and the profane. God was concerned about holiness in everything: "In the major and minor decisions of life, Israel was constantly reminded that she was different; that she was holy, set apart for God's service."[16] Israel was to be a *kingdom* of priests (Exod. 19:6). Prescribed rituals and moral duties were to reflect humility of heart and love for God and neighbor (Ps. 51:15–19). Rites such as "festivals . . . solemn assemblies . . . burnt offerings and . . . grain offerings" were empty if "justice" and "righteousness" were ignored by God's people (Amos 5:21–24).

So we shouldn't see food, clothing, and planting laws as nitpicky commands God gave to oppress Israel. Moses and the prophets reminded the Israelites that God is primarily concerned about justice, mercy, and walking humbly before God (e.g., Deut. 10:12; Mic. 6:8). This underlying *moral* concern, however, didn't obliterate *ritual* prescriptions even much later in theocratic Israel's history after the Babylonian exile.[17] These ritual acts were specifically commanded by God for those living under his theocratic covenant and reign.

Similarly, the Christian living under the reign of God through Christ must look at life with new lenses. After all, we live in a "God-bathed and God-permeated world."[18] God isn't cordoned off to some private, religious realm. God is—either by direct control or by granting divine permission so as not to violate human freedom—sovereignly at work in all the rhythms of creation and workings of human history. He's weaving together his tapestry and bringing all things to their climax in Christ. As the hymnwriter put it, God "speaks to me everywhere."[19]

Fifth, many of the Mosaic commands to Israel reflect a sense of whole-ness, completeness, and integrity; no admixtures were allowed (e.g., in clothing, seeds sown in a field, or the eating of animals that transgressed the individual and distinctive "spheres" of air, water, or land). This badge of holy distinction was to serve as a reminder to Israel to be distinct from surrounding nations rather than "mixed in" with their mindset and ways.[20] Food laws—interwoven with many other Mosaic commands regarding purity—symbolized the boundaries God's people were to keep before them:

- *The sanctuary:* God's visible presence was manifested here; this was his "habitation." God gave laws to remind the people of *his own set-apartness from all creation* and how he is to be approached (e.g., priests as well as sacrificed animals had to be without defect or blemish).
- *The land of Israel:* The land of Israel was set in the midst of pagan nations with false gods, and thus there were certain commands that marked off the *Israelites from other nations*. "Thus, not only what one eats, but where one resides reflects and defines the larger social and theological issues of the community."[21]

Here are some of these boundaries.

God	Sacrifices	Sanctuary
Israelites	Pure (Domesticated) Animals and Game	Israel's Land
Foreign Nations	All Animals	Outside the Land

Many Levitical laws strongly emphasize *semen* and *blood*. Why is this? The reason behind God's commands to wash/be purified after the emission of semen or the discharging of menstrual blood (cf. Lev. 15) appears to be this: *these discharges symbolized what was "outside" the wholeness of the human body—just as unclean foods entering the body would pollute or defile.* Vaginal blood and semen are powerful symbols of life, but *their loss appears to symbolize death.*[22] And the prohibition against the eating of blood in meat metaphorically underscored this regard for life (Lev. 7:27; 17:10–14).

What about Israel's kosher food laws? Some have suggested that the division of clean and unclean animals was for *hygienic/health* reasons: avoid eating vultures because they eat roadkill; don't eat pigs because they could transmit diseases such as trichinosis (and the hare and coney commonly carry tularemia); and don't eat shrimp because they raise one's cholesterol level! But *health* isn't the issue: there's *no hint* of this in the text. And why aren't poisonous *plants* considered unclean? On top of all this, *why did Jesus declare all these foods clean* if they were bad for one's health?[23]

Others have suggested that the animals prohibited from Israel's diet were those that were *associated with non-Israelite religion* in the ancient Near East. However, according to this thinking, the bull should have been an abomination, since it was central to Canaanite and Egyptian religion. But the bull was, in fact, the most valuable of Israel's sacrificial animals.[24] Canaanites, in fact, sacrificed the same sorts of animals in their religious rituals as did the Israelites![25]

Furthermore, ancient Near Easterners generally considered pigs *detestable* and standardly avoided eating them—as well as sacrificing them in their religious rites.[26] Just because pagan neighbors used certain animals in their sacrifices didn't render them unclean in Israel. The hygienic or cultic/ritual explanations don't seem to help us understand why some animals are clean and others aren't.

Recently, many Old Testament scholars have followed the lead of anthropologist Mary Douglas.[27] She has helpfully suggested that *any animal is "clean" that has all the defining features of its class.*[28] Indeed, Genesis 1 divides animals into three "spheres"—animals that *walk on the land*, animals that *swim in water*, animals that *fly in the air*—and Leviticus 11 lists prohibited foods according to animals on the *land* (vv. 2–8), in the *water* (vv. 9–12), and in the *air* (vv. 13–23).[29] *Animals that blurred categories, transgressed boundaries/spheres, and/or overlapped in their characteristics were to be avoided as unclean.*[30]

- *Water:* Aquatic animals must have scales *and* fins (Lev. 11:10; Deut. 14:10); so eels, which didn't fit this category, were unclean and thus prohibited.

- *Land:* Clean animals were four-footed ones that hop, walk, or jump. A clear indication of a land animal's operating according to its sphere is that it *both* (a) has split hooves and (b) is a cud-chewer. These two features made obvious that an animal belonged to the "land" sphere (e.g., sheep and goats). Camels, hares, coneys (which chew the cud but don't have divided hooves), and pigs (which have divided hooves but don't chew the cud) are *borderline cases*; so they're *excluded* as appropriate land animals to eat.

- *Air:* Birds have two wings for flying. Insects that fly but have *many* legs are unclean: they operate in two "spheres"—land and air. However, insects with four feet—two of which are jointed for hopping on the ground—are considered clean (Lev. 11:21–23). These insects—the locust, katydid, cricket, and grasshopper—are like birds of the air, which hop on the ground with two legs. Therefore they are clean.

Swarming animals in any sphere (eels, snakes, flying insects) are considered detestable (Lev. 11:41–42).[31] These swarming creatures cut across the three spheres of classification and are thus unclean.

Of course, God created everything "very good" (Gen. 1:31), and therefore *no animal is inherently "unclean" or "inferior."* But as the people of God, the Israelites were reminded that holiness requires persons to "conform to the class to which they belong."[32] So *what Israelites did in their everyday lives—even down to their eating habits—was to be a reminder that they were God's holy people and distinct from the surrounding nations.* At every meal, Israelites were reminded of their redemption. Their diet, which was limited to certain meats, imitated the action of God, *who limited himself to Israel from among the nations,* choosing them as the means of blessing the world.[33]

So there could be *no religious overlap, blurring distinctions, or compromise between Israel and its neighbors.* Israel was called to integrity and purity of life and to avoid what would restrict or inhibit the worship of God.[34] Holiness involved conformity to God's ordering of things. Just as clean animals belonged to their distinct sphere without "compromise," so *God's holy people were to belong to their distinct sphere,* not mixing their religion with surrounding pagan nations or intermarrying with those who rejected the God of Israel (cf. Ezra 9:1–4; Neh. 13:23–30).

Holiness was not a matter of eating and drinking but a matter of a life devoted to God in every area.

Not only did *animals* have their "spheres." *Other aspects of life* were to conform to a particular order. For example, Leviticus 19:19 and Deuteronomy 22:9–11 prohibit mixed breeding and other attempts at mixing: no crossbreeding of cattle, no planting of different crops ("two kinds of seed") in the same field, no clothing with mixed fibers such as wool and linen[35] (no polyesters!), no plowing with both ox *and* donkey. Now all this seems strange to modern ears. What's behind such commands? The same kind of answer as with clean and unclean animals. Gordon Wenham writes, "In creation God separated between light and darkness, waters and waters. This ban on all mixtures, especially mixed breeding, shows man following in God's steps. He must separate what God created separate."[36]

Mixtures involving cloth, agricultural techniques, or animal breeding were prohibited—as was wrong *sexual* "mixing" such as adultery, incest, bestiality, and homosexuality—since these were viewed as *crossing boundaries* (Lev. 18:6–23; Deut. 21:10–21).[37] In the same way, because God created male and female (Gen. 1:26–27), wearing the clothes of a person of the opposite sex (by which divinely ordained sexual distinctions could be blurred or "spheres" crossed) was prohibited (Deut. 22:5). In all these commands, holiness was also symbolized by *wholeness* and *integrity*; this is why the priest as well as the animal sacrifice weren't allowed to have any physical deformity (Lev. 21:18–24; 22:18–25). The writer of the "open letter" to Dr. Laura misses the powerful symbolism behind such laws.

*Sixth, there was a link between the kinds of **animals** that were permitted or forbidden in the Israelites' diet and the kind of **people** God wanted them to be—they weren't to be "predators" in their human relationships. To symbolize this, (a) predatory animals were to be avoided for food as were (b) ugly, (apparently) defenseless, and odd-looking animals.* Besides keeping food, clothing, planting, and sexual relations in their respective "spheres" as a picture of Israel's set-apartness from the nations, the division between clean and unclean animals *serves as a picture* for how Israelites were to *act* in relationship to their neighbor as well as to God. We see especially in the language of Leviticus how animals serve as a kind of picture or illustration of what God requires from his people.

For example, note the *parallels* between the kinds of *animals* offered in sacrifices in Leviticus 1, 3, and 22 ("without defect" which resulted in a "pleasing aroma to the LORD") and the *priest* who is to be without "defect" (Lev. 21:18–24). The parallel language between the unblemished priest and the unblemished sacrificial animal is striking:

Unblemished priest: Leviticus 21:18–24	Unblemished animal: Leviticus 22:18–26
For no one [of Aaron's priestly line] who has a *defect* shall approach [the altar of sacrifice]: a *blind* man, or a lame man, or he who has a disfigured face, or any deformed limb, or a man who has a broken foot or broken hand, or a hunchback or a dwarf, or one who has a defect in his eye or *eczema* or *scabs* or *crushed testicles*. . . . *He shall not go in to the veil* or come near the altar because he has a defect, so that he will not profane My sanctuaries. For I am the LORD who sanctifies them.	[Anyone] who presents his offering . . . —it must be a male without *defect*. . . . Whatever has a defect, you shall not offer. . . . It must be perfect to be accepted; there shall be no defect in it. Those that are *blind* or fractured or maimed or having a running sore or *eczema* or *scabs*, you shall not offer to the LORD. . . . Also anything with its *testicles bruised or crushed* or torn or cut, *you shall not offer to the LORD*, or sacrifice in your land.

Getting more specific, Mary Douglas writes that in Leviticus there's a connection between the *kinds of animals that are permitted/forbidden* to be eaten and the *kind of people God wants the Israelites to be in their relationships*.[38] The theme of (un)cleanness in Leviticus and Deuteronomy does not only symbolize the orderliness of creation with everything in its own sphere (i.e., unclean animals represent lack of wholeness or integrity in not belonging to their own "sphere"). There's something more going on. It appears that unclean animals are either (a) *predatory animals* or (b) *"vulnerable" animals (defective in appearance or characteristics)*. This has a parallel to human relationships.

Let's look at the predatory aspect. As for *animals of the air* (owls, gulls, hawks, and carrion-eaters such as vultures), they are forbidden in Israel's diet because they themselves have *consumed blood*; they are predatory. (Remember the prohibition of eating blood in Genesis 9:4, suggesting respect for life, which is in the "blood": "The life of all flesh is its blood" [Lev. 17:14]). As for *land animals*, quadruped plant-eaters—rather than carnivores—may be eaten (once their blood has been drained). The fact that they (a) chew the cud and (b) have split hooves (whether domestic or wild; Lev. 11:3) is *a clear indication that they never eat blood and thus are not predatory.* The borderline cases—the pig, the camel, the hare, and the coney/rock badger—are forbidden because they fit one but not both criteria. So land animals that are *predators* must be avoided because of their contact with blood. In a symbolic way, *they "break the law."*[39]

Besides unclean animals that represent (a) *predation*, there are others that represent (b) *victims of predation.* For instance, prohibited *aquatic animals* (without scales and fins) symbolically *lack* something they need—which is a picture of vulnerability. *The distinction between clean and unclean animals serves as a picture of justice and injustice in personal relationships.* Let me quote Douglas at length:

> The forbidden animal species exemplify the predators, on the one hand, that is those who eat blood, and on the other, the sufferers from injustice. Consider the list, especially the swarming insects, the chameleon with its lumpy face, the high humped tortoise and beetle, and the ants labouring under their huge loads. Think of the blindness of worms and bats, the vulnerability of fish without scales. Think of their human parallels, the labourers, the beggars, the orphans, and the defenceless widows. Not themselves but the behavior that reduces them to this state is an abomination. No wonder the Lord made the crawling things and found them good (Gen. 1:31). It is not in the grand style of Leviticus to take time off from cosmic themes to teach that these pathetic creatures are to be shunned because their bodies are disgusting, vile, bad, any more than it is consistent with its theme of justice to teach that the poor are to be shunned. Shunning is not the issue. Predation is wrong, eating is a form of predation, and the poor are not to be a prey.[40]

Holiness and predatory behavior don't mix. Holiness represents respect for human life, and the eating of blood (symbolizing violent death) represents predatory activity. Clean animals don't represent virtues—just as unclean animals don't represent vices—in their own bodies: "They simply keep the rule of avoiding blood."[41] Unclean animals that symbolize vulnerability and defenselessness symbolically point to those who are oppressed—the alien, the widow, and the orphan (Deut. 14:28–29; 16:11; cf. Isa. 1:17). They are to be respected. *Even the very food the Israelites would eat—or would not eat—was to serve as a reminder of the holy and the unholy: Israelites were to avoid the unholy activity of preying upon the vulnerable in society.*

Some may disagree with this assessment, and/or others may still be unclear regarding what makes an animal clean or unclean (or why two types of seed couldn't be used in one field, etc.). However, *the undergirding rationale behind these laws is holiness in everything.* That's why the theme of *holiness* is explicitly mentioned in all the passages where prohibited (or permitted) foods are mentioned (Exod. 22:31; Lev. 11:44–45; 20:25–26; Deut. 14:21).

In the course of God's plan of salvation, certain things are called holy—*land* (Canaan), *person* (priest), *place* (sanctuary), *time* (holy day). This doesn't mean that the rest of creation isn't "very good" (Gen. 1:31). In fact, Jesus later declares all foods clean (Mark 7:19). Rather, Israel was to be a picture of holiness. This meant not only *separation* (Israel was called to holiness, which required being distinct from surrounding nations) and *wholeness* or *integrity*; it also meant the *imitation* of God (being holy as God is holy).[42] The entire existence of Israel expressed its holiness to God.[43]

Seventh, for Christians today, these purity laws—though no longer binding upon the follower of Christ, in whom these purity laws are fulfilled—serve as a reminder that we are to be distinctively cross-centered in our mindset and lifestyle in such a way that sets us apart from unbelievers. We know from Genesis that the animals God created are "good," and Jesus reminds us that no food is inherently unclean (Mark 7:15; cf. Acts 10:14–16; 11:9), but only symbolically so. Jesus proposed a new program centered around his person and work. In his ministry to Israel—and by extension to the whole world—he would take upon himself the curse of sin. In doing so, he broke down old barriers between Jew and non-Jew, between clean and unclean. He, in the spirit of Psalm 24:4 and Psalm 51:17, advocated purity or cleanness of *heart* (Matt. 5:8)—not purity of diet. Indeed, all foods are clean if received with a spirit of gratitude to God (1 Tim. 4:4).[44] In introducing a new order, Jesus himself frequently broke the taboos—for example, by touching and healing "unclean" lepers (Mark 1:40–45) or helping the woman with a hemorrhage which had rendered her permanently ceremonially unclean (Mark 5:25–34). Jesus transmitted purity and cleanness rather than contracting uncleanness.

In the Sermon on the Mount (Matthew 5–7), Jesus tells his disciples that they are to be different (e.g., 6:8: "Do not be like them"). Later in the New Testament, Paul (in Eph. 4:17) tells his audience comprised mostly of Gentile Christians *not to live like the Gentiles* (i.e., unbelievers)! Rather, Christians are to live like *true Jews*, who have been transformed in heart (Rom. 2:28–29). But it is the laws of Sinai—and the salvation-historical context of the Old Testament—that help create a setting by which we can better understand how the inter-ethnic church is to live a life of "holy worldliness"—to be in the world but not of it (John 17:11, 14–19).

Despite the fact that horrendous, anti-Christian things have been done in the name of Christ (the Crusades, the Inquisition, witch-hunting, etc.), the Christian church has played an important part in bringing huge benefits to civilization. These include abolishing of slavery (based on the principle that all people are made in God's image), opposing infanticide/exposure of infants during Roman times, promoting women's rights, building hospitals and hospices, writing great literature (e.g., Milton, Shakespeare), composing great music (e.g., J. S. Bach, Handel), training in literacy, and establishing universities out of medieval monasteries. Alvin Schmidt has documented these remarkable, revolutionary achievements in his excellent book *How Christianity Changed the World*.[45] Though the church isn't a political entity, it has had—and continues to have in many parts of the world—a powerful positive influence as salt and light within society. Through discussion and persuasion in word and deed, we must work to show that the Jewish-Christian worldview actually offers to society the basis for affirming human dignity, worth, and rights as well as the bonds of marriage between husband and wife and the place of "faith-based initiatives" like Prison Fellowship. A secular agenda is unable to ground human rights or the sanctity of marriage. In the "clash of orthodoxies" in the public domain, we Christians should seek to show how a thoughtful faith can have a bearing on public policy. We don't do this by saying "the Bible says" (which many non-Christians today don't take as authoritative anyway). Rather, we appeal to God's general revelation, which is available to all people, to discuss and persuade people by God's grace how many Christian assumptions make good sense and help create better conditions for human flourishing—even in this fallen world.[46]

Today, as Christians—the new community of God's people, true Jews, a royal priesthood and holy nation—we must recognize that God is concerned not just with "getting us to heaven" (or even just with social justice) but with the transformation of every area of life—that all things may be brought under the lordship of Christ.[47]

Despite the sarcastic "open letter" to Dr. Laura regarding Levitical laws, we've seen that many of these (e.g., food, clothing, planting laws) serve an important symbolic purpose with significant theological ramifications. Furthermore, such a letter fails to consider the Christian perspective of the *temporary* theocratic rule under which national Israel was to live. This perspective sees Levitical laws as incomplete—a foreshadowing of and preparation for the substance that was to come in Christ, whose work inaugurated a new inter-ethnic community of believers scattered among the nations.

SUMMARY

- Israel owed its very existence to the saving activity of God in history, and Israel's status as a theocracy was a privilege—and responsibility—rooted in the grace of God.
- Under the authority of Mosaic law, Old Testament Israel uniquely existed as a theocracy (i.e., governed or led by God) in preparation for the coming Messiah. A cultural and theological context needed to be established first to make sense of what Jesus as God's Messiah would do.
- It's helpful to think of many Old Testament laws in terms of a redemptive-movement interpretation within Scripture; we must look beyond the isolated verses in question and observe the underlying spirit and the movement of Scripture.
- The God of holiness wanted his people to be reminded constantly that they were to be holy in every dimension of life.
- Many of the Mosaic commands to Israel reflect a sense of wholeness, completeness, and integrity; no admixtures were allowed (e.g., in clothing, seeds sown in a field, or the eating of animals that transgressed the individual and distinctive "spheres" of air, water, or land). This badge of holy distinction was to serve as a reminder to Israel to be distinct from surrounding nations rather than "mixed in" with their mindset and ways.

- There was a link between the kinds of *animals* that were permitted or forbidden in the Israelites' diet and the kind of *people* God wanted them to be—they weren't to be "predators" in their human relationships. To symbolize this, (a) predatory animals were to be avoided for food as were (b) ugly, (apparently) defenseless, and odd-looking animals, which symbolized the vulnerable in society.

- For Christians today, these purity laws—though no longer binding upon the follower of Christ, in whom these purity laws are fulfilled—serve as a reminder that we are to be distinctively cross-centered in our mindset and lifestyle in such a way that sets us apart from unbelievers.

Further Reading

Douglas, Mary. "The Forbidden Animals in Leviticus." *Journal for the Study of the Old Testament* 59 (1993): 3–23.

Webb, William J. *Slaves, Women, and Homosexuals: Exploring the Hermeneutics of Cultural Analysis.* Downers Grove, IL: InterVarsity, 2003.

Wenham, Gordon J. *Leviticus.* New International Commentary on the Old Testament. Grand Rapids: Eerdmans, 1979.

————. "The Theology of Unclean Food." *Evangelical Quarterly* 53 (1981): 6–15.

Wright, Christopher. *Deuteronomy.* New International Biblical Commentary, Old Testament Series 4. Peabody, MA: Hendrickson, 1996.

13

WHY ARE SOME OLD TESTAMENT LAWS HARSH AND OPPRESSIVE?

In the previous chapter we looked at some of the Levitical laws that seem strange and arbitrary. In this chapter, we want to look at ones that seem harsh and oppressive.

First, there are good reasons for the miscellaneous Levitical laws God gave the people of Israel. Atheist Bertrand Russell believed that the Levitical command "You are not to boil a young goat in the milk of its mother" (Exod. 23:19; 34:26; Deut. 14:21) was simply arbitrary.[1] But was God just giving arbitrary commands? We have already seen that there is a symbolic rationale behind dietary (and clothing and planting) laws. God's commands were intended to remind Israel of their devotion to God and to help Israel keep a distance from its neighbors so that the nation would not be lured away by false religion.[2] *Other commands* in the Mosaic law appear to have this motive behind them. The prohibition against boiling a young goat in its mother's milk seems to have the following reason behind it: *the created order of things would be violated.* "A substance that sustains the life of a creature (milk) should not be fused or confused with a process associated with its death (cooking)."[3] A mother's life-giving milk for her offspring shouldn't be associated with its death.

Or what about cutting one's body for the dead or putting tattoo marks on one's body (Lev. 19:28)? These actions were probably prohibited because of their association with Canaanite/false religion (note 1 Kings 18:28, where prophets of Baal cut themselves). This prohibition against cutting the body applied to priests as well, who were to be holy to their God (Lev. 21:5–6). Furthermore, these acts were seen as a kind of self-imposed alteration—and thus desecration—of the body God had created.[4] The prohibition against men trimming their hair on the sides of their head or the edges of their beard (Lev. 19:27; cf. Deut. 14:1) probably reflects the rejection of the Canaanite practice of making an offering of hair to departed spirits to appease them.

Repeatedly in the Pentateuch (Genesis through Deuteronomy), certain standards are set for the nation of Israel to maintain its theocratic/religious distinctiveness. This is likely reflected in the requirement for a Jewish mother to be separated from the temple for a period of time after giving birth. After this prescribed time elapsed, the mother could come to the tabernacle/temple (Lev. 12). Why have such a restriction? In ancient Near Eastern polytheism, with its strong emphasis on religious fertility rites, the births of gods and goddesses and their sexual unions were dramatized to express the human sexual and reproductive drive. So Israel was to set itself apart from such practices in contrast to the Canaanite fertility rites that closely linked religion and fertility/sexual activity.[5] Excluding the mother from formal religious worship during this time helped create a distance between the birth-event itself and the worship of God.[6]

Mediums and sorcerers were prohibited from living in Israel (Lev. 19:26; Exod. 22:18; 1 Sam. 28:9). Because Israel was a theocracy—not a democracy—worship of the true God was covenantally required, and false religion wasn't permitted. Those who didn't like this arrangement were *free to leave and live among the nations*,[7] but those who remained were bound in a covenant with the God who, through Abraham, called them and later delivered them from slavery in Egypt with signs and wonders.

Whatever the explanation for these laws related to diet, clothing, planting, and the like, Israelites were to obey them because (1) God commanded them to obey out of allegiance to the God who delivered and entered into relationship with them; (2) these commands served as a reminder for Israel to be holy in all aspects of its life; (3) Israel, in both symbol and substance, had to differentiate itself from the false religion surrounding it; (4) these commands served as a reminder that God was to be approached in the way he prescribed rather than the way humans would prefer.

Second, although certain Levitical laws may seem at first to be harsh, unreasonable, and/or unethical to modern ears, the difficulties can be significantly diminished or resolved altogether by achieving, through deeper investigation, a better understanding of the text and appreciating the cultural (ancient Near East) context of Israel. Although there are a number of passages we could discuss, we will look in more detail at a few sample passages to better appreciate the law of Moses in its historical and cultural context.

Exodus 21:20–21 reads: "If a man beats his male or female slave with a rod and the slave dies as a direct result, he must be punished, but he is not to be punished if the slave gets up after a day or two, since the slave is his property [literally, *money*]" (NIV). Is the slave a *person* or merely *property*, as some take this passage as portraying? Although I have dealt with the question of slavery in the Bible elsewhere,[8] I wish to address some important questions that often come up.

The Bible repeatedly speaks of the full humanity—and equality—of slaves with their masters. Both are made in the image of God. For instance, Job says of his slaves (Job 31:13–15 NIV):

> If I have denied justice to my menservants and maidservants
>   when they had a grievance against me,
> what will I do when God confronts me?
>   What will I answer when called to account?
> Did not he who made me in the womb make them?
>   Did not the same one form us both within our mothers?

Contrary to first appearances, the Exodus passage actually supports the full personhood and dignity of human slaves.[9] If the master struck a slave so severely that he died immediately, the master would be tried for capital punishment. Taking "life for life" (Exod. 21:23–24)—which follows on the heels of the slave-beating passage—confirms that the slave was to be treated as a human being with dignity, not as property.

On the other hand, if the slave *didn't* die immediately as a result of this act of using the rod (which wasn't a lethal weapon—like a spear or sword—and therefore required different considerations than if it were a lethal weapon) but happens to die after "a day or two," the master is given the benefit of the doubt that the slave was likely being disciplined and that there was no intention to murder. Of course, if the slave died immediately, no further proof was needed. Keep in mind that later this passage states that if a master injures a slave by blinding an eye or knocking out a tooth, the slave would be entitled to freedom and exemption from any further debt (Exod. 21:26–27).

What about when the passage says that the slave is the master's "property" or "money" (21:21)? The point isn't that slaves were chattel—mere property rather than persons. Rather, "the owner has an investment in this slave that he stands to lose either by death (not to mention capital punishment as well) or by emancipation (vv. 26–27)."[10] To kill a slave would harm the master's moneybag. One Old Testament scholar comments: "This law is unprecedented in the ancient world where a master could treat his slave as he pleased."[11] So the intent of this Exodus passage upholds, rather than tears down, the dignity of the slave.

Not only was the life of the *slave* intrinsically valuable. So was the life of the *unborn* in its mother's womb. Some proabortion advocates looking for some theological proof text for the permissibility of abortion have appealed to Exodus 21:22–25 (NIV).

> If men who are fighting hit a pregnant woman and she gives birth prematurely [some advocate an alternate reading: "she has a miscarriage"] but there is no serious injury, the offender must be fined whatever the woman's husband demands and the court allows. But if there is serious injury, you are to take life for life, eye for eye, tooth for tooth, hand for hand, foot for foot, burn for burn, wound for wound, bruise for bruise.

The issue is whether the Hebrew word *yeled* should be translated "give birth [prematurely]" *or* "have a miscarriage." Was there a low regard for the life of the unborn in the Old Testament? If the mother only *miscarries*, with the result that the offender only has to pay a fine, the implication is that the fetus isn't intrinsically valuable and so isn't deserving of the care normally given to a person outside the womb.

Ironically, the passage says just the opposite! The word *yālad* means "go forth" or "give birth," describing a normal birth (Gen. 25:26; 38:28–30; Job 3:1; 10:18; Jer. 1:5; 20:18). It's *always used of giving birth, not of a miscarriage.* If Moses meant "miscarriage," he could have used the typical word for "miscarry" (*shākal*). "Miscarry" *isn't* used here, though it's used elsewhere in the Old Testament.[12]

Furthermore, *yālad* ("give birth") is always used of a child who has recognizable human form or is capable of surviving outside the womb. The word *gōlem*, which means "fetus," is used only once in the Old Testament: in Psalm 139:16, where God knew the psalmist's "unformed body" (NIV)—yet *another* passage that undermines alleged biblical support for abortion.

This brings us to another question: *Who is injured?* The baby or the mother? The text is silent. It could be *either*, since the feminine pronoun is missing. The gist of the passage seems to be this:

> If two men fight and hit a pregnant woman and the baby is born prematurely, but there is no serious injury [to the child or to the mother], then the offender must be fined whatever the husband demands and the court allows. But if there is serious injury [to the baby or to the mother], you are to take life for life, eye for eye . . .

From these verses we can actually infer the intrinsic value of the unborn child—that the life of the offender is to be taken if the life of the mother or the child is lost. The unborn child is given the same rights as an adult (Gen. 9:6).

Third, many Old Testament laws present a worst-case scenario (and thus appear much more harsh and negative), but biblical authors hoped for virtuous character in the Israelites (love, compassion, generosity, justice) rather than their merely following the letter of the law.[13] The historian Tacitus (AD 55–120) wrote of Rome, "The more corrupt the Republic, the more numerous the laws."[14] In other words, if moral character declines in a culture, law upon law will be issued to make up for this lack. Just think back to transactions between individuals a generation or two ago. Individuals within a community often needed nothing more than a handshake to make an agreement official. Today, bureaucracy, paperwork, and logistical hurdles typically characterize many a transaction.

Old Testament scholar Gordon Wenham writes: "Although the law gives some clues to the [Old Testament] writers' outlook, it represents the *floor* of acceptable behaviour not its *ceiling*."[15] What is socially acceptable or what can be reinforced by the keepers of society doesn't necessarily reflect the ideals of the lawgivers. For example, we're right to recognize adultery as immoral, but our society's laws don't criminalize adulterers—as destructive and treacherous as adultery is. God never intended that *love* be reduced to *obeying the law*. Ideally, Israel was to *love* God wholeheartedly and to *cling* to him. When the psalmist says, "My heart and my flesh sing for joy to the living God" (Ps. 84:2), this goes far beyond following a mere legal code.

Fourth, many Old Testament laws reflect divine permission rather than divine sanction. Since God's ideals were frequently ignored, God made concessions for human hard-heartedness. Many laws in Israel reflected less-than-ideal societal conditions. Once Jesus told his opponents (who asked about Moses's "command" to divorce) that Moses merely *permitted* divorce because of the hardness of human hearts (Matt. 19:8). However, this wasn't God's *intention* from the beginning (Gen. 2:24). God *permitted* slavery and multiple marriages in the Bible, but these weren't God's ideals (Gal. 3:28; Matt. 19:4–6). At a different level, God *permitted* violence—for example, capital punishment, warfare—but this doesn't mean that he *prefers* this to the peaceable kingdom of the new heavens and new earth (Isaiah 11).

Fifth, God ultimately desired an uncomplicated, less restrictive manner of life and worship for Israel—with all Israelites as priests (Exod. 19:6) and offering simple offerings like the patriarchs did. However, Israel's idolatry (Exod. 32—the golden calf; Lev. 17:1–9—the goat idols) led to more stringent laws for Israel; this wasn't God's ultimate intent, however. Paul, in Romans 4 and Galatians 3–4, downplays the prominence of the law of Moses while emphasizing Abraham's *faith/trust in God*.[16] Because of this, Abraham was counted righteous (Gen. 15:6) *before* he and his household were circumcised—and well before the law at Sinai was given.

Paul highlights Abraham in making these important theological points: (1) Abraham was accepted before God not because of self-effort but by *trusting God's promises and provision*; (2) *Abraham's faith enabled him to meet the demands or requirements of the law* (Gen. 26:5); (3) *thus, the law at Sinai is temporary and provisional in nature*: God's requirement of faith was permanent and more fundamental (for all God's people at all times); the law was a short-term arrangement—for a particular period in Israel's history—and it came in response to Israel's disobedience. In the end, Paul argued that if everyone had to follow the law to please God, then this would *exclude* Abraham himself!

Using humble altars, Abraham worshiped like a priest who had intimate access to God. He offered sacrifices wherever he went (Gen. 12:6–9; 13:3–4, 19); Isaac and Jacob would do the same. God had *similar intentions* for Israel's worship as a nation. He wanted them to be a "kingdom of priests" (Exod. 19:6) so that Israel could reflect God's glory and bring blessing to the nations. *Even before* the Aaronic priesthood, "the young men of the sons of Israel" offered burnt offerings and fellowship offerings (Exod. 24:5).

At Sinai, the Israelites agreed to enter into this covenant with God (Exod. 19:8). God's meeting with his nation of priests was anticipated when God told Moses at the burning bush, "When you [singular] have brought the people out of Egypt, you [plural] shall worship God at this mountain [Horeb or Sinai]" (Exod. 3:12).[17] *God's intention, then, was to meet his people as priests—not just Moses alone—on Mount Sinai to enter into a covenant with them without a complex, weighty system of laws.* But as it turns out, Israel, instead of being a kingdom *of* priests, would be a kingdom *with* priests.[18]

Interestingly, *before the golden calf incident* (Exodus 32), God gave *Israel* (Exod. 20:1–7; 20:22–23:33) and the *priests* (Exod. 25:1–31:18) a fairly *simple code of laws* to follow (the "*Covenant* Code"). These weren't elaborate demands or rituals. This covenant reflected the worship of the patriarchs—"earthen altars, burnt offerings, simple devotion."[19] Like their father Abraham, the people of Israel were to *obey God* (Exod. 19:5; cf. Gen. 26:5), *keep his covenant* (Exod. 19:5; cf. Gen. 17:1–14), and *live by faith* (Exod. 19:9; cf. Gen. 15:6). In Exodus 20:24–26, *a simple earthen altar was sufficient.* If a stone altar was desired, it was not to be ornately cut or carved or have elaborate steps. The primary concern in this simple Covenant Code is "the absolute prohibition of idolatry and the simple offering of praise and sacrifice."[20]

After Israel's worship of the golden calf, things change dramatically. In this act of idolatry, *the high priest, Aaron, was* the leading participant (Exodus 32). As a result, *God handed down a more complex set of laws to the priests* (Exodus 35 through Leviticus 16—known as the "*Priestly* Code"). In addition, God selected the Levites (from the tribe of Levi) to assist the priests in their tabernacle service (Exod. 32:29; cf. Num. 3:7–8).

Right after this long section of Scripture (ending at Leviticus 16), the *people of Israel* are said to have engaged in worship of *goat idols* (Lev. 17:1–9)—another act of flagrant disobedience. In similar fashion, *God handed down a complex set of laws for Israel's everyday life* (Lev. 17:10 through Leviticus 26—the "*Holiness* Code").

With the golden calf incident and then goat-idol worship, *God's expectations were no longer straightforward and simple like the earlier Covenant Code was*; rather, this new legislation sought to "ensure Israel's obedience through an elaborate system of priestly requirements."[21] But we should note that the stringency of these laws wasn't God's intention from the beginning. The Old Testament as well as the New bears this out. Jeremiah 7:22 emphasizes this: "For I did not speak to your fathers or command them in the day I brought them out of the land of Egypt, concerning burnt offerings and sacrifices [as with the elaborate requirements and rituals involving a class of priests]. But this is what I commanded them [as with the patriarchs Abraham, Isaac, and Jacob], saying, 'Obey My voice, and I will be your God, and you will be My people; and you will walk in the way which I command you, that it may be well with you.'"

Later in Scripture (Gal. 3:19), Paul expresses this idea of the law of Sinai coming in response to Israel's disobedience, indicating that this was a *temporary measure*: the law was added to the covenant "because of the transgressions" of the people (the golden calf, the goat idols). N. T. Wright observes that the law of Moses was *a necessary part of God's plan, but not his final word. The laws from Sinai were never intended to be permanent.*[22] It was a temporary legal and ceremonial code introduced for a specific purpose; it was to hold sway until the coming of Christ, the seed. The law (of Moses) was added to the promise (made to Abraham)

because of *Israel's transgressions.* He notes that "the Torah [the law of Moses at Sinai] is given for a specific period of time, and is then set aside—not because it was a bad thing now happily abolished, but because it was a good thing whose purpose had now been accomplished."[23] *God had always intended for there to be one single family of Abraham comprised of all the nations* (Gen. 12:3; cf. Gal. 3:8), but many Jews in Jesus's and Paul's day were using the laws of Sinai (food laws, purity laws, holy days, and the temple worship) to maintain a Jewish-Gentile distinction rather than being a light to the nations (Isa. 49:6).[24]

Sixth, even though most of the laws God gave Israel were intended to be severe (due to Israel's rebellion), they still fell far short of other law codes of the ancient Near East (e.g., Hammurabi's). In the second millennium BC, the king of the first Babylonian dynasty, Hammurabi, issued the first series of judicial codes in world history. This influential code exhibited the brute and harsh power of this king. As world historian Paul Johnson notes, "These dreadful laws are notable for the ferocity of their physical punishments, in contrast to the restraint of the Mosaic Code and the enactments of Deuteronomy and Leviticus."[25] So we shouldn't overlook this marked contrast and Israel's own ancient Near East context: Even though the Mosaic law was *intentionally* harsh because of Israel's flagrant repudiation of God's gracious covenant with its simple requirements, it still falls *far short* of the severe Code of Hammurabi.

Seventh, the law of Moses was intended to be temporary—due to Israel's disobedience and hard-heartedness. It shouldn't be seen as the permanent model to follow for all nations at all times. In the last chapter, we looked at the "open letter" to Dr. Laura. We can see more clearly now that this letter *wrongly* presupposed the following about the Mosaic law: (1) the *permanence* of it (the vast majority of laws were given in response to Israel's startling disobedience in the wilderness [the golden calf and goat-idol incidents]); (2) the *ideal nature* of it (many laws were given because of human hard-heartedness and thus don't express God's ultimate desire for Israel); and (3) the *intentions of God* for his people (God, who initially gave much simpler laws, shouldn't be viewed as a harsh despot but as a divine Father dealing with rebellious children [cf. Isaiah 1:2]).

These are just a handful of examples of how Levitical laws uphold human dignity and rights rather than undermining them. But we must take pains to understand and appreciate such laws—and there are plenty of resources available to investigate these matters.

SUMMARY

- There are good reasons for the miscellaneous Levitical laws God gave the people of Israel: (a) God commanded them to obey out of allegiance to the God who delivered and entered into relationship with them; (b) these commands served as a reminder for Israel to be holy in all aspects of its life; (c) Israel would in both symbol and substance differentiate itself from the false religion surrounding it; (d) these commands served as a reminder that God was to be approached in the way he prescribed rather than the way humans would prefer.

- Although certain Levitical laws (e.g., regarding treatment of slaves or of the unborn) may seem at first to be harsh, unreasonable, and/or unethical to modern ears, the difficulties can be significantly diminished or resolved altogether by achieving, through deeper investigation, a better understanding of the text and appreciating the cultural (ancient Near East) context of Israel.

- Many Old Testament laws present a worst-case scenario (and thus appear much more harsh and negative), but biblical authors hoped for virtuous character in the Israelites (love, compassion, generosity, justice) rather than their merely following the letter of the law.

- Many Old Testament laws reflect divine permission rather than divine sanction. Since God's ideals were frequently ignored, God made concessions for human hard-heartedness. Many laws in Israel reflected less-than-ideal societal conditions.

- God ultimately desired an uncomplicated, less-restrictive manner of life and worship for Israel—with all Israelites as priests (Exod. 19:6) and offering simple offerings like the patriarchs did. However, Israel's idolatry (Exodus 32—the golden calf; Lev. 17:1–9—the goat idols) led to more stringent laws for Israel; this wasn't God's ultimate intent, however.

- Even though most of the laws God gave Israel were intended to be severe (due to Israel's rebellion), they still fell far short of other law codes of the ancient Near East (e.g., Hammurabi's).
- The law of Moses was intended to be temporary—due to Israel's disobedience and hard-heartedness. It shouldn't be seen as the permanent model to follow for all nations at all times. It wasn't (a) permanent, (b) ideal, or (c) reflective of God's ultimate intentions for his people.

FURTHER READING

Kaiser, Walter. *Toward Old Testament Ethics.* Grand Rapids: Zondervan, 1986.

Webb, William J. *Slaves, Women, and Homosexuals: Exploring the Hermeneutics of Cultural Analysis.* Downers Grove, IL: InterVarsity, 2003.

Wenham, Gordon J. *Leviticus.* New International Commentary on the Old Testament. Grand Rapids: Eerdmans, 1979.

Wright, Christopher. *An Eye for an Eye.* Downers Grove, IL: InterVarsity, 1983.

_____. *Deuteronomy.* New International Biblical Commentary, Old Testament Series 4. Peabody, MA: Hendrickson, 1996.

_____. *Walking in the Ways of the Lord.* Downers Grove, IL: InterVarsity, 1995.

14

IT'S UNFAIR THAT HUMANS ARE PUNISHED FOR ADAM'S SIN (PART 1)

The first lesson in the old Puritan *New England Primer* declares, "In Adam's fall / We sinned all." Romans 5:12 declares, "Therefore, just as sin entered the world through one man, and death through sin, and in this way death came to all men, because all sinned . . ." (NIV). A certain spiritual infection, known as *original sin*, has been passed on to us from Adam. Edward T. Oakes writes, "No doctrine inside the precincts of the Christian Church is received with greater reserve and hesitation, even to the point of outright denial, than the doctrine of original sin."[1] Is it fair to be held responsible and strapped with the consequences of an act committed by (a) *someone else* (b) *in completely different circumstances* (c) *ages ago*? In this chapter, we'll look at a few preliminaries regarding original sin. Then in the next chapter, we'll offer a response to this *original sin* question.[2]

First, Genesis 1–2 comes before Genesis 3: human nature was created and pronounced good by God but has been corrupted. We should begin our understanding of man as, first of all, God's good creation and only secondarily as a fallen creature. Although we're sinners, we shouldn't begin thinking about ourselves with only that fact in mind. God created humans in his image or likeness (Gen. 1:27; 9:6; James 3:9; cf. Ps. 8). To say we're "just worthless sinners" presents a lopsided picture. While *unworthy* of God's grace, we're not *worthless.* There's a disfigured beauty to us; we're a damaged work of art. We do a disservice to Christian theology by emphasizing human sinfulness and obscuring the goodness of God's creation. We may also damage our Christian witness with, say, a Hindu by emphasizing that we're "just sinners." The Hindu recognizes there's something special or unique about us—though that doesn't make us divine. In addition to Christ as God's own image, Genesis 1–2, not Genesis 3, should be our starting point for properly understanding human nature.

Second, because human beings still possess the divine image, this makes them good in their very nature. But sin—which isn't intrinsic to our nature—has internally damaged and corrupted us so that our soul's faculties are incorrectly aligned. Philosophically speaking, the nature of something is "what makes a thing what it is."[3] Sin doesn't make us what we are as humans. Adam was essentially human (or human by nature) before the fall. Also, Christ was essentially human, being without sin. Furthermore, believers will be fully human but without sin in the new heavens and new earth. So the saying "To err is human" simply speaks of the empirical fact of the depth and universality of sin after the fall. However, it's not essential to who we are as human beings.

To confuse matters, the New International Version (NIV) incorrectly translates the word "flesh [*sarx*]" as "sinful nature" in certain critical places, which can create—and has created—much confusion. New Testament scholar Thomas Schreiner says that the NIV's translation is "unfortunate" and introduces a metaphysical category that's foreign to Paul.[4] A new "entity" or "thing" is being introduced where it shouldn't be. According to Romans 8:9, believers *aren't* "in the flesh"—the this-worldly oriented realm dominated by sin's power; they're now "in the Spirit"—the new realm where believers dwell through Christ, by whom believers can live victoriously (Rom. 6:12–14).

The Lutheran Formula of Concord (1580)[5] makes the helpful distinction between (a) *a philosophically precise use of "nature"*—namely, "the very substance of man, as when we say, 'God created human nature'"—and (b) *a metaphorical, less precise one*—that is, a "temper, condition, defect, or vice of any thing implanted and inhering in the nature, as when we say: 'The serpent's nature is to strike, man's nature is to sin and is sin.'"[6] Much earlier, the philosopher Thomas Aquinas distinguished between "man's nature," which can be similarly understood: (a) human nature "in its integrity, as it was in our first parent before sin" and (b) human nature "as it is corrupted in us after the sin of our first parent."[7] (As an aside, although Romans 1 speaks of the "natural" order of creation, which sinful humans corrupt, the New Testament often uses "nature [*physis*]" in the *less* precise sense to refer to *the condition/state into which we've been born*, e.g., being Jewish "by nature" [Gal. 2:15]; cf. Eph. 2:3.)

Human nature in the *philosophically precise* sense is good; in the *less* philosophically precise sense, it speaks of the sinful condition in which we find ourselves in a post-fall, pre-restoration world. British theologian Alister McGrath has said that it's much less confusing to use the term *sinful condition* or *sinful state*; these terms are to be preferred over the misleading and imprecise term *sinful nature*.[8]

Because of the fall, human nature is out of alignment or out of harmony with itself. Our desires and capacities have been distorted and maladjusted. There's *not* another "thing" that's been added to our nature (contrary to what the NIV suggests).

This point about *human nature* is important for our very salvation. Christ took on our human nature so that he could identify with us to be a true mediator between us and God—the God-man. New Testament scholar F. F. Bruce correctly observes: "It is because man in the creative order bears the image of his Creator that it was possible for the Son of God to become incarnate as man and in His humanity to display the glory of the invisible God."[9] Theologian Harold O. J. Brown rightly comments that if

> man is by nature a sinner, then in the incarnation either Jesus became a sinner or did not truly assume human nature. . . . *If sin belongs to the very nature of man, then Christ cannot be consubstantial* [i.e., sharing in the same nature] *with us, as the Chalcedonian Creed affirms, unless sin also belongs to his nature, which the creed denies.* . . . The mistake lies in thinking that the Fall has so altered human nature that sin is now an

essential component of humanity, so that no one and nothing can be human without thereby partaking in error and even in sin.[10]

The late British theologian Colin Gunton has summarized the matter quite well: because creation—which includes the image of God—is the work and good gift of God, "it is necessary to conclude that evil . . . is not intrinsic to the creation, but some corruption of, or invasion into, that which is essentially good."[11] So human nature is *good* but has been deeply affected and infected by the fall—like poison being mixed into wine. We are good by nature—though marred by the fall.

Third, the exact connection between us and Adam's sin isn't as clear as we would like it to be (or as some say it is). Scripture's lack of clarity on the specifics of original sin can prove to be an open door in defending the doctrine in the face of criticism. Let's look at Romans 5:12 again: "Therefore, just as sin entered the world through one man, and death through sin, and in this way death came to all men, because all sinned. . . ." There are lots of theories attempting to define and describe how Adam's sin has affected us or been transmitted to us. After surveying them, theologian James Leo Garrett observes: "To affirm the universality of sin is easy and to affirm the universality of depravity is not difficult, but to settle on the relationship of the sin of Adam and Eve to our sin is indeed difficult."[12]

One problem is that scholars have sometimes drawn parallels in Romans 5 between Adam and Christ more tightly than they should. For example, although Adam's sin transmitted to us a negative, self-centered *inclination*, this isn't balanced out by Christ's conferring upon us a "good inclination" through justification (being declared righteous by God).[13] This inclination to please God comes by virtue of God's Spirit.

Some who try to prove a tight connection between Adam and the rest of humanity appeal to Hebrews 7:9–10, which speaks of Levi being "in the loins" of Abraham when Abraham gave Melchizedek a tenth of his plunder (Genesis 14). This connection goes way too far, however, as theologian Henri Blocher observes: "All actions of all progenitors would have to be ascribed to each of their descendants, which is nearly absurd."[14]

Or we can ask: Does Christ's death put us in right standing before God regardless of our making a personal and conscious choice in response to God's prevenient (initiating) grace?

On the topic of original sin, *there's a consensus about the lack of consensus* on what the exact connection is between us and Adam's sin. So Romans 5:12 shouldn't be loaded with more theological freight than it's able to bear. The idea of an imputation of an "alien guilt" to Adam's offspring strains things theologically, as Charles Sherlock[15] and Henri Blocher[16] have argued. New Testament scholar Douglas Moo wisely writes:

> Perhaps, indeed, Paul has not provided us with enough data to make a definite decision; and we should probably be content with the conclusion that Paul affirms the reality of a solidarity of all humanity with Adam in his sin without being able to explain the exact nature of that union.[17]

Christians can agree on the "universality, solidarity, stubbornness, and historical momentum of sin."[18] Henri Blocher concludes his book on original sin:

> With all due respect to the Reformed theology to which I am indebted, I have been led to question the doctrine of alien guilt transferred—that is, the doctrine of the imputation to all of Adam's own trespass, his act of transgression. If Scripture definitely taught such a doctrine, however offensive to modern taste, I should readily bow to its authority. But where does Scripture require it? My investigation did not find it in the only passage from which it is drawn, Romans 5. Could it be, then, a case of laying a heavy burden upon people's shoulders, beyond the express demands of God?[19]

So there's a good deal of flexibility in how to understand the relationship of Adam's sin to our predicament.

Fourth, our deeply sinful condition should be understood in terms of **damage/consequences** *rather than* **guilt reckoned** *to all of us as the result of Adam's sin. Otherwise, what do we make of those who die in infancy or who are mentally retarded?* It would be a troublesome thing to claim that the mentally retarded or infants—who can't choose between evil and good (Isa. 7:15)—are automatically condemned through their sheer existence. Romans 5 doesn't seem to have in mind the handicapped or infants. Rather, Paul is apparently writing about those who *knowingly* sin. As Doug Moo writes: "Paul does not seem even to be considering in these verses the special issues created for the doctrine of universal sin and judgment by mentally restricted human beings."[20]

Someone might ask: *If infants or the mentally handicapped are innocent and they die in such a state, why think that the death of Jesus is required on their behalf?*[21] We could reply that the gracious atoning death of Jesus is still necessary for all since the soul of each person has been damaged by sin—even if one never has the opportunity to act sinfully. A certain deformity in the soul (which came through Adam's sin) needs the healing brought about through Christ's death. (We could add that the deformed body is also a condition that Christ's conquering death and resurrection will ultimately make whole in the new heavens and new earth.)

Reformed philosopher Ronald Nash points out that even though we inherit a sinful *condition* as members of the human race, we're *judged* according to our *deeds* done "in the body" (2 Cor. 5:10), which (I would add) are *an outworking of God's grace in one's life—or the absence of appropriating that grace*. Nash makes this point to say that *all* those dying in infancy are saved.[22] Biblical scholar Wayne Grudem writes that final condemnation ultimately falls upon those who have *acted* sinfully and turned away from God; indeed, God will judge us according to what we have *done* (Rom. 2:6; Col. 3:25).[23]

As the Old Testament affirms, the "soul who sins will die" (Ezek. 18:4; cf. 18:20). Under Israel's civic law, only the guilty party was to be punished: "Everyone shall be put to death for his own sin" (Deut. 24:16). Even King Abimelech (after unknowingly taking Abraham's wife Sarah, as his own wife) pleads his innocence before God since he acted unintentionally (Gen. 20:4–7), which God acknowledges—but after thoroughly scaring the tar out of him![24]

Having said this, we should go on to distinguish between *damage* or *consequences* that come from sin and the *guilt* brought about by sin. This will help us further clarify Adam's relationship to us. Think of Achan's sin (with an apparently cooperative family who knew he was hiding plunder from Jericho in his tent). Joshua 7 reveals that the *consequences* of one man's sin affected the well-being of the entire Israelite community (whose army had lost a relatively easy fight at Ai). Consider 2 Samuel 24:17, where David, who had arrogantly demanded that a census be taken, confessed to the Lord: "I am the one who has sinned and done wrong. These are but sheep. What have they done? Let your hand fall upon me and my family" (NIV).

Although we have a tendency to sin and our bodies are corruptible (all *consequences* of Adam's sin), the guilt of Adam's transgression isn't conferred upon us at conception. But, as we've seen, we can't ignore that *one's individual actions can have a powerful effect on others*. We need only think of children of alcoholics or divorce—or AIDS or crack babies—to witness the obvious. Another example is that when a president or king declares war on another country, then the children born during the war would be at war with another nation. They find themselves in such a situation through no choice of their own.[25]

The challenge for the Christian is to put in perspective our *corporate* connection to Adam (something individualistic Westerners resist) while also accounting for *individual* human responsibility (which makes sense of the justice of punishment and personal moral accountability). We mustn't make the connection so tight as to undermine human responsibility.[26]

Christian philosopher Alvin Plantinga speaks of sin in two respects: (1) *sinning*—something for which one is responsible ("He is guilty and warrants blame"), and (2) *being in* sin—a condition in which we find ourselves from birth.[27] Yes, I'm held guilty for a sinful act, but I can't be held guilty for the state of sin into which I've been born: "Insofar as I am born in this predicament, my being in it is not within my control and not up to me."[28] So we can accept original *sin*, but original *guilt* seems theologically and morally problematic.

We're born with an original corruption, a self-centered orientation that permeates all we do. But simply *being born* (or conceived) doesn't render a human being guilty before God—even if atonement is still necessary for removing the lingering stain of sin in the soul. Therefore, though we don't sin *necessarily* (i.e., it's not assured that we must commit this or that particular sin), we sin *inevitably* (i.e., in addition to our propensity to sin, given the vast array of opportunities to sin, we eventually do sin).[29]

*Fifth, **if** it turns out, however, that Adam's **guilt** somehow comes upon us as well, then this should be understood as **conditional**. That is, guilt is reckoned to us **when** we responsibly sin and, by our actions, approve of our sinful condition.* Some noted evangelical theologians want to maintain a tighter (and legal) connection with Adam (as our corporate or "federal" head), but they still want to account clearly for individual responsibility. They have suggested that *conditional guilt* is a plausible way of doing so. Theologian Millard Erickson suggests that if Adam's guilt is somehow reckoned to us, it's not imputed at birth. Rather, guilt comes *when there's a conscious, voluntary decision made on our part to do what's wrong.* Any guilt we would share with Adam (not to mention our own personal guilt) is *conditional,* based upon our response to God's grace as morally accountable agents.[30] Similarly, Gordon Lewis and Bruce Demarest comment on our *conditionally* sharing guilt with Adam:

> In Adam the sentence of condemnation is passed upon the whole human race, but *it is effectually executed only upon those who responsibly sin*; in Christ the verdict of justification is provided for the whole race, but is effectual only for those who trust him and are born again. . . . Although all are justly under the sentence of their natural and legal head [Adam], *none will suffer the execution of the penalty who have not themselves responsibly sinned.* Hence responsible sinful choice and action of a person must have taken place before that person suffers the penalty of eternal death. None will suffer eternally for being born in Adam's fallen race alone.[31]

Erickson puts it this way:

> We become responsible and guilty *when we accept or approve of our corrupt* [*state*]. There is a time in the life of each one of us when we become aware of our own tendency toward sin. At that point we may abhor the sinful [state] that has been there all the time. We would in that case repent of it and might even, if there is an awareness of the gospel, ask God for forgiveness and cleansing. At the very least there would be a rejection of our sinful makeup. But if we acquiesce in the sinful [state], we are in effect saying that it is good. In placing our tacit approval upon the corruption, we are also approving or concurring in the action in the Garden of Eden so long ago.[32]

In Adam, we find ourselves living with the fallout from our predecessor's transgression, but this doesn't imply that *his own* guilt is imputed or transferred to our account.

SUMMARY

- Genesis 1–2 comes before Genesis 3: human nature was created and pronounced good by God but has been corrupted. We should begin our understanding of man as, first of all, God's good creation and only secondarily as a fallen creature.

- Because human beings still possess the divine image, this makes them good in their very nature. But sin—which isn't intrinsic to our nature—has internally damaged and corrupted us so that our soul's faculties are incorrectly aligned.

- We should avoid referring to our "nature" as "sinful" (unless we clarify that "nature" is being used in a philosophically *imprecise* manner). God made human nature to be good—even though it has been deeply damaged by the fall. But because God has created human nature as good, it isn't *intrinsically* sinful. And if it were, then Jesus couldn't truly identify with human beings as the divine-human mediator, and therefore he couldn't bring about salvation for us.

- The exact connection between us and Adam's sin isn't as clear as we would like it to be (or as some say it is). Scripture's lack of clarity on the specifics of original sin can prove to be an open door in defending the doctrine in the face of criticism.

- Our deeply sinful condition should be understood in terms of *damage/consequences* rather than *guilt reckoned* to all of us as the result of Adam's sin. Otherwise, what do we make of those who die in infancy or who are mentally retarded?

- Those who die in infancy (or the mentally handicapped) still require Christ's atonement so that the stain of sin in their souls is removed—even if one never actually sins. But infants and the mentally handicapped aren't automatically condemned simply because they *exist*.

- AIDS and crack babies are clearly affected by the actions of their parents, but this doesn't render the babies guilty. The *consequences* of sin come to them, but not the *guilt* of sin. We're born with "original sin" (*damage* done to us through Adam's transgression—including a self-centered impulse), but we're not born with "original *guilt*" (an "alien guilt" imputed to us). There's a difference between "being in sin" and "sinning."

- *If* it turns out, however, that Adam's *guilt* somehow comes upon us as well, then this should be understood as *conditional*. That is, guilt is reckoned to us *when* we responsibly sin and, by our actions, approve of our sinful condition.

FURTHER READING

Blocher, Henri. *Original Sin: Illuminating the Riddle*. Grand Rapids: Eerdmans, 1997. Now published in a new edition. Downers Grove, IL: InterVarsity, 2001.

Copan, Paul. "Original Sin and Christian Philosophy." *Philosophia Christi* 2, vol. 5, no. 2 (2003): 519–41.

15

It's Unfair That Humans Are Punished for Adam's Sin (Part 2)

We have looked at some of the backdrop to understanding original sin. How then do we deal with the fairness question? How do we defend the plausibility of Christian theism in light of the original sin problem?

First, the doctrine of original sin is empirically verifiable throughout history, across civilizations, and in our own personal experience. This observation supports the realistic Jewish-Christian understanding of human nature rather than a more neutral or optimistic view. G. K. Chesterton is noted for his famous statement: "Certain new theologians dispute original sin, which is the only part of Christian theology which can really be proved."[1] Indeed, the "ancient masters of religion" began with the fact of sin—"a fact as practical as potatoes."[2] Even the naturalistic evolutionist Michael Ruse sees the explanatory power of original sin in the Jewish-Christian tradition:

> I think Christianity is spot on about original sin—how could one think otherwise, when the world's most civilized and advanced people (the

people of Beethoven, Goethe, Kant) embraced that slime-ball Hitler and participated in the Holocaust? I think Saint Paul and the great Christian philosophers had real insights into sin and freedom and responsibility, and I want to build on this rather than turn from it.[3]

The existence of evil seems obvious to our most basic and reliable intuitions.

So when the antagonist asks, "How could a morally respectable God allow human beings to get *this* bad?" we can reply, "If there's no God, why think humans really *are* evil—as opposed to 'abnormal' or socially/biologically determined?" The very existence of *evil* suggests a standard of goodness or a design plan. Evil would be a deviation from or corruption of this standard, or it would be a departure from the way things ought to be (a design plan)—why think things *ought* to be different if God doesn't exist?[4] Naturalism can't very easily account for the existence of evil, whereas Christian theism far more easily can.[5]

So the first point is that the easily verified fact of genuine sin and evil directs us toward a Christian view of humanity. The second point is like unto it.

Second, naturalistic explanations of moral evil (e.g., evil as "abnormal" or "maladjusted" according to psychological/therapeutic categories) are inadequate to capture the depth and horror of evil—as are Eastern views of evil as illusion (maya). The Christian worldview, though, provides a suitable context to understand it. Anna Russell is known for her "Psychiatric Folksong":

> At three I had a feeling of ambivalence toward my brothers;
> And so it follows naturally, I poisoned all my lovers.
> But now I'm happy, I've learned the lesson this has taught,
> That everything I do that's wrong is someone else's fault![6]

Common in naturalistic circles are attempts to get around evil and sin by referring to a "negative environment," to "abnormality," or to "dysfunction." Welcome to what Philip Rieff calls "the triumph of the therapeutic"![7] Are we conditioned by our environment, reduced merely to the causes and effects that preceded us? Do we just need therapy to get us back on the right track?

Now, if we're just products of our genes and environment, then *this view itself* is nothing more than the product of genes and environment! (Of course, the person espousing this view would like to believe she concluded rationally and believed it because it was *true*!) Furthermore, this view eliminates any personal moral responsibility and punishment. Are we truly willing to say that the Columbine killers were simply "abnormal," "maladjusted," or "statistically deviant"—not *evil*?[8] Eastern philosophies might explain away evil as ignorant *illusion (maya)* while some Western philosophies might reduce "evil" to *alienation and class struggle* (Marx), *neurosis* (Freud), or *refusal to choose between available alternatives as I forge my personal identity* (the "bad faith" of existentialism). Even if some of these ideas touch on various aspects of the human condition, they don't capture the core of it. In fact, they seem quite hollow compared to the explanation of original sin. Karl Menninger observed this in his book *Whatever Became of Sin?*

> I believe there is "sin" which is expressed in ways which cannot be subsumed under verbal artifacts such as "crime," "disease," "delinquency," "deviancy." There *is* immorality; there *is* unethical behavior; there *is* wrongdoing. And I hope to show that there is usefulness in retaining the concept, and indeed the SIN, which now shows some sign of returning to public acceptance. I would like to help this trend along.[9]

Theism, not naturalism or Eastern monism, can adequately deal with deep evil.[10]

Third, if we focus only on original sin, however, we're looking at an incomplete picture. Original sin must be understood in the fuller context of grace, redemption, and hope to understand properly its significance and depth. Secular alternatives offer no such hope. Psychologist Paul Vitz asks:

> What do we tell the over-ambitious business man at age forty [whose] career is finished because of a serious—possibly fatal—illness? What do we tell the woman alone in a desperately aging body and with a history of failed relationships? Does one say "go actualize yourself in creative activity"? For people in those circumstances such advice is not just irrelevant, it is an insult. It is exactly suffering, however, which is at the center of the meaning and hope of the religious life.[11]

Hobart Mowrer rightly noted that when we deny the reality of sin, *"we cut ourselves off . . . from the possibility of radical redemption (recovery)."*[12]

Without the language of sin, the language of salvation doesn't make sense. For the relativist, who believes there's no truth for all people (*except* the truth of relativism and the wrongness of intolerance!), there's no moral standard that has been violated. So there's no need for forgiveness. The same goes for much in contemporary psychotherapy: we need to become "self-actualized" or "well adjusted" rather than rightly related to God. The problem is: a person who thinks he's "well adjusted" may be terribly maladjusted to God. Theologian Vernon Grounds once wrote:

> An individual, quite completely free from tension, anxiety, and conflict may be only a well-adjusted sinner who is dangerously maladjusted to God; and it is infinitely better to be a neurotic saint than a healthy-minded sinner. . . . Healthy-mindedness may be a spiritual hazard that keeps an individual from turning to God precisely because he has no acute sense of God. . . . Tension, conflict, and anxiety, even to the point of mental illness, may be a cross voluntarily carried in God's service.[13]

Those who criticize Christianity because of its doctrine of original sin tend not to take seriously the *broader* picture of salvation, which is the *solution* to the original sin problem. As Gary Anderson notes, "Original sin is not a self-contained philosophical doctrine, but depends on the religious experience of redemption. The moment we isolate the sin of Adam from this broader framework we lose its larger meaning."[14] Rather than falling prey to hopelessness and despair because of our moral failings, God's Spirit can point us to the larger picture of the gracious salvation available to us from God through Christ. Sin isn't the total picture in anyone's biography. Human history itself involves not only deep sinfulness but the cross of Christ and the new heavens and new earth.[15] We can't think of the first Adam without thinking of the second Adam. But if we look to secular alternatives to "salvation," we're left without resolution to the human problem.

Fourth, the doctrine of original sin suggests the need for divine grace/ mercy and the insufficiency of our own human resources to deal with our guilt/sin—the "moral gap" between (God's) moral standards and our own performance. Original sin serves as a pointer toward the need for divine grace. This point relates to the previous point: not only do we *need* grace and redemption; they are actually *available* to those who cast themselves upon God's mercy. Our own moral and spiritual failure points us toward the solution. Romans 2:14–15 reminds us that there is a moral law that everyone knows—even if this is suppressed and the heart becomes hardened. Philosopher Thomas Reid correctly pointed out that general virtues and vices (such as treating another person as you want to be treated) "must appear self-evident to every man who has a conscience, and has taken the pains to exercise this natural power of his mind."[16] So even though God's moral law has been violated by each of us, this violation also serves as a sign of hope.

Each of us is aware of a great "moral gap" in our lives.[17] We're aware of (a) a *moral ideal or standard*. We also know of (b) *our own sin and inability to live up to that standard*. What's needed to bridge the gap is (c) *divine assistance/grace*. Original sin serves as a reminder that we have violated the moral law and that we badly need redemption and grace.

The philosopher Immanuel Kant said that "*ought* implies *can*." That is, if we have an *obligation* to do something ("ought"), then this implies that we have the *ability* to do it ("can"). But in light of the moral gap that exists, this should be modified to "*ought* implies *can—with God's available grace*."[18]

The entrance of sin into the world has brought momentous, devastating consequences. We come into the world as "damaged goods"—persons affected deeply by the power of sin and its consequences. The profound awareness of our sin reminds us of our moral *accountability* to God and our moral *inadequacy* before God and thus the need for assistance beyond our own resources. Despite the skeptic's charge that each human stands or falls on her own merits rather than another's, the fact "as practical as potatoes" is that our only real alternative is to cast ourselves upon God's mercy and ask for his grace, which he richly provides in the cross of Christ and the gift of his Spirit, who helps us live as we ought.[19]

Fifth, if God, by his Spirit, gives sufficient grace and opportunity to all people (even if most may reject it), then God isn't being unjust or unloving in allowing us to be damaged by the consequences of Adam's sin. Even though most people reject God's grace (as Romans 1 indicates), God offers sufficient direction to us so that we may cast ourselves upon God's mercy and find salvation. We aren't thrown into this world without available divine resources. God's prevenient grace is available to all through the Holy Spirit. God is near to every one of us (Acts 17:27) and is able to draw people to himself (John 6:44).[20] The fact that God gives humans freedom of the will entails the possibility of "always resisting the Holy Spirit" (Acts 7:51). God desires that all persons come to a knowledge of the truth (2 Peter 3:9).

So persons aren't condemned to hell, which is *the absence of God's presence* (2 Thess. 1:8–9), because they were born at the wrong place or at the wrong time. If a person is condemned, it's because he has resisted God's grace in his life and thus has sealed his own fate. *A person can't point to his sinful condition ("But I was born with original sin") as the basis of his eternal separation from God.* As William Craig observes, God doesn't send people to hell; rather, they *freely choose* to ignore and resist God's initiating grace in their lives so that they end up condemning themselves. Throughout the Scriptures, we see that *God expects/demands repentance and obedience from all persons (Acts 17:30), but surely he doesn't make this demand without supplying the needed grace for doing so.* People can only repent if God opens their eyes and helps them to see this need—although this conviction and illumination can be resisted.

In Isaiah 5, God (the vineyard owner) *expected* the people of Israel (his vineyard) to bear fruit after all he had done for them—"planting" Israel as "the choicest vine" on a fertile hill, digging all around the vineyard, removing the stones. Exasperated, God asks, "What more was there to do for My vineyard that I have not done in it? Why, when I expected it to produce good grapes did it produce worthless ones?" (v. 4; cf. Jer. 2:21, where God planted Israel as a "choice vine" and "faithful seed," but Israel turned away from God). In Jeremiah 3:7, God tells Jeremiah that he *expected* Israel to turn to him, but she continued to rebel. In the New Testament, Christ lamented over the city of Jerusalem, having *longed* to gather her children to himself, but "you were unwilling" (Matt. 23:37). Various religious leaders of Jesus's day "rejected God's purpose for themselves" (Luke 7:30). In Revelation, the risen Christ stated that he had given fair warning to a false prophetess he referred to as "Jezebel": "I gave her time to repent, and she does not want to repent of her immorality" (Rev. 2:21). These (and numerous other) verses[21] suggest that *the only obstacle to universal salvation is human free will and its resistance to God's loving initiative.*[22]

Ultimately, hell is "God's withdrawing of his presence and his blessings from men who have refused to receive them."[23] In the end, C. S. Lewis wrote, there are only two kinds of people: those who say *to God*, "Thy will be done," and those *to whom God says, "Thy* will be done."[24] Scottish pastor and author George MacDonald put it this way: "The one principle of hell is: I am my own."[25]

God doesn't condemn a person without the cooperation of his will. So *this original corruption, by itself, doesn't condemn us.* We are condemned when we align ourselves with it. We must rightly emphasize the *direction* of one's life as shaping one's *destiny*: Am I regularly resisting the grace and the knowledge of God? Or am I moving in a Godward direction? Scripture's emphasis seems to be more on the *direction* or *disposition* of one's heart and will that condemns a person—as opposed to individual *acts* of wrongdoing.[26] William Craig observes:

> The orthodox Christian need not hold that *every* sin merits hell or has hell as its consequence; rather hell is the final consequence (and even just punishment) for those who irrevocably refuse to seek and accept God's forgiveness of their sins. By refusing God's forgiveness they freely separate themselves from God forever. The issue, then, is whether the necessity of making this fundamental decision is too much to ask of a human being.[27]

God hasn't left human beings to make this choice on their own. *God, through his Spirit, is ready to equip anyone for salvation.* It is up to us to respond.

*Sixth, although many have complained that it's not fair that Adam ruined things for everyone else, it may well be that God knew that **any** of us human beings would have sinned in the Garden of Eden just as Adam and Eve did. Though this consideration doesn't address the relationship of Adam's sin to his offspring, it takes a certain presumption out of the discussion.* One particular objection commonly raised regarding Adam's headship of the human race is this: "Why should Adam be my representative head? He really fouled things up, and now, through no fault of anyone else, *everybody* is paying for it." Behind this comment is an unarticulated, arrogant presumption: "If *I* had been in Adam's place, I would have obeyed God's simple command not to take the fruit. I could have prevented the disastrous fallout from the first disobedience."

Think about this, though: perhaps it's the case that had *any* of us human beings been in Adam's place, each of us *would have* freely chosen to eat of the fruit and refused to trust God's word and character. What if *every* human being God created also would have fallen into sin just as Adam and Eve did? Though human sinlessness in the Garden is logically possible, it could be the case that those human beings God has created would have chosen the same Adamic *course*, resulting in the same Adamic *curse*. *The selection of another person would have produced no different outcome.* Had any of the rest of us created humans been in Adam's place, none of us by our free choice would have avoided bringing about the fall and its consequences.

Now this point *doesn't* address the specific connection between Adam and the rest of the human race (e.g., how corruption is transmitted). This point *does* offer perspective, though, about the inappropriateness of blaming Adam, whether expressly or implicitly: "God, I thank You that I am not like [Adam]" (see Luke 18:11). This perspective can help deflate charges of divine injustice regarding Adam being our representative head: *God knows that the rest of us would have acted in the very same way in the same circumstance.* After all, God *could have* placed any arrogant objector in the Garden—and the rest of the human race would still have felt the *same* effects *and* would still have mercilessly beaten up on that objector, just as Adam has been beaten up! Besides exonerating God against charges of injustice, this point can also serve as another important reminder to walk humbly before God and one another.[28]

We've seen that the doctrine of original sin makes the best sense of human experience, and alternative philosophies (abnormality, neurosis, alienation, illusion, etc.) fail to capture the depth of the human condition. Also, original sin isn't the full picture; it points us to the larger context of redemption and hope (which isn't available in secularist models) to help us make sense of the mystery of sin. Original sin reminds us of the need for God's grace in light of the "moral gap" each of us experiences.

Also, we don't fully understand the dramatic consequences that come from sin. We simply aren't in a good position to assess what the limits of the consequences of Adam's sin should be. And it just may be the case that, had *any* of us humans been in the Garden of Eden, we too would have disobeyed God's command and taken the fruit.

Furthermore, even if the Christian can't supply full answers, he can point to the love of God in Christ by saying, "If God is willing to go to such great lengths to bring us to reconciliation with himself by experiencing weakness, facing injustice, and enduring horrible suffering for our sakes, then surely we can leave in his hands such difficult questions as original sin." Indeed, the biblical tradition offers us a foothold—a context—for understanding original sin as well as a solution for overcoming it. The humanistic/secularistic and Eastern alternatives fail to capture the depth of sin and evil as does the Christian doctrine of original sin.

SUMMARY

- The doctrine of original sin is empirically verifiable throughout history, across civilizations, and in our own personal experience. It's "a fact as practical as potatoes." This observation supports the realistic Jewish-Christian understanding of human nature rather than a more neutral or optimistic view.
- Naturalistic explanations of moral evil (e.g., evil as "abnormal" or "maladjusted" according to psychological/therapeutic categories) are inadequate to capture the depth and horror of evil—as are the Eastern view of evil as illusory (*maya*). The Christian worldview, though, provides a suitable context to understand it.
- If we focus only on original sin, however, we're looking at an incomplete picture. Original sin must be understood in the fuller context of grace, redemption, and hope to understand properly its significance and depth. Secular alternatives offer no such hope.
- The doctrine of original sin suggests the need for divine grace/ mercy and the insufficiency of our own human resources to deal with our guilt/sin—the "moral gap" between (God's) moral stan-

dards and our own performance. Original sin serves as a pointer toward the need for divine grace.

- If God, by his Spirit, gives sufficient grace and opportunity to all people (even if most may reject it), then God isn't being unjust or unloving in allowing us to be damaged by the consequences of Adam's sin.

- God expects/demands repentance and obedience from all persons (Acts 17:30), but surely he doesn't make this demand without supplying the needed grace for doing so. Repentance requires God's initiating grace.

- Although many have complained that it's not fair that Adam ruined things for everyone else, it may well be that God knew that *any* of us human beings would have sinned in the Garden of Eden just as Adam and Eve did. Though this consideration doesn't address the relationship of Adam's sin to his offspring, it takes a certain presumption out of the discussion ("If *I* had been in Adam's place, things would have been different for the human race").

FURTHER READING

Blocher, Henri. *Original Sin: Illuminating the Riddle*. Grand Rapids: Eerdmans, 1997. Now published in a new edition. Downers Grove, IL: InterVarsity, 2001.

Copan, Paul. "Original Sin and Christian Philosophy." *Philosophia Christi* 2, vol. 5, no. 2 (2003): 519–41.

Klein, William. *The New Chosen People: A Corporate View of Election*. Grand Rapids: Zondervan, 1990. Now reprinted. Eugene, OR: Wipf and Stock, 2001.

16

WHY WERE CERTAIN TEXTS ARBITRARILY EXCLUDED FROM THE NEW TESTAMENT CANON?

In 1945 in Upper Egypt, an Arab peasant accidentally discovered ancient texts known as the Nag Hammadi Library (named after the town Naj 'Hammādī). Fifty-two different papyrus texts (which can be dated to AD 400) were found there. The most notable discovery was the *Gospel of Thomas*—an alleged "Gospel" containing sayings of Jesus.

Many of these documents are "Gnostic" writings, dating from the second/early third century AD.[1] Back then Gnosticism (from the Greek word *gnōsis*, "knowledge") was an amazingly varied belief-system/ religious movement in the Mediterranean world. It emphasized the following elements:

1. A secret, saving knowledge (*gnōsis*) or illumination is available only to a select "enlightened" few; ignorance, not sin, is the ultimate human problem.
2. The body/matter is evil, and the spirit/soul is good—a belief that tended to produce extreme self-denial (asceticism).

3. An eternal dualism exists between a good Being/God and an inferior evil being/god (who created matter); so the creator in Genesis is an inferior intermediary between the ultimate/true God (the Pleroma—"Fullness") and this world.

4. History is unimportant and insignificant; if Jesus played any part in Gnostic systems, he only appeared to be human but was really divine; God couldn't take on an evil human body or suffer on a cross. (This view is known as Docetism, derived from the Greek *dokeō*, which means "(I) appear, seem.")

In her book *The Gnostic Gospels*, Elaine Pagels claims there were many diverse, legitimate expressions of Christianity in the early centuries AD—not just one strand. She alleges that the book of Acts wrongly portrays a virtually unified early Christianity.[2] As the whims of history would have it, the "orthodox" happened to have the power to keep the "heretics" in check. The "orthodox" engaged in "suppression" of these "banned documents" of Nag Hammadi.[3] Those embracing the "official" version of Christianity suppressed these diverse texts.

Pagels claims that church leaders such as Irenaeus (bishop of Lyons in the late second century) "politicized" orthodoxy. Gnostics rejected monotheism—belief in the one supreme God and Creator. Therefore they were called "heretics." Pagels charges that philosophical or doctrinal differences aren't enough to account for the theological bullying of Gnostics. We have to consider the social and political context of "orthodoxy" (e.g., Christian bishops claiming they were spiritual authorities).[4] "Ecclesiastical Christians first defined the terms," naming themselves "orthodox" and their opponents "heterodox" or "unorthodox."[5] Thus these "suppressed" texts never made it into the biblical (Christian) canon. (By the way, *canon*—from the Greek word *kanōn*—meant a straight rod to measure units of length, like our rulers for marking inches. So *canon* means "rule" [cf. Gal. 6:16—"those who will walk by this *rule*" (my emphasis)] or "[standard of] measure.")

Did the early church—perhaps arbitrarily—*determine* which books and letters were to be the Word of God? How do we know which books should be included in the biblical canon? Let's look at the following points that respond to these questions. In the next chapter, we'll look at the specific matter of the *Gospel of Thomas*, which gets plenty of attention these days.

First, the body of Old Testament Scriptures was fairly well established before Christ's day and was confirmed by Christ. By Jesus's time, no official pronouncement by Jewish authorities had been made on what the official scriptural canon was. However, the Scriptures we know *were* generally recognized to be inspired and authoritative revelation from God. Moses read "all the words of the LORD" and "the book of the covenant" in Exodus 24:3–7. After the Babylonian exile, Ezra read publicly from the "book of the law of Moses" (cf. Neh. 8:1–9:38). The postexilic prophet Zechariah writes of the "former" preexilic prophets (Zech. 1:4; 7:7). And Daniel (9:2) looked to Jeremiah's prophecy (in chapter 25) regarding the return from exile.

In addition to the divine authority (direct or implied) behind many Old Testament texts, Jesus pronounced the Old Testament authoritative. In Luke 24:44, Jesus affirmed a particular body of Scripture—"the Law of Moses and the Prophets and the Psalms"—as speaking prophetically of him. He appears to endorse this very body of authoritative Scripture in Matthew 23:35: he referred to the *beginning* and the *end* of the Hebrew Old Testament canon—serving as bookmarks or brackets—when he spoke of the "blood of righteous Abel [Genesis 4] to the blood of Zechariah son of Berekiah [2 Chron. 24:20–22]" (NIV).[6] Here we have the Hebrew Scripture's first and last martyrs. This is equivalent to our saying "from Genesis to Malachi" (for the Old Testament) or "from Genesis to Revelation" (for the entire Bible).[7]

When Jesus spoke of the Old Testament, he said that the Word of God could not be "broken" (John 10:35). Even though he was here speaking to Jewish religious leaders about "your Law," he meant something much broader, since he had just cited Psalm 82:6. Often, to establish a point, Jesus would say, "It is written" (e.g., Matt. 4:4, 7, 10). In theological disputes, Jesus and his opponents appeared to *assume the same body of authoritative writings*—even if we don't know of any formal canonization procedures.

In Jewish synagogues, it was typical to read from "the Law and the Prophets" (Acts 13:15). Even though Jesus and other New Testament writers typically referred to "the Law" or "the Law and the Prophets"—rather than "the Law of Moses and the Prophets and the Psalms," as Jesus did in Luke 24:44—they apparently referred to a typical categorization of an authoritative body of Old Testament Scripture (cf. Matt. 5:17–18; 7:12; 22:40; Rom. 3:21). Sometimes the word *Scripture* is used to refer to this divinely inspired collection of writings (John 13:18; Gal. 3:8). While we cannot be absolutely certain that there was an already fixed, set-in-stone Old Testament canon in Jesus's time, the New Testament clearly implies that there was a body of authoritative Scripture by which one could safely say, "It is written."

Second, not only does the New Testament affirm that a body of authoritative writings existed (the Old Testament), but various extrabiblical writings suggest this idea as well. The Qumran community (the Essenes), which produced the Dead Sea Scrolls from 250 BC through AD 70, also acknowledged as Scripture the Pentateuch ("Law"), the prophetic writings, and the Psalms ("the book of Moses, the words of the prophets and of David")—as well as Daniel and Job.[8] While extrabiblical books such as Tobit, Jubilees, and Enoch were used, we don't have enough evidence to determine whether the Essenes believed these to be Scripture or not.[9]

In addition, the Jewish historian Josephus (AD 37–100) wrote about an apparent canon:

> We do not possess myriads of inconsistent books conflicting with each other. Our [inspired] books, those which are justly accredited, are but two and twenty [perhaps equivalent to the thirty-nine Old Testament books we're familiar with], and contain the record of all time (*Against Apion*, 1:37–42).

Further evidence dates back to the end of the first century AD: the pseudonymous (i.e., written under an assumed name) 4 Ezra (or 4 Esdras) 14:44–48 speaks of "twenty-four books" (which were written "first") that are distinguished from another "seventy" (which were written "last"). Could these twenty-four books be the same body of writing (though differently numbered) as those Josephus mentions? This seems to be the case, as Josephus may have believed Ruth to be an appendix to Judges and Lamentations an appendix to Jeremiah.[10] Also, the grandson of Joshua ben Sirach (author of the apocryphal book Sirach) translated this work into Greek around 116–110 BC (possibly earlier). In the preface to this translation, he wrote that his grandfather devoted himself to the reading of "the Law and the Prophets and the other books of our ancestors"—or, worded a bit differently "the Law itself, the Prophecies, and the rest of the books." In both cases, a closed Old Testament canon appears to be assumed.[11]

When the Old Testament canon is discussed, two topics typically come up—the council at Jamnia at the end of the first century AD and the Apocrypha. Let's take these in order.

Around AD 90, there was a rabbinic gathering at Jamnia (Yavneh), which was a city between Jaffa and Ashdod. At this meeting, Old Testament books such as the Song of Solomon and Ecclesiastes were discussed in relation to authoritative Scripture. Some people appeal to this event in support of the claim that the Old Testament canon was still not fixed. But this is too hasty for the following reasons: (a) Jamnia wasn't a decree-making council like the Christian councils of Nicea or Chalcedon. (b) It's likely that rabbis discussed the *role* of these books in public or liturgical use, not whether they should be withdrawn from the canon. They were *already* considered canonical. (c) The Jamnia gathering also discussed Ezekiel, which was a well-established prophetic and *canonical* book. The fact is: we simply know of no decision to establish the Old Testament canon. By the first century AD, it appears to have been firmly fixed.[12]

With regard to the Apocrypha, the Catholic Church included other writings as canonical (in April 1546) at the Council of Trent, which gathered in response to the Protestant Reformation.[13] This, of course, raises questions about whether these books had implicit authority or simply supported Catholic doctrines over against Protestant beliefs. In the Eastern Orthodox Church, these writings are more frequently read and used than in Protestantism, but the Orthodox do not esteem these works as having the kind of authority as the books traditionally accepted by Jews and Protestants. Furthermore, New Testament writers didn't acknowledge these books as Scripture, nor did a significant number of early church fathers (who generally viewed the Hebrew tradition of twenty-two biblical books as authoritative).[14] Even Jerome (AD 342–420), who translated the Hebrew/Aramaic and Greek Scriptures into the Latin Vulgate (which was used by the Catholic Church), didn't recognize these apocryphal books as canonical. He basically follows the Hebrew canon.[15] Furthermore, the Jews never accepted the apocryphal books as part of their Scriptures.

Third, the books of the New Testament—like those of the Old Testament—had an authority that was **recognized** *rather than* **bestowed**. *Canonicity—not to mention orthodoxy—wasn't arbitrary but was based on the divinely authoritative tone of these texts.* It's not unusual to hear the claim that the church fathers arbitrarily picked out authoritative books (leaving aside other perfectly legitimate candidates for the canon), compiled them, and pronounced them authoritative. ("This book is God's word. Let's just say that one isn't. . . .") But this isn't at all an accurate depiction of what happened.

Lists of scriptural books began to be compiled in the second and third centuries. By AD 130, thirteen letters of Paul and the four Gospels had already been received as divinely authoritative by many churches in the East and West. In 324, the church historian Eusebius, in his *Ecclesiastical History*, distinguished between "recognized" books, "disputed" books, and "heretical" texts.[16] In 367, Athanasius of Alexandria, Egypt, finalized a significantly more definitive list, which was approved at the Third Council of Carthage (397) and ratified by papal decree in 405. It's ironic that the finalized list was compiled by an Egyptian (Athanasius), and in his list he mentions *none* of the Nag Hammadi texts found in Egypt as canonical!

What, then, does the evidence show regarding the New Testament canon? Against Pagels's revisionist claim that there were plenty of noncanonical texts that were arbitrarily excluded by the powerful, self-proclaimed "orthodox," we see an *early orthodoxy already in place in the New Testament*. Paul, in the Pastoral Epistles, is frequently speaking of "sound [healthy] teaching" or "sound words" (e.g., 1 Tim. 1:10; 2 Tim. 1:13) or grace-denying heresies ("doctrines of demons" [1 Tim. 4:1]). The apostle John, writing in the AD 90s, uses "us-them" language: "We are from God; he who knows God listens to us; he who is not from God does not listen to us" (1 John 4:6). John distinguishes between true prophecy and erroneous prophecy. He affirms the divine Son Jesus's coming "in the flesh"—that the incarnation of the Son of God was real, not merely the *appearance* of being human—and opposes the spirit of "antichrist" because it denies this teaching.

Furthermore, there are plenty of references *within* the New Testament books regarding their own *divine origin and authority*. Let's just look at a few:

- *Jesus* told his disciples that the Spirit would bring to mind what Jesus had said (John 14:26), that he would "guide" these apostles "into all the truth" and "disclose . . . what is to come" (John 16:13). (Keep in mind this promise is primarily for Jesus's disciples *back then*, but we today indirectly benefit from the Spirit's working through them and the message they left to us.)
- *Paul* declared that his message was "not according to man," but was received directly from Christ (Gal. 1:11–12). Paul said that he spoke "the word of God's message" to the Thessalonians (1 Thess. 2:13). His message was authoritative because he had been "taught by the Spirit" (1 Cor. 2:13). Paul wrote with an awareness that his written words were nothing short of the Lord's (1 Cor. 14:37–38). Now, Paul would admit to being ignorant of certain things (e.g., exactly whom he baptized [1 Cor. 1:14–16]), reminding us that the treasure of the gospel was communicated by "earthen vessels" (2 Cor. 4:7). However, Paul was still expressing what is true. In fact, by the time 2 Peter was written, Paul's own writings were considered "Scriptures" (2 Pet. 3:15–16)—a word *not* used of nonsacred/noncanonical writings in the New Testament.
- *Peter* writes of his being an eyewitness of Christ's life and teaching and claims to have "the prophetic word" from God (2 Pet. 1:16–21).
- *John* (as we just saw) makes the claim: "We are from God; he who knows God listens to us" (1 John 4:6)—a powerful statement regarding John's apostolic authority. The book of Revelation itself is a prophecy given to John by Jesus Christ (Rev. 1:1–3), and serious warnings are issued against anyone who would add to or take away from the book's message (Rev. 22:18–19).

While noting the New Testament's witness about itself, we should also look at church history to better discern the process of discovering which writings were considered canonical. While there wasn't utter unanimity on every book in the canon, and while the canonization process appears to be murky at times,[17] we can draw some firm conclusions, as we've already seen (and we'll see more below).

But we *can* say that Pagels's claim can't even get off the ground. Gnostic texts such as the second- and third-century "Gospels" of Thomas and Philip and Peter and Mary come well *after* the New Testament documents were written. And these New Testament documents were *already* talking about truth and error, sound doctrine and erroneous doctrine, genuine prophecy and false prophecy.

*Fourth, from very early on, church fathers, while **not** deliberately trying to establish a canon, recognized New Testament writings as having inherent authority; these fathers didn't **select** them to be authoritative—contrary to Pagels's claim that these texts were just arbitrarily chosen and declared authoritative.* Many church fathers heard in the New Testament writings a divine voice—well before Gnostic texts started to appear. What's more, these fathers didn't claim their own writings were divinely authoritative. Rather, they appealed to the words of Christ and his apostles as their authority.

- The *Epistle of Barnabas*, a pseudonymous work (ca. AD 90–130), cites Jesus's words from Matthew 22:14: "Let us take heed lest, as it is written, we be found [as] 'many called but few chosen'" (4:14).
- **Clement of Rome** (ca. AD 96) cites both Jesus and the Old Testament as divinely authoritative, speaking of "the blessed Paul the apostle" (*1 Clement* 47:1). In 42:1–2, he states that the apostles received the gospel from Christ, who came from God: "The Christ therefore is from God and the Apostles from the Christ."
- **Ignatius of Antioch** (d. AD 107?) wrote: "I do not command you like Peter and Paul . . . they were apostles; I am a convict" (*To the Romans* 8:3; 4:3).
- **Polycarp**, writing to the Philippians (ca. AD 140–55), quotes Ephesians 4:26 and refers to it as "these Scriptures" (12:1).[18]
- **Irenaeus** (c. AD 180) assumed four fixed and authoritative Gospels (*Against Heresies* 3.11.8).

This process of recognizing divinely inspired texts—and thus "orthodox" ones—and the circulation of these books took place long before key Gnostic texts were written. As Ben Witherington asserts, "There was never a time when a wide selection of books, including Gnostic ones, were widely deemed acceptable."[19] Contrary to the pseudo-historical claims made in the *Da Vinci Code* novel (which many have taken to be a serious historical work),[20] this process also took place well before the church fathers sought to compile these writings into a canon or to pronounce them authoritative in an official council such as Nicea in AD 325.

Fifth, the basic characteristics for discerning divine authority and canonicity of New Testament books are (a) apostolicity, (b) orthodoxy, (c) antiquity, and (d) universality. It seems that—whether intended consciously or not—the canonical writings achieved their status because they possessed the following characteristics:

Apostolicity	Orthodoxy	Antiquity	Universality
Having their source in Christ's teaching and ministry and those in (and associated with) his authoritative apostolic circle.	Not contradicting previous divinely revealed truth.	Belonging to the era of the apostles.	Being widely accepted as authoritative.

Let's look at these in a bit more detail.

Criterion 1: Apostolicity: This is the *primary* mark of canonicity. Christ alone and his appointed witnesses constitute what is authoritative. Therefore, a document had to be written by an apostle or by one who was in immediate contact with the apostles. As we have seen, Peter considered Paul's writings to have equal authority to Old Testament Scripture (2 Pet. 3:16). Also, in 1 Timothy 5:18, Paul writes, "For the Scripture says . . ." and then he quotes two Scriptures—one from the Old Testament and the other from the New: (a) Deuteronomy 25:4 ("You shall not muzzle the ox while he is threshing") and (b) Luke 10:7—a saying of Jesus ("The laborer is worthy of his wages").

Except for six books (Mark, Luke, Acts, Hebrews, James, and Jude), all New Testament books were written by apostles. Mark, Luke, and Acts were recognized as authoritative very early: according to the church father Papias, Mark was the *amenuensis* (scribe) for the apostle Peter,[21]and

Luke (who wrote Luke and Acts) was *a close associate of the apostle Paul,* often traveling with him (e.g., note the "we" passages in Acts 16:10–17; 20:5–15; 21:1–18; 27:1–29; 28:1–16). The book of James was accepted as James was the half brother of Jesus. The book of Jude was accepted because Jude was the brother of James (Jude 1) as well as the half brother of Jesus (Matt. 13:55). Hebrews (which was perhaps written by Apollos; cf. 1 Cor. 1:12) has an authoritative, self-attesting nature to its divine origin (cf. Heb. 1:1–2) and has an association with the apostles (Heb. 2:3).[22] This book was delayed in becoming accepted due to its anonymous nature.

Criterion 2: Orthodoxy: We have already seen that standards of biblical orthodoxy existed well before Gnostic texts emerged. As we'll note in the next chapter, the *Gospel of Thomas* makes heretical statements, such as, "Simon Peter said to them, 'Make Mary leave us, for females do not deserve life'" (§114)—a passage clearly at odds with God making male *and female* in his image (Gen. 1:26–27) and with there being neither male nor female in Christ (Gal. 3:28). The Gnostic *Apocalypse of Peter* 81.10–11 portrays a human "substitute" placed on the cross while Jesus is "glad and laughing" at ignorant human beings. Another text, the sometimes unorthodox *Shepherd of Hermas,* was included in an early list known as the Muratorian Canon (ca. AD 170). The compiler acknowledged that it had been written "quite recently"—"in our own times," which removes it from the time of apostolic authority. The important point here, however, deals with the criterion of orthodoxy: the *Shepherd* teaches the necessity of doing good deeds to obtain forgiveness ("penance"), which poses theological problems.[23] This text also appears to teach that the Holy Spirit and the Son of God were one and the same before Jesus was born in Bethlehem ("For that Spirit is the Son of God").[24]

Christ and his gospel are central to the formation of the canon. Jesus was the final and full revelation of God "in these last days" (Heb. 1:1–2). If a writing did not conform to "this rule" (Gal. 6:16)—that is, the gospel of grace)—and "the faithful word" (Titus 1:9) and "the faith which was once for all handed down to the saints" (Jude 3), it wasn't deemed acceptable as Scripture.

Criterion 3: Antiquity: F. F. Bruce writes that if "a writing was the work of an apostle or of someone closely associated with an apostle, it must belong to the apostolic age."[25] Writings of a later date, whatever their merit, would not be included in the canon. This is the key reason the *Shepherd of Hermas* was excluded from an early compilation in AD 170 (the Muratorian Canon). This criterion goes hand in hand with apostolicity (a document had to written by an apostle or by someone in immediate contact with the apostles) for obvious reasons.

Apocryphal New Testament writings, which were written well after the death of the apostles (from the second century AD and beyond), tend to add embellishments that are fanciful and legendary. For example, the *Gospel of Peter* is clearly "doctored up" as opposed to the straightforwardly simple resurrection narratives in the four Gospels. A sound rings out from heaven in the night, the stone rolls back all by itself away from the tomb's door, and two men descend from out of heaven and enter the tomb. Three men then exit the tomb, two of them supporting the third. The men's heads reach to the clouds, but the head of the third rises above the clouds. A cross follows them out of the tomb. A voice from heaven asks, "Hast thou preached to them that sleep?" And the cross answers, "Yea!" No wonder such fictitious additions were rejected by churches!

Now the New Testament sometimes quotes or alludes to apocryphal (or pseudepigraphal) books. For example, 1 Peter 3:19–20 refers to *1 Enoch* 10:12–13; 12:4. Jude 9, when speaking of the devil's dispute with the archangel Michael over the body of Moses, refers to *The Assumption of Moses*. Enoch's prophecy in Jude 14–15 is a quotation from *1 Enoch* 1:9: "See, the Lord is coming with thousands upon thousands of his holy ones to judge everyone, and to convict all the ungodly of all the ungodly acts they have done in the ungodly way" (NIV). Does this mean these books should be accepted into the biblical canon as authoritative? This doesn't follow. As R. T. France comments,

> There is no suggestion that [citing apocryphal books] confers canonical status on the book concerned, any more than when Paul quotes from the pagan poets Menander, Aratus, and Epimenides (1 Cor. 15:33; Acts 17:28; Titus 1:12), or when we quote anything from Calvin's *Institutes* to *Winnie the Pooh* in the course of a sermon.[26]

France reminds us that the biblical writers spoke out of an environment which was far broader than the Bible itself, and we must let them speak out of the literature and culture with which they were familiar.

But weren't there debates regarding the inspiration of various books? Yes, the status of works such as the *Shepherd of Hermas, 1 Clement,* Ignatius's letters, and even the Wisdom of Solomon were debated. This shouldn't throw us off track, however. Ben Witherington remarks: "It is noteworthy that not a single document written after about 120 was ever considered for inclusion in the canon, not least because such documents were not written by people in direct touch with the apostolic tradition, much less with the apostles themselves."[27] (Note that the *Gospel of Thomas* wasn't even considered!) It seems that *if there was strong doubt, the book in question would be left out of the canon: when in doubt, leave it out.*

Criterion 4: Universality: Some scholars have given the impression that the recognition of the New Testament canon took an inordinately long amount of time. However, we must distinguish between *the formal, universal recognition* of a closed list of New Testament documents (which came in the fourth century) and *the recognition of their authority* (which came very early in the church). Time was needed before the recognition of authority could be worked into official canonization.

A canonical document was to have had *widespread* and *continuous* usage by the churches. The formula for the acceptability of a tradition in the history of the church was *ubique, semper, ab omnibus*—[confessed] "everywhere, always, by all." That is, the universality, antiquity, and consensus of a tradition gave it validity. In some sense, the "everywhere" and "by all" apply to the biblical canon's acceptance. In fact, this criterion, D. A. Carson reminds us, "requires the passage of time to be useful, and helps to explain why so much time elapsed before the 'closing' of the canon."[28]

What's really remarkable is that without any hierarchy or ecclesiastical machinery to make sweeping decisions for Christians (e.g., bishops, popes, or councils), "eventually all of the universal church came to recognize the same twenty-seven books" of the New Testament. So without any "official recognition," the people of God in many different places came to "recognize what other believers elsewhere found to be true."[29]

This is further indication that *the resulting canon was not contrived* but was the result of a wide consensus. The church, then, did not *confer* canonical status upon certain documents but only *recognized* what God had authoritatively revealed about his Son through the apostles and their associates. Again, some canonical books took a longer time to be recognized, and there were (as we've seen) disagreements on other books (*The Shepherd of Hermas, 1 Clement,* etc.).

So, yes, the process of canonization (particularly the New Testament) had some bumps and hiccups along the way. But this is a far cry from the claims made by Pagels and others that these books were arbitrarily chosen by those in power, the self-proclaimed "orthodox," who suppressed the writings of—here comes an oxymoron—"Christian Gnostics."

SUMMARY

- The body of our Old Testament Scriptures was fairly well established before Christ's time and was confirmed by Christ.
- Not only does the New Testament affirm that a body of authoritative writings existed (the Old Testament), but various extrabiblical writings (e.g., various early church fathers) suggest this idea as well.
- The meeting of Jewish authorities at Jamnia in the late first century wasn't a matter of determining which books should be in the Old Testament canon. Rather, it was an attempt to understand their *function* or *role* in the canon.
- The books of the New Testament—like those of the Old Testament—had an authority that was *recognized* rather than *bestowed*. Canonicity—not to mention orthodoxy—wasn't arbitrary but was based on the divinely authoritative tone of these texts.
- From very early on, church fathers, while *not* deliberately trying to establish a canon, *recognized* New Testament writings as having inherent authority; these fathers didn't *select* them to be authoritative—a far cry from Pagels's claim that these texts were just arbitrarily chosen and declared authoritative.
- The basic characteristics for discerning divine authority and canonicity of New Testament books are (a) apostolicity, (b) orthodoxy, (c) antiquity, and (d) universality.

FURTHER READING

Bruce, F. F. *The Canon of Scripture.* Downers Grove, IL: InterVarsity, 1988.

Dunbar, David C. "The Biblical Canon," in *Hermeneutics, Authority, and Canon.* Edited by D. A. Carson and John D. Woodbridge. Grand Rapids: Zondervan, 1988.

Wenham, David. *Christ and the Bible.* 3rd ed. Grand Rapids: Baker Books, 1994.

17

ISN'T THE *GOSPEL OF THOMAS* A LEGITIMATE SOURCE ABOUT THE HISTORICAL JESUS?

The *Gospel of Thomas* begins: "These are the secret words which the living Jesus spoke, and which Didymus Judas Thomas wrote." *Thomas* is a text (one of the Nag Hammadi writings) containing 114 alleged sayings (*logia*) of Jesus. These texts don't emphasize Jesus's humanity or the historical facts surrounding his life. A third of those sayings are clearly *Gnostic* (see the previous chapter)—even if *Thomas*'s Gnosticism isn't as fully developed as later versions—with arrays of intermediaries or demiurges between God and the evil material world.[1] *Thomas* has gotten a lot of press through the Jesus Seminar, which accepts it as a legitimate—and even more reliable—source for historical-Jesus studies.[2] Jesus Seminar members, with whom the mainstream media tends to be very friendly, have claimed that *Thomas* dates to the AD 50s—rather than the AD 150 date more standardly accepted by most scholars. (A mediating position is taken by Risto Uro, who allows for an earlier dating of AD 100–140.)[3]

In her book *Beyond Belief*, Harvard historian Elaine Pagels suggests that the respective authors of John's Gospel and the *Gospel of Thomas* used the same Jesus-sources, but these authors drew different conclusions. John is responding to the teachings in the *Gospel of Thomas*. So John "invents" Doubting Thomas, who demands to see in order to believe (John 20:24–29). Pagels claims that there was a group of "Thomas Christians" who followed this type of approach. So John's goal is to expose Thomas's thinking as "faithless and false."[4] Pagels declares that despite the "diversity within the Christian movement," *Thomas* was one of the texts suppressed by "official" versions of Christianity.[5] So why not accept this text as legitimately Christian? Why accept the "orthodox" version of Christianity when it was the result of power-players who called all others "heretics"?

I've heard many questions about the legitimacy of these claims—often asserted as factual without much support (for, say, an early date of writing). Before responding to these claims, perhaps we should look a bit more closely at what the assumed worldview of *Thomas* involves.

Thomas stresses secret knowledge hidden from the masses but made known to the elite enlightened ones. It expresses antagonism toward the body, childbirth (and women, because of their association with it), creation, and history. These are inferior and evil; spirit—especially disembodied spirit—is good. *Thomas*'s Gnosticism also stresses preexistence of the soul and the hope of *returning* to that state of "the All"—the "spiritual universe of divine beings" which were once united with the divine—rather than anticipating future *restoration* of all things.

Salvation (or, more accurately, *self*-salvation) in *Thomas* is, according to historical-Jesus scholar John Meier, "ahistorical, atemporal, amaterial."[6] It's in some ways like the monism or pantheism of certain Eastern philosophies.[7] Salvation for *Thomas* is the freedom that comes from the elite/chosen person simply realizing he belongs to another world (he "wakes up" so that he can go back to the "place" or "rest" of the Father); he recognizes the illusion of the material world. Salvation comes through "self-knowledge and ascetic detachment from this material world."[8]

Note the following passages from *Thomas* that reflect these themes:

§27   [*Denial of material world*]: (Jesus said:) "If you do not abstain from the world, you will not find the kingdom."

§75   [*Elitist salvation*]: Jesus said, "Many are standing at the door, but it is the solitary one [the truly enlightened one] who will enter the bridal chamber [initiated into Gnostic secrets]."

§77   [*Original oneness with "the All"*]: Jesus said, "It is I who am the All; it is from me that the All has come, and to me that the All goes."

§87   [*Soul trapped in a material body*]: Jesus said, "Wretched is the body that is dependent upon a body, and wretched is the soul that is dependent on these two."

§108 [*The pursuit of the original uniting with "the All"*]: Jesus said, "Whoever drinks from my mouth will become like me. I, too, will become that person."

§112 [*Inferiority/evil of the body*]: Jesus said, "Woe to the flesh that depends on the soul; woe to the soul that depends on the flesh."

§114 [*Inferiority of women*]: Simon Peter said to them, "Make Mary leave us, for females do not deserve life." Jesus said, "Look, I will guide her to make her male, so that she too may become a living spirit resembling you males. For every female who makes herself male will enter the kingdom of Heaven."

These passages reflect a "borrowing" of Jesus's authority and a reshaping of his words to buttress a worldview completely alien to Jesus. This syncretism—or blending of two differing worldviews—is known as "Gnostic Christianity," which came into full bloom much later than the writing of the New Testament books.

So then, was this text arbitrarily excluded as "heretical" from the biblical canon by the self-proclaimed "orthodox" church leaders, as Pagels charges? This charge is an example of historical revisionism. There are a number of responses that can be offered.

First, introducing political motives regarding the "orthodox" pronouncements on the "heretics" is simply unnecessary; this matter of canonicity can be resolved based on divinely authoritative teaching preceding Thomas. The *simpler* approach is that texts like *Thomas* were in fact deviations from what the Old Testament, Jesus, and Jesus's appointed apostles taught. Introducing politics is unnecessary and only muddies the waters; the worldview of Gnosticism and the whole of the Jewish-Christian Scriptures are vastly different. Introducing "orthodox" power-players adds extra entities unnecessarily; it's a kind of distraction from the more basic issues, such as *Which better matches up to the Old Testament—the canonical Gospels or the* Gospel of Thomas?

Imagine a Muslim cleric living around AD 800 in Saudi Arabia—let's call him Mullah Abdullah. He proclaims he's the founder of a new, enlightened school of Islam. He claims that his version of Islam is "just as legitimate" as the Sunni or Shi'a schools. There's a catch, however: Mullah Abdullah *denies* that Muhammad is the final prophet of Allah. In fact, he denies that *any* of the respected prophets of Islam are legitimate. (This claim would make Islam a *nonprophet organization*!) Only *he* is the authority on Islam. But we would rightly observe that if a self-proclaimed Muslim declares that Muhammad isn't the final prophet, then he's no longer a Muslim.

Similarly, to say that "Gnostic Christianity" is just one of many legitimate versions of Christianity is plainly false because it denies themes essential to the Jewish-Christian worldview: God created the material world and the human body as good; God reveals himself in human history; Jesus's death is necessary for our salvation; our hope is a future bodily resurrection in a restored (material) creation; and so on. To say *Thomas*'s version of Christianity is one of many is to make Christianity utterly unrecognizable. Surely *the apostle Paul had a much better handle on first-century Christianity than Pagels and the Jesus Seminar do!* In 1 Corinthians 15:14, Paul declared: "If Christ has not been raised, then our preaching is vain, your faith also is vain." For Pagels and various Jesus Seminar members, Paul is dead wrong!

Second (and this builds on the first point), thinkers like Pagels haven't gone back far enough in comparing Gnostic "Gospels" like Thomas with the four canonical Gospels. The more fundamental question is: Which text is more clearly rooted in the **Old Testament**—*Thomas or the canonical Gospels and the rest of the New Testament? Not surprisingly, Gnostic texts like Thomas rarely refer to the Old Testament; this should prompt us to give the New Testament canon priority over the anti–Old Testament Gnostic documents.* There's no reason to accept *Thomas* as a primary source for historical-Jesus studies. It clearly defies the doctrinal teachings of earlier New Testament writings. But writers like Pagels (or Harvard's Karen L. King)[9] ignore the place of the Old Testament, which Gnostic texts hardly *ever* cite—a massive oversight, since Jesus is clearly conscious that he is fulfilling and embodying themes, figures, and institutions from the Old Testament. The problem with Pagels's thesis is this: The Old Testament—like the New—expresses an appreciation for (a) God's involvement in history; (b) the goodness of material creation, the human body, sexuality; (c) the future hope of bodily resurrection and a new heavens and new earth; (d) God's publicly accessible revelation and his concern for the salvation of all peoples—not "hidden words"[10] given to an elite few; (e) the central problem of human sinfulness (not simply ignorance). By pitting *Thomas* against the "accepted" New Testament Gospels, Pagels doesn't go back far enough! *The reason these Gnostic texts were rightly excluded from the New Testament canon is because they are in conflict with the Old Testament worldview, on which the New Testament builds.* Because Gnosticism rejects all that the Old Testament Scriptures stand for, we should reject texts like *Thomas* as inauthentic reflections of Jesus's teaching.

Third, it's a curious (and humorous) irony that scholars like Pagels endorse a text that's appallingly politically incorrect. As we've seen, *Thomas* endorses a worldview that is *antihistory*, denying the importance of human history and God's working through it. *Thomas's* Gnosticism is *anticreation*, rejecting the goodness of the created world. Contrary to the Jesus of the canonical Gospels, Gnosticism is an *elitist* belief system that's only for a select few. Enlightened knowledge isn't available to all people.

Thomas is also *antiwoman*. Remember Saying 114—where Peter says, "Make Mary leave us, for females do not deserve life," and Jesus replies that he would make her into a male since females can't enter the kingdom of heaven. One reason women were put down or considered undesirable by Gnostics is their association with childbirth and bodily existence; Gnostics wanted to be freed from such "burdens."[11] New Testament scholar Raymond Brown says the tone of *Thomas* reflects "antifeminism," which "has no place in the canonical Gospels."[12] Gnosticism is also *antisex*: human sexuality—though despised by Gnostics—is God's good gift to human beings.

Jesus scholar N. T. Wright observes that *Thomas* is "explicitly anti-creational" and opposed to bodily resurrection (in advocating how to escape bodily existence and return to one's previously enjoyed state of disembodiment).[13] *Isn't this antimaterialism the sort of attitude that would oppose caring for the environment rather than the biblical emphasis on humans as stewards or caretakers of the earth?*

So why give implicit support to such a shocking set of beliefs in *Thomas* when we have in the Jewish-Christian Scriptures support for the goodness of the physical creation, the body, female equality, sex, childbirth, the importance of history (and God's involvement in it), and the like?

Without sufficient support, the Jesus Seminar dates *Thomas* a century earlier than most scholars (AD 50 rather than 150). This strategy of favoring an ahistorical "Gospel" undercuts the canonical Gospels as reliable historical sources. Ironically, the Jesus Seminar *virtually ignores Mark*, our earliest Gospel, as a reliable source of historical-Jesus material. The Jesus Seminar consistently rejects the historical authenticity of Jesus's miracles (*Thomas* mentions no miracles by Jesus), his exalted identity claims (also lacking in *Thomas*), and the like—reflecting an antisupernaturalistic bias. But favoring *Thomas* over Mark is both arbitrary and unwarranted. Historical-Jesus scholar John Meier declares that calling upon *Thomas* as a historical-Jesus source is "to broaden out our pool of resources from the difficult to the incredible."[14]

Fourth, the weight of the evidence suggests that rather than the Gospels building on Thomas, Thomas *builds on the canonical Gospels by loosely citing them to suit its Gnostic purposes. In addition, the writer of* Thomas *doesn't use the same Jesus-sources as other Gospel writers.* No evidence exists that the Gospel writers even had access to *Thomas.* Elements of *Thomas* not found in the Gospels are best explained as later Gnostic sayings (such as "solitary one" or "bridal chamber" in Saying 75).[15] Pagels's hypothesis that Thomas and John wrote different Gospels based on the same Jesus-sources is inadequate; a better explanation is Thomas's exposure to and use of all four of the Gospels but shaping (and distorting) them "within a very different worldview."[16]

We can find some similarities and parallels between *Thomas* and *each* of the four Gospels, which utilized different sources (cf. Luke 1:1–4). Craig Blomberg points out that it would be highly unlikely that every Gospel source would independently use *Thomas* at an early date. Instead, "it is far more probable that *Thomas* knew and relied on the later fourfold Gospel collection."[17]

In other places, *Thomas* follows the sequence of phrases mentioned in the narrative flow of the Synoptic Gospels (Matthew, Mark, Luke), but there's no coherent connection between them. Saying 65 refers to the parable of the wicked tenants (cf. Mark 12:1–8 and parallels). *Thomas's* next saying (66) mentions the "cornerstone"—a clear reference to Mark 12:10–11. Here's the rub: *there's no connection between Sayings 65 and 66, while they are clearly connected in Mark 12.* If we didn't have Mark 12:9 to connect them, we wouldn't know that these sayings in *Thomas* had any relation to each other. The most reasonable conclusion is that the writer of *Thomas* is borrowing from the Synoptics (and not vice versa), using this passage for his own purposes.[18] Additionally, unlike the Synoptics, *Thomas* tends to view discipleship in *individualistic*—not *communal*—terms: the "you" in *Thomas* tends to be *singular*; it tends to be *plural* in the Synoptics.[19]

Let's look at a couple of passages that reveal how *Thomas* borrows from the Beatitudes in both Matthew 5 and Luke 6, revealing that *Thomas* is significantly later than the canonical Gospels. *Thomas's* Saying 54 reads: "Blessed are the poor, for yours is the kingdom of heaven." Saying 68 reads: "Blessed are you [plural] whenever they hate you and persecute you." In light of *Thomas's* use of these verses, we should note the following points:

1. *Borrowing from Matthew's "kingdom of heaven"*: Matthew's Gospel utilizes "kingdom of heaven." Of course, there's no difference in meaning from Luke's "kingdom of God." Matthew follows the Jewish method of "circumlocution" ("talking around" the name of God by using "Heaven," "Power," or "the Majesty"), whereas Luke doesn't. *Thomas's* favoring "kingdom of heaven" reflects a second-century development, in which Matthew exerted a greater influence than Luke.[20]

2. *Combining Matthew's beatitudes with Luke's: Thomas* combines or conflates sayings from Luke *and* Matthew (rather than just citing one or the other). Thomas helps himself to both traditions as it suits his purposes. Matthew *alone* uses a particular word

for *persecute* (*diōkō*), and Luke alone uses *hate* (*miseō*). *Both* appear in Thomas's version, which indicates Thomas's picking and choosing.

John Meier observes that *Thomas's* method of combining and harmonizing the Gospels is a typical *second*-century phenomenon—not a first-century one: "Rather than representing an independent stream of Jesus' sayings, the *Gospel of Thomas* fits perfectly into the [second]-century phenomenon of Gospel conflation and harmonization."[21] Also, if *Thomas* is so early, why isn't Mark (the earlier Gospel) being cited? Why is the later Gospel of Luke being used? And, for reasons I can't go into, *Thomas* is clearly using Tatian's *Diatesseron* (ca. mid-second century AD)—which combines the four canonical Gospels into one narrative.[22]

John Meier concludes that it's "much more probable" that *Thomas* has borrowed material from the canonical Gospels and arranged them—often using "catchwords" to link one saying to the next—than that the wide range of independent sources used in the four Gospels draws from *Thomas*.[23] We're on much firmer ground in taking *Thomas* to be a later, significantly less reliable record of the sayings of Jesus than the canonical Gospels are.

We've seen that giving priority to *Thomas* over the canonical Gospels is seriously misguided. New Testament scholar Craig Evans points out: "Although it is possible that *Thomas* may contain a few primitive sayings [of Jesus], it has little to offer Jesus research."[24] N. T. Wright considers the Jesus Seminar's (particularly John Dominic Crossan's) methodology involving assumptions regarding *Thomas's* priority as "extremely shaky" and "tenuous in the extreme."[25]

SUMMARY

- Introducing political motives regarding the "orthodox" pronouncements on the "heretics" is simply unnecessary; this matter of canonicity can be resolved based on divinely authoritative teaching preceding *Thomas* (Old Testament and New Testament writings).

- Thinkers like Pagels haven't gone back far enough in comparing Gnostic "Gospels" like *Thomas* with the four canonical Gospels. The more fundamental question is: Which text is more clearly rooted in the *Old Testament—Thomas* or the canonical Gospels and the rest of the New Testament? Not surprisingly, Gnostic texts like *Thomas* rarely refer to the Old Testament; this should prompt us to give the New Testament canon priority over the anti-Old Testament Gnostic documents.

- Gnostic texts like *Thomas* were rightly excluded from the New Testament canon because they're in conflict with the Old Testament worldview, on which the New Testament builds.

- It's a rather curious irony that some scholars endorse texts like *Thomas* that are appallingly politically incorrect (antiwoman, anticreational, antisex, elitist, etc.).

- The weight of the evidence suggests that rather than the Gospels building on *Thomas*, *Thomas* builds on the canonical Gospels by loosely citing them for its Gnostic purposes. In addition, the writer of *Thomas* doesn't use the same Jesus-sources as other Gospel writers.

FURTHER READING

Copan, Paul, ed. *Will the Real Jesus Please Stand Up? A Debate between William Lane Craig and John Dominic Crossan.* Grand Rapids: Baker Books, 1998.

Copan, Paul, and Ronald Tacelli, eds. *Jesus' Resurrection: Fact or Figment? A Debate between William Lane Craig and Gerd Lüdemann.* Downers Grove, IL: InterVarsity, 2000.

Meier, John P. *A Marginal Jew: Rethinking the Historical Jesus.* Vol. 1. New York: Doubleday, 1991 (cf. 123–39).

Wilkins, Michael J., and J. P. Moreland. *Jesus under Fire: Modern Scholarship Reinvents the Historical Jesus.* Grand Rapids: Zondervan, 1995. (See especially Craig Blomberg's essay, "Where Do We Start Studying Jesus?")

Notes

Introduction

1. H. L. Mencken, *Minority Report: H. L. Mencken's Notebooks* (Baltimore: Johns Hopkins University Press, 1956; repr., 1997), 48.

2. Douglas Groothuis, *On Jesus* (Belmont, CA: Wadsworth, 2003), 5.

3. Dallas Willard, "Jesus the Logician," *Christian Scholar's Review* 28, no. 4 (1999): 605–14. Willard also discusses this in *The Divine Conspiracy* (San Francisco: HarperSanFrancisco, 1998).

4. Michael Martin, *Atheism, Morality, and Meaning* (Amherst, NY: Prometheus, 2002), 165. See my response to Martin's book in "Morality and Meaning without God: Another Failed Attempt," in *Philosophia Christi* 2, vol. 6, no. 2 (2004): 105–14.

5. R. T. France, "God and Mammon," *Evangelical Quarterly* 51 (1979): 3–21. See also Craig Blomberg, *Neither Poverty nor Riches* (Downers Grove, IL: InterVarsity, 2001).

6. C. S. Lewis, "Learning in War-Time," in *The Weight of Glory* (New York: Macmillan, 1965), 28.

7. C. S. Lewis, "Is Theology Poetry?" in *Weight of Glory*, 140.

8. Randy Newman, *Questioning Evangelism: Engaging People's Hearts the Way Jesus Did* (Grand Rapids: Kregel, 2004).

9. Dallas Willard, *Renovation of the Heart: Putting on the Character of Christ* (Colorado Springs: NavPress, 2002), 11.

Chapter 1 How Do You Know You're Not Wrong?

1. See chap. 1 of Hilary Putnam, *Reason, Truth, and History* (Cambridge: Cambridge University Press, 1981).

2. See Paul K. Moser, Dwayne H. Mulder, and J. D. Trout, *The Theory of Knowledge: A Thematic Introduction* (New York: Oxford University Press, 1998), 7–11, 149–64.

3. Ibid., 10–11.

4. Groothuis, *On Jesus*, 51.

5. L. S. Carrier, "Direct Realism," in *A Companion to Epistemology*, ed. Jonathan Dancy and Ernest Sosa (Cambridge: Blackwell, 1992), 105–6.

6. Colin E. Gunton, *Act and Being: Toward a Theology of the Divine Attributes* (Grand Rapids: Eerdmans, 2003), 47.

7. Josiah Royce, "The Possibility of Error," in *The Basic Writings of Josiah Royce*, vol. 1, ed. John J. McDermott (Chicago: University of Chicago Press, 1969), 321–53.

8. Roderick M. Chisholm emphasizes the priority of *particularism* (we begin the knowledge process with particular beliefs) over *methodism* (which requires following a method [e.g., "the scientific method"] before a belief can pass for "knowledge"). The problem with methodism is *How does one know that this is a good criterion?* I must know at least three things before formulating a criterion for knowledge:

I must know *P* (e.g., that there is a computer in front of me);
I must know *Q* (e.g., a criterion such as "Knowledge comes through testing by the senses");
I must know *R*—namely, that *P* satisfies *Q* (e.g., that seeing the computer in front of me is a sufficient example for meeting the criterion).

Criteria are helpful in borderline cases, but we can clearly know things *before* we apply a criterion to them. See Roderick M. Chisholm, *The Problem of the Criterion* (Milwaukee: Marquette University Press, 1973).

9. See Brendan Sweetman, "The Pseudo-Problem of Skepticism," in *The Failure of Modernism: The Cartesian Legacy and Contemporary Pluralism*, ed. Brendan Sweetman (Mishawaka, IN: American Maritain Association, 1999), 228–41.

10. *Hannah and Her Sisters*, produced by Robert Greenhut, written and directed by Woody Allen (Orion Pictures, 1986).

11. Roderick M. Chisholm, *Theory of Knowledge*, 3rd ed. (Englewood Cliffs, NJ: Prentice-Hall, 1987), 16.

12. This point is taken from Jim Beilby and David K. Clark, *Why Bother with Truth?* (Norcross, GA: Ravi Zacharias International Ministries, 2000), 25–26.

13. Alvin Plantinga, "Warrant and Accidentally True Belief," *Analysis* 57 (April 1997): 142.

14. Moser et al., *Theory of Knowledge*, 98. William Alston asserts that in such situations there must be some *accessibility requirement* for justification (or warrant). That is, there must be *adequate grounds* sufficiently indicative of the truth of a proposition in order to be justified. William P. Alston, "An Internalist Externalism," *Synthese* 74, no. 3 (March 1998): 269, 270.

15. Sweetman, "Pseudo-Problem of Skepticism," 239.

16. Keith Lehrer and Ronald E. Beanblossom, eds., *Thomas Reid's Inquiry and Essays* (Indianapolis: Bobbs-Merrill, 1975), 84–85.

17. Sweetman, "Pseudo-Problem of Skepticism," 241.

18. See Peter Lipton, *Inference to the Best Explanation* (London: Routledge, 1991). By *simpler*, I mean less convoluted or ad hoc. By *more powerful*, I mean being able to explain larger numbers of things and different kinds of things. For example, the theistic hypothesis offers a sufficient explanatory context for *all* of the *wide-ranging* features listed above. There's also the criterion of being *more familiar*, which means that certain parallels or analogies are available to us to help explain other phenomena. For instance, I infer that a personal cause must have brought about the universe and physical time from a state of nothingness and changelessness, and I have the familiar experience of seeing personal human agents initiating or bringing about events.

19. Taken from Dallas Willard, "Toward a Phenomenology for the Correspondence Theory of Truth," *Discipline filosofiche* 1 (1991): 125–47. Found online at www.dallaswillard.com.

20. This point is taken from Sweetman, "Pseudo-Problem of Skepticism," 228–41.

Chapter 2 Whatever Works for You

1. See William Dyrness, *How Does America Hear the Gospel?* (Grand Rapids: Eerdmans, 1989).

2. Stephen P. Stich, *The Fragmentation of Reason* (Cambridge, MA: MIT Press, 1990).

3. Richard Rorty, *Philosophy and the Mirror of Nature* (Princeton: Princeton University Press, 1979), 176.

4. Stephen Hawking, "The Objections of an Unashamed Positivist," in Roger Penrose, *The Large, the Small, and the Human* ed. Malcalm Longair (Cambridge: Cambridge University Press, 1997), 169.

5. Caroline Davies, "'Pregnancy came as a shock. Now I'm happy to give up the Olympics,'" *The Telegraph* (May 13, 2004), http://www.telegraph.co.uk/news/main .jhtml?xml=/news/2004/05/13/ntash13.xml&sS. See also, http://www.pfm.org/AM/Tem plate.cfm?Section=BreakPoint_Home&Template=/ContentManagement/ContentDisplay .cfm&ContentID=12672.

6. Paul C. Vitz, *Censorship: Evidence of Bias in Our Children's Textbooks* (Ann Arbor, MI: Servant, 1986), 3, 18, 19.

7. David K. Clark, *To Know and Love God: Method for Theology* (Wheaton: Crossway, 2003), 109.

8. Richard Rorty, *Consequences of Pragmatism* (Minneapolis: University of Minnesota Press, 1982), 166.

9. I've noted the logical/philosophical problems of relativism in Paul Copan, *"True for You, but Not for Me"* (Minneapolis: Bethany House, 1998), and Paul Copan, *"That's Just Your Interpretation": Responding to Skeptics Who Challenge Your Faith* (Grand Rapids: Baker Books, 2001).

10. Richard Rorty, "Science as Solidarity," in *Objectivity, Relativism, and Truth*, vol. 1, *Philosophical Papers* (Cambridge: Cambridge University Press, 1991), 39, 45.

11. Ibid., xvii.

12. Carl F. H. Henry, *God, Revelation, and Authority* (Waco: Word, 1976), 3:453.

13. David K. Clark, "Beyond Inerrancy: A Speech Act Proposal for a Holistic View of Scripture" (paper presented at the Evangelical Theological Society meeting in Toronto, Ontario, November 2002). For further discussion, see David K. Clark's fine book, *To Know and Love God.*

14. J. L. Austin speaks of this in *How to Do Things with Words*, 2nd ed., ed. J. O. Urmson and Marina Sbisà (Cambridge: Harvard University Press, 1975). Speech-act theory involves more than just mere description or propositions. Take the statement "The store is closing in fifteen minutes." This statement operates at a number of different levels: (a) the act *of* saying something, (b) what one does *in* saying it, and (c) what one does *by* saying it. The first aspect speaks of (a) *locutionary* acts: this statement or utterance by the store manager has a specific meaning or sense to it—namely, the particular store he's managing and you're visiting will be closed fifteen minutes after this act of speaking. But that's not all. Statements have (b) *illocutionary* force: the manager is also trying to help his audience *understand* or is *informing* them about the store's closing soon. Utterances also have (c) *perlocutionary* force: customers can infer from the store manager's utterance that they should *do* something—namely, make their final purchasing decisions soon and head promptly to the checkout counter. So this store manager's speech-act involves all three levels—not simply uttering truth-statements. See also Kevin J. Vanhoozer, *Is There Meaning in This Text?* (Grand Rapids: Zondervan, 1998).

15. This and other comments below are taken from Kevin J. Vanhoozer, "From Speech Acts to Scripture Acts: The Covenant of Discourse and the Discourse of Covenant," in *After*

Pentecost: Language and Biblical Interpretation, ed. Craig Bartholomew, Colin Greene, and Karl Miller, Scripture and Hermeneutics Series, vol. 2 (Grand Rapids: Zondervan, 2001), 1–49.

16. Augustine, *On Christian Doctrine*, trans. D. W. Robertson Jr. (Indianapolis: Bobbs-Merrill, 1958), 86–87.

17. Karl Barth, *Church Dogmatics*, trans. Geoffrey R. Bromiley (Edinburgh: T&T Clark, 1957–75), vol. 1, pt. 1, 147.

18. Some of these comments are taken from Anthony C. Thiselton, *Interpreting God and the Postmodern Self: On Meaning, Manipulation and Promise* (Grand Rapids: Eerdmans, 1995), 63–66.

Chapter 3 Naturalism Is a Simpler Explanation Than Theism

1. David Papineau, *Philosophical Naturalism* (Oxford: Blackwell, 1993), 1.

2. John Lucas, personal email, February 14, 2005.

3. Carl Sagan, *Cosmos* (New York: Random House, 1980), 4.

4. See William Lane Craig and J. P. Moreland, preface to their coedited volume, *Naturalism: A Critical Analysis* (London: Routledge, 2000), xi–xv. See also Vance G. Morgan, "The Metaphysics of Naturalism," *American Catholic Philosophical Quarterly* 75 (Summer 2001): 409–31.

5. Paul M. Churchland and Patricia S. Churchland, "Intertheoretic Reduction: A Neuroscientist's Field Guide," in Paul M. Churchland and Patricia S. Churchland, *On the Contrary* (Cambridge, MA: MIT Press, 1998), 77.

6. *Substance* dualists would maintain that the body and soul/mind are distinct and the soul can potentially survive bodily death.

7. Jaegwon Kim, "Mental Causation and Two Conceptions of Mental Properties" (paper presented at the American Philosophical Association Eastern Division meeting, December 1993), 2–23.

8. *Groundhog Day*, written by Danny Rubin, directed by Harold Ramis (Columbia/Tristar, 1993).

9. See my chapter on God and evil in Paul Copan, *"That's Just Your Interpretation,"* 90–100.

10. Dallas Willard, "Language, Being, God, and the Three Stages of Theistic Evidence," in J. P. Moreland and Kai Nielsen, *Does God Exist? The Great Debate* (Nashville: Thomas Nelson, 1990; Amherst, NY: Prometheus, 1993), 207. Citations are to the Nelson edition.

11. For further discussion on this, see Paul Copan and Paul K. Moser, eds., *The Rationality of Theism* (London: Routledge, 2003), 1–14.

12. Alvin Plantinga, "Natural Theology," in *Companion to Metaphysics*, ed. Jaegwon Kim and Ernest Sosa (Cambridge: Blackwell, 1995), 347.

13. Kai Nielsen, *Reason and Practice* (New York: Harper & Row, 1971), 48.

14. To deny the principle of sufficient reason (*everything that exists has a reason for its existence*) is to utilize it or assume it, since one presumably has a sufficient reason for denying it! To deny it is to use it. (Of course, God, by his very nature, must exist; so the reason for God's existence is that he is by nature self-sufficient—unlike any other entities.) For a defense of the principle of sufficient reason in the context of the cosmological argument for God's existence, see Stephen T. Davis, "The Cosmological Argument and the Epistemic Status of Belief in God," *Philosophia Christi* 2, vol. 1, no. 1 (1999): 5–15.

15. Michael Martin, *Atheism: A Philosophical Justification* (Philadelphia: Temple University Press, 1990), 106.

16. See William Lane Craig's responses to Martin and other critics on the beginning of the universe and other topics in Moreland and Nielsen, *Does God Exist?*

17. Willard, "Language, Being, God," 206.

18. John Locke, *An Essay Concerning Human Understanding* 4.10.

19. Martin, *Atheism, Morality, and Meaning*, 45. Martin himself, however, holds to the view that moral values emerge from matter (supervenience) but aren't constituted by matter.

20. Steven Weinberg, *Dreams of a Final Theory* (New York: Pantheon, 1992), 52.

21. Lewis, "Is Theology Poetry?" 140.

Chapter 4 Unless You Can Scientifically Verify or Falsify Your Belief, It's Meaningless

1. C. P. Snow, "The Two Cultures," in *The World Treasury of Physics, Astronomy, and Mathematics*, ed. Timothy Ferris (Boston: Little, Brown, and Co., 1991), 742.

2. Richard Dawkins, *River Out of Eden: A Darwinian View of Life* (New York: Basic Books, 1995), 33.

3. Mikael Stenmark discusses the various forms of scientism such as *epistemic, rationalistic, ontological, axiological, redemptive, comprehensive*, etc. Mikael Stenmark, "What Is Scientism?" *Religious Studies* 33 (1992): 15–32; see also Stenmark's book *Scientism: Science, Ethics and Religion* (Burlington, VT: Ashgate, 2004). Some of my comments in this section reflect Stenmark's insights and observations.

4. Stephen Hawking, *A Brief History of Time* (New York: Bantam, 1988), 13.

5. See Richard Lewontin's article "Billions and Billions of Demons," *New York Review of Books*, January 9, 1997, 28–32, from which this quotation is taken.

6. See Stephen Jay Gould, *Rocks of Ages: Science and Religion in the Fullness of Life* (New York: Ballantine, 1999).

7. Taken from an online version of *A Christmas Carol* at http://www.classicbookshelf .com/library/charles_dickens/a_christmas_carol/0/.

8. Paul Horwich, "Review of J. R. Lucas, *The Future*," *British Journal for the Philosophy of Science* 44 (1993): 579.

9. John Post, *Metaphysics: A Contemporary Introduction* (New York: Paragon House, 1991), 85.

10. John J. O'Dwyer, *College Physics*, 3rd ed. (1981; repr., Belmont, CA: Wadsworth, 1984; Pacific Grove, CA: Brooks/Cole, 1990): 2, quoted in J. P. Moreland, *Christianity and the Nature of Science* (Grand Rapids: Baker Academic, 1989), 21 (my italics). Citation is to the Brooks/Cole edition.

11. David Hume, *Enquiry Concerning Human Understanding*, ed. L. A. Selby-Bigge (1900; repr., Oxford: Clarendon, 1951), 7.3, 165.

12. For a recent response to this line of reasoning, see William P. Alston, "Religious Language and Verificationism," in *The Rationality of Theism*, ed. Paul Copan and Paul K. Moser (London: Routledge, 2003), 17–34.

13. Del Ratzsch, *Philosophy of Science* (Downers Grove, IL: InterVarsity, 1986), 15. (The second edition of this book is retitled *Science and Its Limits* [Downers Grove, IL: InterVarsity, 2000].)

14. Antony Flew, "Theology and Falsification," in *New Essays in Philosophical Theology*, ed. Antony Flew and Alasdair MacIntyre (London: SCM, 1955), 106.

15. Stephen C. Meyer, "The Methodological Equivalence of Design and Descent," in *The Creation Hypothesis*, ed. J. P. Moreland (Downers Grove, IL: InterVarsity, 1994), 74–75.

Chapter 5 You Can't Prove That Scientifically

1. See Alvin Plantinga's discussion of the proposed "demarcation criteria" in Alvin Plantinga, "Methodological Naturalism?" *Perspectives on Science and the Christian Faith* 49 (September 1997): 143–54; reprinted as Alvin Plantinga, "Should Methodological Naturalism Constrain Science?" in *Science: Christian Perspectives for the New Millennium*, ed. Scott Luley, Paul Copan, and Stan W. Wallace (Dallas/Atlanta: Christian Leadership Ministries/Ravi Zacharias International Ministries, 2003), 107–34.

2. For example, see Larry Laudan, "Science at the Bar—Causes for Concern," in *But Is It Science?* ed. Michael Ruse (Buffalo: Prometheus Books, 1988), 351–55; also see Philip Quinn, "The Philosopher of Science as Expert Witness," in *But Is It Science?* 367–85.

3. Richard Swinburne, *The Existence of God* (Oxford: Oxford University Press, 1979), 3.

4. Robert C. Koons, "Science and Theism," in *The Rationality of Theism*, ed. Paul Copan and Paul K. Moser (London: Routledge, 2003), 75–76.

5. See Francis Beckwith, *Law, Darwinism, and Public Education: The Establishment Clause and the Challenge of Intelligent Design* (Lanham, MD: Rowman and Littlefield, 2003). Here Beckwith shows that atheists or secular humanists or scientific materialists shouldn't be favored by the First Amendment over against theists. The teaching of intelligent design has an appropriate place in public education. See also Del Ratzsch's excellent book *Nature, Design, and Science: The Status of Design in Natural Science* (Albany, NY: SUNY, 2001).

6. William C. Dembski, "On the Very Possibility of Intelligent Design," in *The Creation Hypothesis*, ed. J. P. Moreland (Downers Grove, IL: InterVarsity, 1994), 133.

7. Richard Lewontin, "Review of Carl Sagan, *The Demon-Haunted World*," *New York Review of Books*, January 9, 1997, 28, 31.

8. See Hoyle's "testimony" in Sir Fred Hoyle, *The Origin of the Universe and the Origin of Life* (New York: Moyer Bell, 1994).

9. Daniel C. Dennett, *Darwin's Dangerous Idea: Evolution and the Meaning of Life* (New York: Simon & Schuster, 1995), 519.

10. Roger Trigg, *Rationality and Science* (Oxford: Blackwell, 1993), 4.

11. Philosopher Alfred North Whitehead spoke of "neglecting the degree of abstraction involved when an actual entity is considered merely so far as it exemplifies certain categories of thought." Alfred North Whitehead, *Process and Reality* (New York: Harper, 1929), 11.

12. Edwards maintained that "spirits are only properly substance" ("Of Being," Corollary 1, 206)—although God is "substance" in the truest sense of the word: "There is no proper substance but God himself" ("Of Atoms," Corollary 11, 215). Edwards said that the "material universe exists nowhere but in the mind" ("The Mind," no. 34, 353). Edwards held an idealistic version of the correspondence theory of truth: "Truth . . . may be defined after the most strict and metaphysical manner: 'the consistency and agreement of our ideas with the ideas of God'" ("The Mind," no. 10, 341–42). Citations are taken from *The Works of Jonathan Edwards: Scientific and Philosophical Writings*, ed. Wallace E. Anderson (New Haven: Yale University Press, 1980).

13. Stephen Hawking and Roger Penrose, *The Nature of Space and Time*, The Isaac Newton Institute Series of Lectures (Princeton, NJ: Princeton University Press, 1996), 121. Earlier in the book, he asserts: "I take the positivist view point that a physical theory is just a mathematical model and that it is meaningless to ask whether it corresponds to reality" (ibid., 3–4). Elsewhere, Hawking says, "I . . . am a positivist who believes that physical theories are just mathematical models we construct, and that it is meaningless to ask if they correspond to reality, just whether they predict observations." Stephen Hawking, "The Objections of an

Unashamed Positivist," in Roger Penrose, *The Large, the Small, and the Human* (Cambridge: Cambridge University Press, 1997), 169.

14. Dallas Willard, "Space, Color, Sense Perception and the Epistemology of Logic," *The Monist* 72 (January 1989): 122.

15. Ian Barbour, "Ways of Relating Science and Theology," in *Physics, Philosophy, and Theology*, ed. R. J. Russell et al. (Rome: Vatican Observatory, 1988), 23.

16. Taken from Ratzsch, *Philosophy of Science*, 17.

17. Steven Weinberg, *The First Three Minutes: A Modern View of the Origin of the Universe* (New York: HarperCollins, 1993), 154–55.

18. Peter van Inwagen, "Genesis and Evolution," in *Reasoned Faith*, ed. Eleonore Stump (Ithaca: Cornell University Press, 1993), 104–5.

19. William J. Macquorn Rankine, "The Mathematician in Love," in *Songs and Fables* (Glasgow: James Maclehose, 1874), 3–6, lines 1–5, 26–40, http://eir.library.utoronto.ca/rpo/display/poem1699.html.

20. Edward O. Wilson, *Consilience: The Unity of Knowledge* (New York: Knopf, 1998), 266.

21. Richard Dawkins, *The Blind Watchmaker* (New York: Norton, 1986), 1.

22. Francis Crick, *What Mad Pursuit* (New York: Basic Books, 1988), 138.

23. We could also throw "irreducible complexity" into the mix. Michael Behe has argued that, at a cellular level, a number of interworking components need to be in place all at once in order for a cell to function at all. A gradualistic development of, say, a bacterium (with flagellum) is unworkable. See Michael J. Behe, *Darwin's Black Box* (New York: Free Press, 1996).

24. "The Political Christopher Reeve," *CBS News.com* (October 31, 2000), http://www.cbsnews.com/stories/2000/10/31/entertainment/main245551.shtml; see also "Christopher Reeve Addresses Vt. Graduates," *MSN Entertainment* (May 23, 2003), http://entertainment.msn.com/celebs/article.aspx?news=159187.

25. See "Christopher Reeve Addresses Vt. Graduates."

26. Leon R. Kass, *Toward a More Natural Science* (New York: Free Press, 1985), 78.

27. Ibid., 46.

28. C. S. Lewis, *The Abolition of Man* (New York: Macmillan, 1965), 69–71.

29. Aldous Huxley, *Ends and Means* (London: Chatto and Windus, 1969), 270, 273 (my italics).

30. Michael Polanyi, *Personal Knowledge: Towards a Post-critical Philosophy* (Chicago: University of Chicago Press, 1958), 203–45.

31. John Polkinghorne, *One World: The Interaction of Science and Theology* (Princeton: Princeton University Press, 1986), 12.

32. Thomas S. Kuhn, *The Structure of Scientific Revolutions* (Chicago: University of Chicago Press, 1962; 2nd ed., 1970). Note that Kuhn, at least when he first wrote his highly influential book, believed that science operates according to one "paradigm"—like the Aristotelian or Newtonian models of the universe—before it is displaced by another through a scientific "revolution." Kuhn neglected to note that each successive "paradigm" *builds on the foundation of scientific work that preceded it*; a new theory absorbs part of the old theory and doesn't simply discard it wholesale. Richard Purtill, "Kuhn on Scientific Revolutions," *Philosophy of Science* 34 (1967): 53. There's most certainly objectivity involved in moving from one paradigm to another. On the other hand, Kuhn does show us the importance of studying the history of science for understanding the philosophy of science. See Mikael Stenmark, *Rationality in Science, Religion, and Everyday Life* (Notre Dame: University of Notre Dame Press, 1996), 115–39.

33. Stephen C. Meyer, "A Scopes Trial for the '90s," *Wall Street Journal*, December 6, 1993, A14.

34. William Hasker, *Metaphysics* (Downers Grove, IL: InterVarsity, 1983), 26–28.

35. Nancy Pearcey and Charles Thaxton, *The Soul of Science: Christian Faith and Natural Philosophy* (Wheaton, IL: Crossway Books, 1994), 19.

36. Andrew Dickson White, *A History of the Warfare of Science with Theology in Christendom* (New York: D. Appleton, 1908).

37. John William Draper, *History of the Conflict between Religion and Science* (New York: D. Appleton, 1902).

38. Stanley L. Jaki, *The Savior of Science* (Washington: Regnery Gateway, 1988); Robert C. Koons, "Science and Theism," in *The Rationality of Theism*, ed. Copan and Moser, 72–90.

39. Pearcey and Thaxton, *The Soul of Science*.

40. The following is taken from Pearcey and Thaxton, *Soul of Science*, 59–78, 259: **Aristotelianism** (the God-as-Architect perspective) (1) stressed God's *transcendence*, his *rationality*, and his *purposes* in nature ("final causes"); (2) emphasized creation as *below God* in the hierarchy of being; (3) promoted *geocentrism*; (4) claimed that planets' orbits were *perfect spheres*, and the stars were *changeless*; (5) emphasized the importance of *rationality/logical reasoning* as scientific; (6) viewed the universe as an *organism*; (7) inspired *astronomy*. On the other hand, **Neoplatonism** (the God-as-Artisan view) (1) stressed God's *immanence*, his *indwelling Spirit operating through natural processes*; (2) emphasized the creation as *"God's body"*; (3) promoted *heliocentrism*; (4) claimed the planetary orbits were "less-perfect" *ellipses*; (5) emphasized the importance of *mystical insight* or *spiritual inspiration* (which God bestows) as scientific; (6) viewed the universe as being somewhat *magical*; planets had their own built-in homing devices; (7) inspired *chemistry* ("spirits").

41. Mark Kalthoff, "God and Creation: An Historical Look at Encounters between Christianity and Science," in Michael Bauman, ed., *Man and Creation: Perspectives in Science and Theology* (Hillsdale, MI: Hillsdale College Press, 1993), 15–17.

42. Galileo, letter to the Grand Duchess Christina of Tuscany, quoted in Mark Noll, *The Scandal of the Evangelical Mind* (Grand Rapids: Eerdmans, 1994), 205–6 (my italics).

43. Barbour, "Ways of Relating Science and Theology," 25.

44. Jaki, *The Savior of Science*, 11–45. Alfred North Whitehead, *Science and the Modern World* (New York: Macmillan, 1925); Michael Foster, "The Christian Doctrine of Creation and the Rise of Modern Science," *Mind* 43 (1934): 446–68; and "Christian Theology and the Rise of Modern Science I and II," *Mind* 44 (1935): 439–83 and *Mind* 45 (1936): 1–27; Christopher Kaiser, *Creation and the History of Science* (Grand Rapids: Eerdmans, 1981); A. R. Hall, *The Scientific Revolution, 1500–1800: The Formation of the Modern Scientific Attitude* (Boston: Beacon, 1954); Joseph Needham, *The Grand Titration: Science and Society in East and West* (Toronto: University of Toronto Press, 1969), 327; Stanley L. Jaki, *The Road of Science and the Ways to God* (Chicago: University of Chicago Press, 1978); Eugene M. Klaaren, *Religious Origins of Modern Science* (Grand Rapids: Eerdmans, 1977); Loren C. Eiseley, *Darwin's Century: Evolution and the Men Who Discovered It* (New York: Doubleday, 1958), 62; Margaret Osler and Paul Lawrence Barber, eds., *Religion, Science and Worldview* (Cambridge: Cambridge University Press, 1985); Margaret Osler, *Rethinking the Scientific Revolution* (Cambridge: Cambridge University Press, 2000). Thanks to Robert Koons for these references.

45. Polkinghorne, *One World*, 4.

46. Paul Davies, *Are We Alone?* (New York: Basic Books, 1995), 96.

47. Immanuel Kant, *The Critique of Pure Reason*, 2nd ed., trans. Norman Kemp Smith (New York: St. Martin's Press, 1929), 521 (A 625-26/B 653-54). On this, see Del Ratzsch, "Stenmark, Plantinga, and Scientific Neutrality," *Faith and Philosophy* 21, no. 3 (July 2004): 353–64.

Chapter 6 The Soul Is Nothing More Than the Brain

1. Dr. Seuss, *Happy Birthday to You!* (New York: Random House, 1959), n.p.

2. Dalai Lama, *Kindness, Clarity and Insight* (New York: Snow Lion, 1984), 45.

3. J. P. Moreland, "An Enduring Self: The Achilles' Heel of Process Philosophy," *Process Studies* 17 (Fall 1988): 193.

4. Peter van Inwagen, *Metaphysics* (Boulder, CO: Westview, 1993), 172. Van Inwagen, however, claims that we are *material beings* (a nonreductive materialist). He takes the tack that persons do not *persist through time* (what he calls "three-dimensional beings," who simply occupy space) but rather are *extended in time* ("four-dimensional beings," inhabiting four-dimensional space-time). A common example is Theseus's ship, whose boards are replaced one at a time. Is this ship the same at point B as it was before all of its boards were replaced (point A)? According to van Inwagen, yes: the ship is four-dimensional; it extends in time between points A and B. However, it's helpful to distinguish between an *artifact* (e.g., a ship) and an *organism/substance* (e.g., a human person) at this point. There also is a certain *psychological unity* for human beings that can account for identity.

5. Francis Crick, *The Astonishing Hypothesis: The Scientific Search for the Soul* (New York: Charles Scribner's Sons, 1994), 3.

6. Owen Flanagan, *The Problem of the Soul: Two Visions of the Mind and How to Reconcile Them* (New York: Basic Books, 2002), 3.

7. Ibid., 77.

8. Jaegwon Kim, *Philosophy of Mind* (Boulder, CO: Westview, 1996), 3. Peter van Inwagen is a Christian philosopher who would call himself a nonreductive materialist. He brings up this "interaction argument" too: it seems difficult to see how two completely different substances could interact with each other. See van Inwagen, *Metaphysics*, 178–79.

9. Kim, *Philosophy of Mind*, 4.

10. Jaegwon Kim, "Mind, Problems of the Philosophy of," in *The Oxford Companion to Philosophy*, ed. Ted Honderich (New York: Oxford University Press, 1995), 576.

11. Descartes wrote, "On the one hand, I have a clear and distinct idea of myself, in as far as I am only a thinking and unextended thing, and as, on the other hand, I possess a distinct idea of body, in as far as it is only an extended and unthinking thing. It is certain that I, (that is, my mind, by which I am what I am), is entirely and truly distinct from my body, and may exist without it." Descartes, "Meditation VI," in *The Meditations and Selections from the Principles of René Descartes*, trans. John Veitch, (Chicago: Open Court, 1927), 91.

12. See the discussion in J. P. Moreland and Scott B. Rae, *Body and Soul: Human Nature and the Crisis in Ethics* (Downers Grove, IL: InterVarsity, 2000).

13. See Moreland and Rae, *Body and Soul*, chap. 2. Although we can't go into a lot of detail on what a substance is, here's a start:

A substance has *a deep, basic unity* rooted in the very *nature* of a thing. (A nature or essence *makes a thing what it is*; without this underlying essence, this thing wouldn't exist or would be something else.) When a tadpole turns into a frog, this is because the frog has an internal nature that directs this change.

There's a certain *goal-orientedness* (or teleology) of substances; substances carry out particular tendencies that are in keeping with their nature. The tadpole has a *potential* that can become *actualized* (or realized).

A substance isn't simply a conglomeration or bundle of parts or properties; rather, it *has* properties (e.g., a lion has *brown* fur) rather than *being had* by something else.

A substance also has *continuity over time*; while certain characteristics or properties change, these *changes presuppose sameness* (e.g., an oak grows from an acorn, but there's a continuity of substance). We can't make sense of change unless we presuppose sameness.

A substance can *act on things*; even small substances such as atoms can act on each other. (The properties that substances have—roundness, hardness, whiteness—are inert and cannot act on something else or produce something.)

American philosopher and theologian Jonathan Edwards took the view that with respect to bodies, "there is no proper substance but God himself" ("Of Atoms," Corollary 11, in *Works of Jonathan Edwards*, 215). More precisely, however, Edwards considers those beings that have "knowledge and consciousness" to be the "only proper and real and substantial beings" ("Of Being," Corollary 1, in ibid., 206). In contrast to those who think that material things have true substance whereas spirits are more like shadows, Edwards argues that "spirits are only properly substance" (ibid.). The material universe "exists nowhere but in the mind" ("The Mind," no. 34, in ibid., 353). The existence of the material universe is "absolutely dependent on idea" (ibid.). Of course, this view (known as *idealism*) has never really even *seemed true*. It appears too counterintuitive to be affirmed; it's a very impractical view of reality.

14. Taken from J. P. Moreland, "Restoring the Substance of the Soul to Psychology," *Journal of Psychology and Theology* 26 (1998): 29–43.

15. J. P. Moreland, *Love Your God with All Your Mind* (Colorado Springs: NavPress, 1997), 68–69.

16. Paul K. Moser, "Jesus on Knowledge of God," *Christian Scholar's Review* 28 (Summer 1999): 590. The entirety of the article is excellent.

17. Joseph A. Fitzmyer, *The Gospel according to Luke*, Anchor Bible Commentary 28a (Garden City, NY: Doubleday, 1985), 1306–7. Compare 4 Maccabees 7:19 and 16:25, which argue in this fashion.

18. Moser, "Jesus on Knowledge of God," 587.

19. For example, Joel B. Green takes the view of *nonreductive physicalism*—that a human being is a "unitary physical entity without a separate, nonphysical soul, with capacities that are incapable of being reduced to the behavior of nerve cells and their related molecules. In such a view, 'soul' is not an ontological [or really distinct] entity but an embodied capacity and vocation to relate to others, to self, and to God" (Joel B. Green, "Scripture and the Human Person: Further Reflections," *Science and Christian Belief* 11 [1999]: 58). Thus Green maintains that this passage is not referring to a state of disembodiment. Green argues that 1 Corinthians 15:38–58 gives us guidance on this matter. There is a "profound continuity" between this present life and life everlasting with God. For believers, this continuity has to do with bodily existence. Green adds: "Paul cannot think in terms of a free-floating soul from a body" (61). See also Warren Brown, Nancey Murphy, and Newton Maloney, eds., *Whatever Happened to the Soul?* (Minneapolis: Fortress, 1998).

20. Ben Witherington III, *Conflict and Community in Corinth* (Grand Rapids: Eerdmans, 1995), 391.

21. Colin Kruse, *2 Corinthians*, Tyndale Series (Grand Rapids: Eerdmans; Downers Grove, IL: InterVarsity, 1987), 114.

22. Charles Taliaferro, "Philosophy of Mind and the Christian," in *Christian Theism and the Problems of Philosophy*, ed. Michael D. Beaty (Notre Dame: University of Notre Dame Press, 1990), 238. Substance dualism doesn't entail that a resurrection body must be "re-assembled" atom-for-atom from a mortal body incinerated in an explosion (or from the deceased body of a converted cannibal)—*contra* Kevin J. Corcoran's allegation in "Dualism, Materialism, and the Problem of Postmortem Survival," *Philosophia Christi* 2, vol. 4, no. 2 (2002): 411–25.

23. Taliaferro, "Philosophy of Mind and the Christian," 239. See David F. Siemens Jr., "Thoughts on Non-Reductive Materialism: A New Heresy?" *Philosophia Christi* 2, vol. 4, no. 2 (2002): 522.

24. Robert Gundry, *Matthew*, 2nd ed. (Grand Rapids: Eerdmans, 1994), 197. See Gundry's various supporting references.

25. See Stephen T. Davis, *Risen Indeed* (Grand Rapids: Eerdmans, 1993), chap. 7.

26. Jaroslav Pelikan, *The Emergence of the Catholic Tradition (100–600): The Christian Tradition*, vol. 1 (Chicago: University of Chicago Press, 1971), 51.

27. Murray J. Harris, "Resurrection and Immortality in the Pauline Corpus," in *Life in the Face of Death: The Resurrection Message of the New Testament*, ed. Richard N. Longenecker (Grand Rapids: Eerdmans, 1998), 160.

28. Ibid., 153.

29. See N. T. Wright's comments in *The Resurrection of the Son of God* (Minneapolis: Fortress, 2003) in chaps. 2–3. Despite Stanley Porter's observations, "Resurrection, the Greeks, and the New Testament," in *Resurrection*, ed. Stanley E. Porter, Michael A. Hayes, and David Tombs (Sheffield: Sheffield Academic, 1999), 52–81, see Wright, *Resurrection*, 35, 66, 68, etc.

30. The Westminster Confession speaks of the souls of persons as having "an immortal subsistence" (33.1), but this is inaccurate. *Immortality for humans is a divine gift gained through bodily resurrection:* "According to Paul and the New Testament, what is immortal when one uses that term with regard to humanity is the resurrected believer" (Harris, "Resurrection and Immortality," 165).

31. For further reading on this, see N. T. Wright, *The Millennium Myth* (Louisville: Westminster John Knox, 1999). Wright nicely summarized this point in his Evangelical Philosophical Society address "Resurrection in History and Theology" at the Evangelical Theological Society meeting in Atlanta, Georgia (November 2003).

32. Taken from George E. Ladd, *A Theology of the New Testament* (Grand Rapids: Eerdmans, 1974), 457–64.

33. For a general discussion of these three views, see Gregory A. Boyd and Paul R. Eddy, *Across the Spectrum* (Grand Rapids: Baker Academic, 2002), 87–100.

34. C. Stephen Evans, *The Quest for Faith* (Downers Grove, IL: InterVarsity, 1996), 123. This has been reprinted as *Why Believe?* by Eerdmans.

Chapter 7 Why Think Immaterial Things Like Souls Exist?

1. Colin McGinn, *The Mysterious Flame: Conscious Minds in a Material World* (New York: Basic Books, 1999), 13, 15.

2. Ned Block, "Consciousness," in *A Companion to the Philosophy of Mind*, ed. Samuel Guttenplan (Malden, MA: Blackwell, 1994), 211.

3. Charles Taliaferro, "Mysterious Flames in Philosophy of Mind," *Philosophia Christi* 2, vol. 1, no. 2 (1999): 29.

4. *Supervenience* has been something of a buzzword in the vocabulary of many philosophers of mind. According to the idea of supervenience, *the mental is anchored in the physical and biological world*—without identifying one with the other. Supervenience doesn't imply that a *psychological* property must be *physical* but that *nothing can have a mental property without having some physical property* (and hence without being a physical thing). This is the view of property dualism—the view that the mental and the physical are two distinct properties, but the physical serves as the basis for the mental, and the mental can't be reduced to it. Mental properties are *grounded in* physical ones but are *not identical* to them. Kim, *Philosophy of Mind*, 11.

5. See J. P. Moreland's booklet *What Is the Soul?* (Atlanta: Ravi Zacharias International Ministries, 2001).

6. There are various approaches to the mind-body problem—eliminative materialism, identity theory, functionalism, property dualism, idealism. We can't address them all here, though some of my arguments will address eliminative materialism, and others will be directed more specifically at nonreductive materialism (property dualism). But see Charles Taliaferro, "Philosophy of Mind and the Christian," 233–35.

7. Ibid., 241.

8. Produced by Ben & Jerry's, Waterbury, Vermont.

9. Philip E. Devine, *Natural Law Ethics* (Westport, CT: Greenwood, 2000), 36.

10. C. S. Lewis, *Christian Reflections* (Grand Rapids: Eerdmans, 1967), 64.

11. Robert Audi, "Theism and Scientific Understanding," *Companion to Philosophy of Religion*, ed. Phillip Quinn and Charles Taliaferro (Cambridge: Blackwell, 1997), 436.

12. Consider the identity statement that "Mark Twain = Samuel Langhorne Clemens." Every characteristic or property that Twain has is the same one that Clemens has; so they are identical. The law of identity states that for any object O and any object O', O is identical with O' if and only if every property that O has O' also has (and vice versa). That is, O = O'.

13. Taliaferro, "Philosophy of Mind and the Christian," 244.

14. Colin McGinn, *The Problem of Consciousness* (Oxford: Basil Blackwell, 1990), 1.

15. Jerry A. Fodor, "The Big Idea: Can There Be a Science of the Mind?" *Times Literary Supplement,* July 3, 1992, 5.

16. Michael Martin writes: "Atheism is not committed to materialism and even if it were, there would be no a priori reason why in an objective morality values could not be constituted by matter." Martin, *Atheism, Morality, and Meaning,* 45.

17. Charles Taliaferro, *Contemporary Philosophy of Religion* (Malden, MA: Blackwell, 1997), 94.

18. Taken from "Egyptian Mummies" from the Smithsonian Institution's website: http://www.si.edu/resource/faq/nmnh/mummies.htm.

19. Taliaferro, *Contemporary Philosophy of Religion,* 94.

20. Ibid., 96. In fact, Stewart Goetz remarks that "if nonreductive physicalism is correct, our first-person experience must be illusory and, thus, the ordinary person's view of the world must be radically different." Review of Brown, Murphy, and Maloney, eds., *Whatever Happened to the Soul? Philosophia Christi* 2, vol. 1, no. 2 (1999): 128.

21. C. S. Lewis, *Studies in Medieval and Renaissance Literature,* ed. W. Hooper (Cambridge: Cambridge University Press, 1966), 3, 4.

22. Thanks to Charles Taliaferro's discussion on this in his fine booklet *Does the Idea of God Make Sense?* (Atlanta: Ravi Zacharias International Ministries, 2001).

23. A. J. Ayer, "What I Saw When I Was Dead," appendix in Terry Meithe and Antony Flew, *Does God Exist?* (San Francisco: HarperSanFrancisco, 1991), 225.

24. Melvin Morse with Paul Perry, *Closer to the Light: Learning from the Near-Death Experiences of Children* (New York: Random House/Villard, 1990), 3–9, quoted in Gary R. Habermas and J. P. Moreland, *Beyond Death: Exploring the Evidence for Immortality* (Wheaton: Crossway, 1998), 163.

25. Michael B. Sabom, M.D., F.A.C.C., *Recollections of Death: A Medical Investigation* (New York: Harper & Row, 1982), 87–91. See also Kenneth Ring and Sharon Cooper, *Mindsight: Near-Death and Out-of-Body Experiences in the Blind* (Palo Alto, CA: William James Center for Consciousness Studies, 1999). Thanks to Kris Key for furnishing me with these resources.

26. Sabom, *Recollections of Death,* 104.

27. Michael Sabom, M.D., *Light and Death: One Doctor's Fascinating Account of Near-Death Experiences* (Grand Rapids: Zondervan, 1998), 56–57. NDE authority Raymond Moody (author of *Life after Life*) endorses this book (back cover), declaring that Sabom's study has become a "benchmark in the field of near-death research."

28. Taliaferro, *Contemporary Philosophy of Religion*, 94.

29. Stewart Goetz, "Naturalism and Libertarian Agency," in *Naturalism: A Critical Analysis*, ed. William Lane Craig and J. P. Moreland (London: Routledge, 2000), 157.

30. Some see *freedom* as compatible with *determinism* (compatibilists). From a theological point of view, this links God too closely to evil; philosophically speaking, compatibilism doesn't afford a robust view of personal agency. Thus I would opt for an *incompatibilist* approach in which freedom and determinism are incompatible.

31. J. P. Moreland discusses this in *Love Your God with All Your Mind*, 71–73. A person might be in a rut of bad habits (constantly eating chocolate, say) that seem to enslave him so that he can't break out of this pattern *right now*. But that in no way means that the chocoholic doesn't have freedom of will to *develop* the ability to refrain from indulging certain negative impulses and engaging in positive ones in the future. We have the capacity to *grow in our freedom or diminish it*.

32. For a useful book on the subject of freedom (endorsing an incompatibilist view), see James W. Felt, *Making Sense of Your Freedom: Philosophy for the Perplexed* (Ithaca: Cornell University Press, 1994).

33. Roderick Chisholm, "Human Freedom and the Self," in *Free Will*, ed. Gary Watson (Oxford: Oxford University Press, 1982), 32.

34. See Paul Copan, *"That's Just Your Interpretation,"* chap. 8, for a further discussion of this topic.

35. See Viktor E. Frankl, *Man's Search for Meaning*, trans. Ilse Lasch (New York: Simon & Schuster, 1963), 105.

36. Some philosophers tend to present a false dilemma of choices/events either being (a) *rigidly determined* or else (b) *utterly random*. (What is meant by "determinism" is that for everything that happens, there are prior conditions that necessitate certain events rather than others.) But (c) *personal agency* offers a third alternative. *So my reasons—not necessarily my inner states, motivations, background, genetics—are the basis for my actions; therefore my actions can be free but still have a reason.*

We must distinguish between *efficient* causality (causes that *produce* effects) and *final* causality (the *goal, end,* or *reason* for which something is done).

37. Thomas Nagel, *The View from Nowhere* (New York: Oxford University Press, 1986), 111.

38. Ibid.

39. John Searle, *Minds, Brains, and Science* (1984; repr., Cambridge: Harvard University Press, 1986), 87, 88. Elsewhere, Searle claims that a necessary condition for rationality requires at least that *there seems to be a "causal gap" between the agent's reasons and performing an action*. See John Searle, *Rationality in Action* (Cambridge, MA: MIT Press, 2001).

40. Searle, *Minds, Brains, and Science*, 92.

41. Nagel, *The View from Nowhere*, 113.

42. For a good overview of substance dualism, see J. P. Moreland and William Lane Craig, *Philosophical Foundations for a Christian Worldview* (Downers Grove, IL: InterVarsity, 2003), 228–303.

43. See Daniel Dennett's book by this title: *Elbow Room: The Varieties of Free Will Worth Wanting* (Cambridge, MA: MIT Press, 1984). Dennett simply writes off libertarianism as

an invention by philosophers, claiming that no reasonable person would even bring up the possibility of libertarian free will.

44. Derk Pereboom, *Living without Free Will* (Cambridge: Cambridge University Press, 2001), xiii.

45. Ibid., xiv.

46. Keith M. Parsons, "Defending Objectivity," *Philo* 2 (Spring–Summer 1999): 84.

47. Victor Reppert, *C. S. Lewis's Dangerous Idea: In Defense of the Argument from Reason* (Downers Grove, IL: InterVarsity, 2003), 107–8.

48. Evans, *Quest for Faith*, 122.

49. Goetz, review of Brown, Murphy, and Maloney, eds., *Whatever Happened to the Soul?* 127.

50. The physicalist might ask the question: How could the soul exist in a disembodied state and engage with other disembodied human beings? H. H. Price has maintained that a world of mental images (visual, auditory, and telepathic) is possible; by these images souls are aware of each other's presence, live in a real world (consisting of mental images rather than material objects), communicate with each other telepathically, and have dreamlike (as opposed to bodily) perceptions of their world. See H. H. Price, "Survival and the Idea of 'Another World,'" *Proceedings of the Society for Psychical Research* 50 (1953): 1–25. According to Stephen Davis, it is widely held by philosophers that Price's article "goes a long way toward establishing the coherence of disembodied survival of death." Stephen T. Davis, "Survival of Death," in *Companion to Philosophy of Religion*, 559.

51. Goetz, "Naturalism and Libertarian Agency," 158.

52. Moreland, "Restoring the Substance," 38.

Chapter 8 How Can an Immaterial Soul Influence a Material Body?

1. Kim, "Mind, Problems of the Philosophy of," 576; Kim, *Philosophy of Mind*, 4.

2. C. D. Broad, *The Mind and Its Place in Nature* (London: Routledge and Kegan Paul, 1925), 98. Note that C. D. Broad, though a dualist, was an *agnostic* about whether consciousness continues after death. C. J. Ducasse held a similar position. The point to be grasped here is that annihilation of the *body* doesn't entail annihilation of the *mind/soul*. Charles Taliaferro makes this point in his essay "Mysterious Flames in Philosophy of Mind," 27.

3. In an article written in 1935, Albert Einstein, Boris Podolsky, and Nathan Rosen (hence, EPR) opposed Niels Bohr's quantum indeterminacy (that we can't simultaneously figure out the momentum *and* the location of elementary particles such as electrons) in favor of the idea of "hidden variables." They proposed: "If, without in any way disturbing a system, we can predict with certainty (i.e., with probability equal to unity) the value of a physical quantity, then there exists an element of physical reality corresponding to this physical quality." Albert Einstein, Boris Poldosky, and Nathan Rosen, "Can Quantum Mechanical Description of Physical Reality Be Considered Complete?" *Physical Review* 47 (1935): 777.

4. A bootstrap model in science is antiholistic in its approach to scientific theories. Instead of claiming to argue for or against whole theories, bootstrapping is designed to show how evidence (derived deductively or probabilistically) counts for or against a single hypothesis rather than the whole theory it belongs to.

5. Bas van Fraassen, "Empiricism in the Philosophy of Science," in *Images of Science*, ed. Paul Churchland (Chicago: University of Chicago Press, 1985), 258.

6. Colin E. Gunton, *Act and Being: Towards a Theology of the Divine Attributes* (Grand Rapids: Eerdmans, 2003), 113–16.

7. See Paul Copan and William Lane Craig, *Creation Out of Nothing: A Biblical, Philosophical, and Scientific Exploration* (Grand Rapids: Baker Academic, 2004).

8. Stephen T. Davis, "God's Actions," in *In Defense of Miracles*, ed. R. Douglas Geivett and Gary Habermas (Downers Grove, IL: InterVarsity, 1997). Davis acknowledges: "Of course, there are different senses of the word *conceive*, so I do not wish to place great emphasis on this argument" (ibid., 170).

9. Taliaferro, "Mysterious Flames in Philosophy of Mind," 26.

10. Kim, "Mind, Problems of the Philosophy of," 578.

11. William Rowe, *Philosophy of Religion: An Introduction*, 2nd ed. (Belmont, CA: Wadsworth, 1993), 100.

12. Paul Edwards, "Some Notes on Anthropomorphic Theology," in *Religious Experience and Truth*, ed. Sidney Hook (New York: New York University Press, 1961), 243.

13. Davis, "God's Actions," 169. See also Taliaferro, *Contemporary Philosophy of Religion*, 96.

14. Martin, *Atheism: A Philosophical Justification*, 11.

15. See Charles Taliaferro, *Consciousness and the Mind of God* (Cambridge: Cambridge University Press, 1994); Richard Swinburne, *The Evolution of the Soul* (Oxford: Clarendon, 1986).

16. Davis, "God's Actions," 169.

Chapter 9 You're a *Speciesist* If You Think Humans Are Superior to Nonhuman Animals

1. "Germany Guarantees Animal Rights," *CNN.com*, June 21, 2002, http://www.cnn.com/2002/WORLD/europe/06/21/germany.animals/index.html.

2. Found at http://www.peta.com/.

3. Found at http://www.mtd.com/tasty/.

4. Tom Regan, *The Case for Animal Rights* (Berkeley: University of California Press, 1983), 329.

5. Peter Singer, *Animal Liberation: A New Ethics for Our Treatment of Animals* (New York: Random House, 1975), vii. Singer follows eighteenth-century utilitarian philosopher Jeremy Bentham, who said this of animals: "The question is not, can they reason? Nor can they talk? But, can they suffer?"

6. This is a summary (an expansion) of material mentioned in Copan, *"That's Just Your Interpretation,"* 150–52 (and extensive endnotes).

7. Pattle P. T. Pun, "First Response," in *Evangelical Affirmations*, ed. Kenneth Kantzer and Carl Henry (Grand Rapids: Zondervan, 1990), 429. Davis Young, *Creation and the Flood: An Alternative to Flood Geology and Theistic Evolution* (Grand Rapids: Baker Books, 1977), 161, 175.

8. Alfred Lord Tennyson, *In Memoriam* (London: E. Moxon, 1850), quoted online in Alfred Lord Tennyson, *In Memoriam A. H. H. OBIIT MDCCCXXXIII: 56*, line 15, http://eir.library.utoronto.ca/rpo/display/poem2141.html.

9. How does belief in Adam and Eve square with scientific discovery? Here we must be tentative. In a book series edited by D. A. Carson (now republished by InterVarsity), theologian Henri Blocher calls Adam the "first theological man"—he had the capacities of relating to God and probably belonged to the category of the *Paleolithic (or Stone Age) man*, noted for their cave drawings. Blocher asserts: "Modern prejudice may tempt us to underestimate the mental powers and sensitivities of palaeolithic man; the artists who painted the cave walls of Lascaux, Altamira, and the Grotte Chauvet near Vallon-Pont-d'Arc, discovered in December 1994, were masters at least equal to the greatest in our times. How do we measure culture?

We should, moreover, beware of presupposing too close a link between cultural refinement and spiritual competence. . . . [Even] children reach profound understandings. Though we feel uncomfortable with all the uncertainties when we try to correlate scientific data and the results of a sensible interpretation of Genesis 1–4, therefore, we maintain as plausible the hypothesis that the biblical Adam and Eve were the first parents of our race, some 40,000 years ago; and we may posit an initial period of fellowship with God in their lives before they apostatized." Henri Blocher, *Original Sin* (Grand Rapids: Eerdmans, 1997), 41–42.

See the following websites on these cave drawings: http://www.culture.gouv.fr/culture/ arcnat/chauvet/en/; http://www.hominids.com/donsmaps/chauvetcave.html; http://campus .northpark.edu/history/WebChron/Prehistory/Altamira.html; http://www.culture.fr/culture/ arcnat/lascaux/en/index4.html. Blocher also notes that Genesis 4 seems to correspond to the *Neolithic* period—about thirty millennia later.

10. Gordon J. Wenham, *Genesis 1–15*, Word Biblical Commentary 1 (Dallas: Word, 1987), 34.

11. Gordon J. Wenham, "Genesis," in *The New Bible Commentary*, ed. Gordon Wenham et al. (Downers Grove, IL: InterVarsity, 1994), 61.

12. Henri Blocher, *In the Beginning: The Opening Chapters of Genesis* (Downers Grove, IL: InterVarsity, 1984), 209n.

13. John Goldingay, *Old Testament Theology: Israel's Story*, vol. 1 (Downers Grove, IL: InterVarsity, 2003), 111.

14. See Kenneth S. Bailey's excellent study of this in *Jacob and the Prodigal* (Downers Grove, IL: InterVarsity, 2003).

15. As commentator John Oswalt argues, the text of Isaiah 11:7 makes *an overarching point* that in Messiah's reign, "the fears associated with insecurity, danger, and evil will be removed." John Oswalt, *Isaiah 1–39*, New International Commentary on the Old Testament (Grand Rapids: Eerdmans, 1986), 283.

16. C. F. D. Moule, *Man and Nature in the New Testament* (Philadelphia: Fortress, 1964), 11.

17. See chapter 3 on naturalism in this book. See also Copan and Moser, eds., *The Rationality of Theism*. I address some popular-level questions related to naturalism in Copan, *"That's Just Your Interpretation."* See also Craig and Moreland, *Naturalism: A Critical Analysis*; William Lane Craig and J. P. Moreland, eds., *Philosophy of Religion: A Reader and Guide* (Edinburgh: University of Edinburgh Press, 2002); Taliaferro, *Contemporary Philosophy of Religion*; Michael C. Rea, *World without Design: The Ontological Consequences of Naturalism* (Oxford: Oxford University Press, 2003); Thomas Crisp et al., eds., *Knowledge and Reality* (Dordrecht: Kluwer, 2004).

18. One who takes such a view is Terence Penelhum. See his *Christian Ethics and Human Nature* (Harrisburg, PA: Trinity, 1999), 75–99.

19. Dawkins, *The Blind Watchmaker*, 6.

20. Hawking and Penrose, *The Nature of Space and Time*, 20.

21. Peter Ward and Donald Brownlee, *Rare Earth: Why Complex Life Is Uncommon in the Universe* (New York: Copernicus, 2000).

22. See Charles B. Thaxton, Walter L. Bradley, and Roger L. Olsen, *The Mystery of Life's Origin: Reassessing Current Theories* (New York: Philosophical Library, 1984). See Walter Bradley's revisiting of this issue in "Does the Scientific Evidence Support an Intelligently Designed Universe?" in *Science: Christian Perspectives in the New Millennium*, ed. Scott B. Luley, Paul Copan, and Stan W. Wallace (Atlanta: Ravi Zacharias International Ministries, 2003).

23. Stephen Jay Gould, *Ever Since Darwin: Reflections in Natural History* (London: Norton, 1973), 130.

24. Behe, *Darwin's Black Box.*

25. These quotations are from Peter Singer, "Heavy Petting: A review of Midas Dekker's Book *Dearest Pet: On Bestiality*," http://www.nerve.com/Opinions/Singer/heavyPetting/main.asp.

26. See http://www.princeton.edu/Ombuds/fairness.html.

27. Jenny Teichman, "The False Philosophy of Peter Singer," *The New Criterion*, http://www.newcriterion.com/archive/11/apr93/jenny.htm.

28. Another utilitarian who holds similar views to Singer is Jonathan Glover. See Jonathan Glover, *Humanity: A Moral History of the Twentieth Century* (London: Jonathan Cape, 1999); Jonathan Glover, *Causing Death and Saving Lives* (New York: Penguin, 1977).

29. Michael Shermer, *The Science of Good and Evil* (New York: Henry Holt, 2004), 19. Shermer calls his view "transcendent empiricism"—morality, though not supernatural, is a human universal and thus transcendent. It's empirical in that it is a "testable hypothesis" (ibid., 18, 19).

30. Tom Regan, "The Case for Animal Rights," in *People, Penguins and Plastic Trees*, ed. Christine Pierce and Donald VanDeVeer (Belmont, CA: Wadsworth, 1995), 75.

31. This section on Cora Singer is taken from Michael Specter, "The Dangerous Philosopher," *New Yorker* (September 6, 1999), http://www.michaelspecter.com/ny/1999/1999_09_06_philosopher.html.

32. Ibid.

33. Philosopher Simon Blackburn offers a number of caricatures and rather surprising misrepresentations of biblical texts in order to dismiss God from consideration as the source of ethics (Simon Blackburn, *Being Good: A Short Introduction to Ethics* [Oxford: Oxford University Press, 2001], 10–14)—a problem that's unfortunately quite commonplace amongst naturalistic philosophers.

34. See appendix in C. S. Lewis, *The Abolition of Man* (San Francisco: Harper, 2001), 83–101.

35. Kai Nielsen, *Ethics without God*, rev. ed. (Buffalo: Prometheus, 1990), 10–11.

36. Paul Draper, "Craig's Case for God's Existence," in *Does God Exist? The Craig-Flew Debate* (Burlington, VT: Ashgate, 2003), 147.

37. William Lane Craig, "A Reply to Objections," in *Does God Exist?* ed. Stan W. Wallace, 171.

38. Simon Blackburn, *Being Good*, 133, 134.

39. These quotations are documented in *Jeffrey Dahmer: The Monster Within*, A&E Biography (1996).

40. For example, see Copan and Moser, *The Rationality of Theism*; Taliaferro, *Contemporary Philosophy of Religion*; Craig and Moreland, *Philosophy of Religion*.

Chapter 10 Animals Have Rights Just Like Humans Do

1. Tom Regan, *The Case for Animal Rights* (London: Routledge, 1984), 243.

2. David S. Oderberg, *Applied Ethics* (Malden, MA: Blackwell, 2000), 105.

3. United Nations, "The Universal Declaration of Human Rights," General Assembly resolution 217A (III), December 10, 1948, http://www.unchr.ch/udhrlang/eng.htm.

4. All these citations are taken from Charles Darwin, *The Descent of Man*, 1.5. See http://etext.library.adelaide.edu.au/d/d22d/. For a discussion on Darwin, see Philip J. Sampson, *Six Modern Myths about Christianity and Western Civilization* (Downers Grove, IL: InterVarsity, 2001), 46–70.

5. Mary Midgley, *Beasts and Man: The Roots of Human Nature* (Ithaca: Cornell University Press, 1978), 34–35, 145, 146, 150.

6. James Reichmann, *Evolution, Animal "Rights," and the Environment* (Washington: Catholic University of America Press, 2000), 264–65.

7. Oderberg, *Applied Ethics*, 113.

8. Ibid., 110. See Oderberg's other comments in this segment of his book.

9. Ibid., 111.

10. Steve Pinker, *The Language Instinct* (London: Penguin, 1994), 339.

11. See "Jane Goodall's Wild Chimpanzees" at http://www.pbs.org/wnet/nature/goodall/relatives.html.

12. Jane Goodall, *Through a Window: My Thirty Years with the Chimpanzees of Gombe* (Boston: Houghton Mifflin, 1990), 109.

13. Ibid., 206. David Oderberg cites the example of a study in which primates engaged in "intelligent deception"—as though this implies a moral understanding and an intelligence comparable to that of humans (cf. R. Byrne and H. Whiten, "The Thinking Primates' Guide to Deception," *New Scientist* [December 3, 1987]: 54–57). However, he cautions that we be careful here: *Why think that primate deception is different from other animal deception in nature?* For example, the trapdoor spider which builds a trap in the sand to capture its prey or the chameleon which blends in with its surroundings so that it can more readily catch its prey. Oderberg comments on the primate "deception" study: "It would have been surprising if apes were *not* capable of such behaviour." Oderberg, *Applied Ethics,* 118.

14. Oderberg, *Applied Ethics*, 116–17.

15. Reichmann, *Evolution, Animal "Rights," and the Environment*, 254–55. Reichmann states that the human being brings about events as an uncaused cause; nothing *causes* it to react to its physical or intellectual environment the way it does. Nonhuman animals are *caused causes* in that their thinking and actions are "a spontaneous response to the automatic internal calculus determined by its own nature" (ibid., 159).

16. Richard Rorty, "Untruth and Consequences," *The New Republic*, July 31, 1995, 32–36.

17. *Turner and Hooch*, directed by Roger Spotiswoode (Touchstone Pictures, 1989).

18. Reichmann, *Evolution, Animal "Rights," and the Environment*, 261.

19. Peter Singer, "Living and Dying: Animal Rights Activist Peter Singer," *Psychology Today*, June 1999, http://articles.findarticles.com/p/articles/mi_m1175/is_1_32/ai_534 79124.

20. Oderberg, *Applied Ethics*, 98.

21. I owe this point to Taliaferro, *Contemporary Philosophy of Religion*, 227.

22. Richard Bauckham, "Jesus and the Wild Animals (Mark 1:13): A Christological Image for an Ecological Age," in *Jesus of Nazareth: Lord and Christ: Essays on the Historical Jesus and New Testament Christology*, ed. Joel B. Green and Max Turner (Grand Rapids: Eerdmans; Carlisle, U.K.: Paternoster, 1994), 20–21.

23. Oderberg, *Applied Ethics*, 141.

24. Robert Wennberg's *God, Humans, and Animals: An Invitation to Enlarge Our Moral Universe* (Grand Rapids: Eerdmans, 2003) offers some helpful perspectives on showing greater regard for animals (although I don't fully agree with Wennberg's perspective). Writing in a similar vein is Matthew Scully, *Dominion: The Power of Man, the Suffering of Animals, and the Call to Mercy* (New York: St. Martin's, 2002).

25. *As Good as It Gets*, directed by James L. Brooks (Columbia/Tri-Star, 1997).

26. C. Stephen Layman, *The Shape of the Good: Christian Reflections on the Foundation of Ethics* (Notre Dame: University of Notre Dame Press, 1991), 200.

27. Taken from Oderberg, *Applied Ethics*, 139–40.

28. John Stott, *The Birds Our Teachers: Biblical Lessons from a Lifelong Bird Watcher* (Grand Rapids: Baker Books, 2001).

29. Oderberg, *Applied Ethics*, 142.

30. Ibid., 143.

Chapter 11 How Could God Command Abraham to Sacrifice Isaac?

1. See C. S. Evans, "Is Kierkegaard an Irrationalist? Reason, Paradox, and Faith," *Religious Studies* 25 (September 1989): 347–62. Evans writes that the charge of Kierkegaard's faith being an arbitrary leap (fideism) is "profoundly mistaken" (ibid., 347). When he calls upon us to embrace the "paradox" of, say, the incarnation, he doesn't mean that this is a formal contradiction. In many of his writings, Kierkegaard opposes Hegel's philosophy, in which the either-or (thesis-antithesis) can become a both-and (synthesis); Kierkegaard rejects the idea that every opposition can achieve a Hegelian synthesis. What Kierkegaard means by "paradox" is *apparent contradiction*. It's one's *constricted conception* of God that leads a person to conclude that the incarnation is a contradiction (ibid., 354).

2. Søren Kierkegaard, *Fear and Trembling* and *The Sickness unto Death*, trans. Walter Lowrie (Garden City, NY: Doubleday, 1954), 41.

3. Walter Kaiser, *Toward Old Testament Ethics* (Grand Rapids: Zondervan, 1983), 262.

4. E. A. Speiser, *Genesis*, Anchor Bible Commentary 1 (Garden City, NY: Doubleday, 1964), 166.

5. Roland de Vaux, *Ancient Israel* (New York: McGraw-Hill, 1965), 443.

6. William L. Lane, *Hebrews 9–13*, Word Biblical Commentary 47B (Dallas: Word, 1991), 360.

7. Some comments from this section are taken from John H. Sailhamer, *The Pentateuch as Narrative* (Grand Rapids: Zondervan, 1992), 33–79; John H. Sailhamer, "The Mosaic Law and the Theology of the Pentateuch," *Westminster Theological Journal* 53 (1991): 24–61.

8. See Douglas Moo, *The Epistle to the Romans*, New International Commentary on the New Testament (Grand Rapids: Eerdmans, 1996), 423–67.

9. Some of this is taken from Eleonore Stump's excellent discussion in her "Evil and the Nature of Faith"—part of her Gifford Lectures series. This will be published as *Wandering in Darkness: Narrative and the Problem of Evil* by Oxford University Press.

10. The Hebrew word *nā'* ("please") is in view. Gordon Wenham, *Genesis 16–20*, Word Biblical Commentary 2 (Dallas: Word, 1994), 104.

11. Ibid., 105. Of course, 2 Chronicles 3:1 informs us that Mount Moriah is the location of the Jerusalem temple.

12. John H. Walton and Victor H. Matthews, *The Bible Background Commentary: Genesis–Deuteronomy* (Downers Grove, IL: InterVarsity, 1997), 49.

13. Taliaferro, *Contemporary Philosophy of Religion*, 317.

14. Norman Geisler and Thomas Howe, *When Skeptics Ask* (Wheaton: Victor, 1992), 51.

15. I have modified the NASB translation, since the same word used in Romans 8:32 ("spare" [*pheidomai*]) is used in the Septuagint (the Greek translation of the Old Testament).

16. James D. G. Dunn, *The Theology of the Apostle Paul* (Grand Rapids: Eerdmans, 1998), 225.

17. Thomas Torrance, *The Christian Doctrine of God: One Being, Three Persons* (Edinburgh: T&T Clark, 1996), 244.

260

Chapter 12 Many Old Testament Laws Are Strange and Arbitrary

1. One site with this letter is http://www.thehumorarchives.com/humor/0001065.html.

2. For a useful overview of the Pentateuch (especially the purpose of Levitical laws), see Gordon J. Wenham, *Exploring the Old Testament: A Guide to the Pentateuch* (Downers Grove, IL: InterVarsity, 2003).

3. J. K. Bruckner, "Ethics," in *Dictionary of the Old Testament: Pentateuch*, ed. T. Desmond Alexander and David W. Baker (Downers Grove, IL: InterVarsity, 2003), 229.

4. Christopher J. H. Wright, *An Eye for an Eye: The Place of Old Testament Ethics Today* (Downers Grove, IL: InterVarsity, 1983), 26–27.

5. Ibid., 29.

6. C. S. Lewis speaks of "chronological snobbery" (the "uncritical acceptance of the intellectual climate common to our age and the assumption that whatever has gone out of date is on that count discredited") in *Surprised by Joy* (New York: Harcourt Brace, 1956), 207.

7. Mencken erroneously applied this to Puritanism—a gross distortion which needs serious correcting. For a corrective, see J. I. Packer, *The Quest for Godliness* (Wheaton: Crossway, 1990).

8. William Webb, *Slaves, Women, and Homosexuals: Explaining the Hermeneutics of Cultural Analysis* (Downers Grove, IL: InterVarsity, 2001).

9. Ibid., 43.

10. Ibid., 42–43.

11. R. T. France, "From Romans to the Real World," in *Romans and the People of God*, ed. Sven K. Soderlund and N. T. Wright (Grand Rapids: Eerdmans, 1999), 245.

12. Victor P. Hamilton, *Handbook on the Pentateuch* (Grand Rapids: Baker Academic, 1982), 246.

13. William Dyrness, *Themes in Old Testament Theology* (Downers Grove, IL: InterVarsity, 1979), 51.

14. Richard Bauckham, *The Bible in Politics: How to Read the Bible Politically* (Louisville: Westminster/John Knox, 1989), 23.

15. Ibid.

16. Gordon J. Wenham, *Leviticus*, New International Commentary on the Old Testament (Grand Rapids: Eerdmans, 1979), 270.

17. For example, demanding genealogical evidence to serve as a priest (Ezra 2:62; Neh. 7:64), observing Passover and the Feast of Unleavened Bread (Ezra 6:19–22), affirming that unclean food and carcasses are defiling (Hag. 2:11–13).

18. Dallas Willard, *The Divine Conspiracy*, 61.

19. Maltbie D. Babcock, "This Is My Father's World."

20. Wenham, *Leviticus*, 23.

21. David P. Wright, "Unclean and Clean (OT)," *Anchor Bible Dictionary* (New York: Doubleday, 1992), 6:740.

22. Timothy A. Lenchak, "Clean and Unclean," in *Eerdmans Dictionary of the Bible*, ed. David Noel Freedman (Grand Rapids: Eerdmans, 2000), 263.

23. Wenham, *Leviticus*, 167–68.

24. Gordon J. Wenham, "The Theology of Unclean Food," *Evangelical Quarterly* 53 (1981): 7.

25. Wenham, *Leviticus*, 167.

26. J. G. McConville, *Deuteronomy*, Apollos Old Testament Commentary (Downers Grove, IL: InterVarsity, 2002), 249.

27. Mary Douglas, *Purity and Danger* (London: Routledge, 1966). Jacob Milgrom has asserted that Douglas's earlier writings in particular are "replete with errors." Jacob Milgrom,

Leviticus 1–16, Anchor Bible Commentary 3 (New York: Doubleday, 1991), 721. See some of Milgrom's comments on pages 718–36. Douglas has modified and corrected some of her assertions, but she has suggested a very fruitful direction in understanding apparently obscure Levitical laws.

28. Mary Douglas, *Implicit Meanings: Essays in Anthropology* (Boston: Routledge and Kegan, 1975), 266, 284.

29. Deuteronomy 14 also utilizes this threefold division: land animals (vv. 4–8), aquatic animals (vv. 9–10), and animals of the air (vv. 11–20).

30. Raymond B. Dillard and Tremper Longman III, *An Introduction to the Old Testament* (Grand Rapids: Zondervan, 1994), 81. Note too that not all the animals mentioned in Leviticus 11 and Deuteronomy 14 can be identified with reasonable certainty.

31. John H. Sailhamer, *The Pentateuch as Narrative* (Grand Rapids: Zondervan, 1992), 333.

32. Douglas, *Purity and Danger*, 53.

33. Wenham, "The Theology of Unclean Food," 11; Wenham, *Leviticus*, 170.

34. Sailhamer says, "Uncleanness meant one was barred from the worship life of the covenant community. Uncleanness meant separation from the sacred and the tabernacle." Sailhamer, *Pentateuch as Narrative*, 335.

35. However, priestly clothing (cf. Exod. 39) was exempted from this, being made of both wool and linen. Wool didn't dye very well, so it was combined with linen.

36. Wenham, *Leviticus*, 269.

37. Lenchak, "Clean and Unclean," 263.

38. Mary Douglas, "The Forbidden Animals in Leviticus," *Journal for the Study of the Old Testament* 59 (1993): 3–23. I follow Douglas in the following paragraphs. Notice the very structure of Leviticus, which serves as a reminder for the themes she discusses (ibid., 11).

39. Wenham, *Leviticus*, 174–75.

40. Douglas, "Forbidden Animals in Leviticus," 22.

41. Ibid., 23.

42. Milgrom, *Leviticus 1–16*, 730–31.

43. McConville, *Deuteronomy*, 250.

44. Hans Hübner, "Unclean and Clean (NT)," *Anchor Bible Dictionary* (New York: Doubleday, 1992), 6:742.

45. For thorough documentation on these phenomena, see Alvin J. Schmidt, *How Christianity Changed the World* (Grand Rapids: Zondervan, 2004).

46. On articulating our faith in the public square, see Robert P. George, *The Clash of Orthodoxies: Laws, Religion, and Morality in Crisis* (Wilmington, DE: ISI Books, 2001); J. Budziszewski, *What We Can't Not Know* (Dallas: Spence, 2004).

47. On this, see Willard, *The Divine Conspiracy*.

Chapter 13 Why Are Some Old Testament Laws Harsh and Oppressive?

1. Russell mentions this in passing in Bertrand Russell, "Science and Ethics," in *Religion and Science* (Oxford: Oxford University Press, 1961).

2. Baruch A. Levine, *Leviticus*, JPS Commentary (New York: Jewish Publication Society, 1989), 256.

3. Milgrom, *Leviticus 1–16*, 740–41.

4. The mark of circumcision, however, is an exception commanded by God as a mark of God's covenant for all males. Though Arab and Egyptian adult males (or those on the verge of manhood) were circumcised, they weren't circumcised as infant boys.

5. Levine, *Leviticus*, 58–59.

6. Ibid., 250. The reason for the varying lengths of ceremonial separation (thirty-three days after a boy's birth, sixty-six after a girl's) isn't clear. However, it doesn't reflect less social worth. After all, a human corpse defiles just as does a dead pig, but this doesn't mean the pig has value equal to that of the human (Milgrom, *Leviticus 1–16*, 752). R. K. Harrison suggests that the difference may be symbolic (the daughter would eventually experience the same uncleanness herself later on when she gives birth; perhaps circumcision reduces the attendant uncleanness) or practical (in the patriarchal ancient Near East, the tendency may have been for the father to favor the son and ignore the daughter; thus the longer time the mother spends at home with her newborn daughter would be a positive compensation). R. K. Harrison, "Leviticus," in *Expositor's Bible Commentary*, vol. 2, ed. Frank E. Gaebelein (Grand Rapids: Zondervan, 1990), 574.

7. Harrison, "Leviticus," 608.

8. See the chapter "Doesn't the Bible Condone Slavery?" in Copan, *"That's Just Your Interpretation,"* 171–78.

9. Some of my comments come from Walter Kaiser, "Exodus," in *Expositor's Bible Commentary*, vol. 2, 433–35.

10. Ibid., 435.

11. Ibid., 433.

12. For example, Gen. 31:38; Exod. 23:26; Job 21:10; Hosea 9:14.

13. Gordon J. Wenham, *Story as Torah: Reading Old Testament Narrative Ethically* (Grand Rapids: Baker Academic, 2000), 109.

14. Tacitus, *Annals* 3.27 (or "And now bills were passed, not only for national objects but for individual cases, and laws were most numerous when the Republic was most corrupt").

15. Wenham, *Story as Torah*, 109 (my emphasis). I am grateful to Wenham's book for other insights in these paragraphs.

16. These comments are taken from Sailhamer, *The Pentateuch as Narrative*; John Sailhamer, *Introduction to Theology: A Canonical Approach* (Grand Rapids: Zondervan, 1995), 272–89. I can only summarize here.

17. So when the Israelites finally arrived at Sinai, they had to wait three days—not beforehand—when the ram's horn sounded. Only then could they all "go up to [literally, 'up in'] the mountain" (Exod. 19:13). When the third day finally came and Israel "heard the trumpet," they didn't go up to the mountain, because they were frightened when God displayed his presence in thunder, lightning, and smoke (vv. 16, 18). The Israelites told Moses to go up in their place to speak with God as a priest. They resisted God's invitation; so Moses went up. Only *after* this point did God bar them from going up the mountain (v. 21). As a result, God would (a) *reestablish his Sinai covenant* in Exod. 24. He would also (b) *make a provision for this failure/refusal in establishing the tabernacle* (chaps. 25–31) *and a priesthood* (through Aaron's family) for the people.

18. Sailhamer, *Pentateuch as Narrative*, 57.

19. Ibid., 289.

20. Ibid., 58.

21. Ibid.

22. N. T. Wright, *The Climax of the Covenant* (Minneapolis: Fortress, 1991), 168.

23. Ibid., 181.

24. Leviticus 1–16 deals with *priestly* responsibilities (which continues the Priestly Code from Exodus) and reaches its climax with the *Day of Atonement* (chap. 16). There is also an *object lesson* in chap. 10, where the priests Nadab and Abihu are destroyed for offering

"strange fire" (perhaps some form of pagan worship). Leviticus 18–27 (the Holiness Code) deals with the *people's* responsibilities, reaching its climax with the *Year of Jubilee* (chap. 25), in which relationships were restored. There is an object lesson for the people: a lay Israelite is stoned to death for blasphemy (chap. 24). See Christopher Wright, "Leviticus," in *New Bible Commentary*, ed. G. Wenham et al. (Downers Grove, IL: InterVarsity, 1996), 122.

25. Paul Johnson, *Art: A New History* (New York: HarperCollins, 2003), 33.

Chapter 14 It's Unfair That Humans Are Punished for Adam's Sin (Part 1)

1. Edward T. Oakes, "Original Sin: A Disputation," *First Things* 87 (1998): 16.

2. These two chapters are a summary of my essay, "Original Sin and Christian Philosophy," *Philosophia Christi* 2, vol. 5, no. 2 (2003): 519–41.

3. Alvin Plantinga puts it this way: "An object has a property *essentially* if it has it in such a way that it is not even possible that it exist but *fail* to have it." Alvin Plantinga, "Essence and Essentialism," in *A Companion to Metaphysics*, 138.

4. Thomas R. Schreiner, *Paul: Apostle of God's Glory in Christ: A Pauline Theology* (Downers Grove, IL: InterVarsity, 2001), 143. Schreiner cites the work of Walter B. Russell regarding how "flesh" should be understood salvation-historically: Walter B. Russell, "The Apostle Paul's View of the 'Sin Nature'/'New Nature' Struggle," in *Christian Perspectives on Being Human*, ed. J. P. Moreland and David Ciocchi (Grand Rapids: Baker Books, 1993), 210; Walter B. Russell, "Does the Christian Have 'Flesh' in Gal. 5:13–26?" *Journal for the Evangelical Theological Society* 36 (June 1993): 179–87. See also Gordon Fee, *God's Empowering Presence: The Holy Spirit in the Letters of Paul* (Peabody, MA: Hendrickson, 1994), 434–45.

5. See Phillip Schaff, *The Creeds of Christendom*, vol. 3 (New York: Harper, 1877), 1.1.

6. Ibid., 1.12.

7. Thomas Aquinas, *Summa Theologica* I/II, 109.2.

8. Personal conversation with Alister McGrath in Atlanta, Georgia, on June 22, 2000.

9. In E. K. Simpson and F. F. Bruce, *The Epistles of Paul to the Ephesians and to the Colossians*, New International Commentary on the New Testament (Grand Rapids: Eerdmans, 1957), 194.

10. Harold O. J. Brown, *Heresies* (Garden City, NY: Doubleday, 1984), 344 (my emphasis).

11. Colin E. Gunton, *The Triune Creator: A Historical and Systematic Study* (Grand Rapids: Eerdmans, 1998), 203.

12. James Leo Garrett Jr., *Systematic Theology*, vol. 1 (Grand Rapids: Eerdmans, 1990), 493.

13. Henri Blocher, *Original Sin: Illuminating the Riddle* (Grand Rapids: Eerdmans, 1997), 67.

14. Ibid., 115.

15. Sherlock states that "a full-blown Augustinian position is not supported by the actual Greek text of Romans 5:12." Charles Sherlock, *The Doctrine of Humanity* (Downers Grove, IL: InterVarsity, 1996), 65. It has been noted by many that Augustine wrongly took the *in quo* (from the Greek *eph' hō*) to mean "in whom [i.e., Adam]" instead of "in that" or "because." Schreiner sees in this text a reference to all people sinning personally and individually because they enter the world spiritually dead because they are born in Adam. Thomas Schreiner, *Paul: Apostle of God's Glory in Christ*, 148. Schreiner follows Joseph A. Fitzmyer, "The Consecutive Meaning of *eph' hō* in Romans 5:12," *New Testament Studies* 39 (1993): 321–39.

16. Blocher, *Original Sin*, 74. Blocher asks if this reading is even the most natural. And *if* the imputation of alien guilt is in Romans 5:12, then it must be understood that "nowhere else is that thought distinctly expressed." Blocher rejects "the unattested and difficult thesis

of the imputation of an *alien* sin" without downplaying "the tragic realism of the Augustinian human predicament" (ibid., 80).

17. Douglas Moo, *The Epistle to the Romans*, New International Commentary on the New Testament (Grand Rapids: Eerdmans, 1996), 328n.

18. Cornelius Plantinga Jr., *Not the Way It's Supposed to Be: A Breviary of Sin* (Grand Rapids: Eerdmans; Leicester, U.K.: Apollos, 1995), 33.

19. Blocher, *Original Sin*, 128.

20. Moo, *The Epistle to the Romans*, 331. Regarding various theories of how sin is transmitted, see Sherlock, *Doctrine of Humanity*, 233–38.

21. Blocher, *Original Sin*, 24.

22. Or, as Nash puts it, part of the "elect." Ronald Nash, *When a Baby Dies: Answers to Comfort Grieving Parents* (Grand Rapids: Zondervan, 1999), 60–65. One Reformed theologian once asked me (in the context of my defending my "De-formed"—non-Reformed—theology!): "If spiritual salvation is the greatest gift possible and all infants who die are saved [he believed in 'elect infants'], then why not (purely hypothetically speaking) have all infants physically killed before they reach some 'age of accountability'? After all, at that point they would sin, and they may never turn to God, which would mean they'd be everlastingly lost." My response was: "Why couldn't it be the case that any infants who die are those who *would have* put their trust in God/Christ had they had the opportunity?"

23. Wayne Grudem, *Systematic Theology* (Grand Rapids: Zondervan, 1994), 495. The repeated point that God will reward each person according to what he or she has done is found in various places: Job 34:11; Ps. 62:12; Prov. 24:12; Jer. 17:10; 32:19; Matt. 16:27; Rom. 2:6; 1 Cor. 3:8; 2 Cor. 5:10; 1 Peter 1:17.

24. "Behold, you are a dead man . . ." (Gen. 20:3).

25. Blocher, *Original Sin*, 129.

26. Blocher points out that John Calvin and Jonathan Edwards were not always consistent in their handling of original sin. Blocher wisely admonishes: "When giants stumble, we should look out for slippery stones in our path" (ibid., 119).

27. Alvin Plantinga, *Warranted Christian Belief* (New York: Oxford University Press, 2000), 206–7.

28. Ibid., 207. Richard Swinburne, in *Responsibility and Atonement* (Oxford: Clarendon, 1989), agrees that we have a propensity toward sin, but he (erroneously) denies that "the proneness was caused by the sin of the first sinner" (143).

29. This paragraph is based on a discussion with Alvin Plantinga in Madison, Wisconsin, sometime in October 1996. Swinburne argues that "bad desires incline," but "they do not (as such) necessitate." Swinburne, *Responsibility and Atonement*, 138.

30. Erickson says, "We were all involved in Adam's sin, and thus we receive both the corrupted [state] that was his after the fall, and the guilt and condemnation that attach to his sin." Millard Erickson, *Christian Theology* (Grand Rapids: Baker Books, 1983–85), 639.

31. Gordon R. Lewis and Bruce A. Demarest, *Integrative Theology* (Grand Rapids: Zondervan, 1996), 2:235 (my emphasis). This is also the view of David L. Smith, *With Willful Intent: A Theology of Sin* (Grand Rapids: Baker Books, 1994). He concludes, after surveying Scripture on the topic of sin, that the biblical teaching stresses our being born with a propensity to sin, but this by itself does not bring condemnation (which comes when this propensity is acted upon). On the broad views regarding the transmission of sin (legal, federal, biological, social, etc.) and its key proponents, see Smith's summary on p. 367.

32. Erickson, *Christian Theology*, 639 (my emphasis). (Erickson uses the word *nature*. I have used *state* to prevent confusion.)

Chapter 15 It's Unfair That Humans Are Punished for Adam's Sin (Part 2)

1. G. K. Chesterton, *Orthodoxy*, repr. ed. (Garden City, NY: Image/Doubleday, 1959), 15.

2. Ibid.

3. Michael Ruse, "Darwinism and Christianity Redux: A Response to My Critics," *Philosophia Christi* 2, vol. 4, no. 1 (2002): 192.

4. Cf. Romans 1–3.

5. Layman, *The Shape of the Good*, 140.

6. Quoted in Paul C. Vitz, *Psychology as Religion: The Cult of Self-Worship*, 2nd ed. (Grand Rapids: Eerdmans, 1994), 61n.

7. Philip Rieff, *The Triumph of the Therapeutic: Uses of Faith after Freud* (Chicago: University of Chicago Press, 1987).

8. On this, see Gordon Graham's excellent book *Evil and Christian Ethics* (Cambridge: Cambridge University Press, 2001).

9. Karl Menninger, *Whatever Became of Sin?* (New York: Hawthorn Books, 1973), 46.

10. This is not to deny that there is a theological irrationality and abnormality involved in sin. Because, as Aquinas declared, the "guilty character of sin consists in the fact that it is committed against God" (*Summa Theologica* III, 46.2 and 3); sin is an irrationality that flies in the face of how we were designed to function. Thus for Aquinas sin is both *contra naturam* (against nature) and *actus contra rationem* (an act against reason). See *Summa Theologica* I/II, 78.3; II/II, 153.2; II/II, 168.4).

11. Vitz, *Psychology as Religion*, 104.

12. O. Hobart Mowrer, *The Crisis in Psychiatry and Religion* (Princeton, NJ: D. Van Nostrand, 1961), 40 (my italics).

13. Vernon Grounds, "Called to Be Saints—Not Well-Adjusted Sinners," *Christianity Today*, January 17, 1986, 28.

14. Gary Anderson, "*Necesarium Adae Peccatum*: The Problem of Original Sin," in *Sin, Death, and the Devil*, ed. Carl E. Braaten and Robert W. Jenson (Grand Rapids: Eerdmans, 2000), 38.

15. Stephen J. Duffy, "Our Hearts of Darkness: Original Sin Revisited," *Theological Studies* 49 (1988): 618.

16. Thomas Reid, "Of the First Principles of Morals," essay 3 in *Essays on the Active Powers of the Human Mind*, intro. Baruch A. Brody (Cambridge, MA: MIT Press, 1969), 364–67.

17. John E. Hare, *The Moral Gap: Kantian Ethics, Human Limits, and God's Assistance*, Oxford Studies in Theological Ethics (Oxford: Oxford University Press, 1997).

18. Hare makes this point in "Naturalism and Morality," in *Naturalism: A Critical Analysis*, 194.

19. Terence Penelhum, *Christian Ethics and Human Nature* (Harrisburg, PA: Trinity Press International, 2000), 22, 41. I would disagree, however, with Penelhum's revised understanding of original sin, which is shaped by his belief in the evolution of the human species.

20. I discuss the question of God's desire for all to be saved as it pertains to the unevangelized in Paul Copan, *"True for You, but Not for Me"* (Minneapolis: Bethany House, 1998), 123–63.

21. See Copan, *"That's Just Your Interpretation,"* 84–89. See also William Klein's *The New Chosen People: A Corporate View of Election* (Grand Rapids: Zondervan, 1990; Eugene, OR: Wipf and Stock, 2001).

22. Taken from William Lane Craig (debate with Ray Bradley), "Can a Loving God Send People to Hell?" http://www.leaderu.com/offices/billcraig/docs/craig-bradley0.html.

23. Stephen Travis, "The Problem of Judgment," *Themelios* 11 (January 1986): 53.

24. C. S. Lewis, *The Great Divorce* (Macmillan, 1946), 72.

25. C. S. Lewis, *George MacDonald: An Anthology* (New York: Macmillan, 1948), 85.

26. Joel B. Green and Mark D. Baker, *Recovering the Scandal of the Cross* (Downers Grove, IL: InterVarsity, 2000), 54–55; cf. 95.

27. William Lane Craig, "Politically Incorrect Salvation," in *Christian Apologetics in the Postmodern World*, ed. Timothy R. Phillips and Dennis L. Okholm (Downers Grove, IL: InterVarsity, 1995), 88.

28. Thanks to Frank Beckwith and Bill Craig for their discussions on this point.

Chapter 16 Why Were Certain Texts Arbitrarily Excluded from the New Testament Canon?

1. D. M. Scholer, "Gnosis, Gnosticism," in *Dictionary of the Later New Testament and Its Developments*, ed. Ralph P. Martin and Peter H. Davids (Downers Grove, IL: InterVarsity, 1997), 400. Some points used in the numbered list in the text are taken from Scholer's article.

2. Elaine Pagels, *The Gnostic Gospels* (New York: Vintage/Random House, 1979), xxii.

3. Ibid., xvii.

4. Ibid., 33–56.

5. Ibid., 170. See Pagels's more recent work, *Beyond Belief: The Secret Gospel of Thomas* (New York: Random House, 2003).

6. In 2 Chronicles, another ancestor, Jehoiada, is mentioned. This isn't a contradiction but rather reflects Scripture's use of the phrase "son of" in a flexible way. For example, Jesus was called the "son of David."

7. Some question that 2 Chronicles is the last part of the Hebrew Old Testament. David Noel Freedman claims that the "Writings [Psalms]" end with Ezra/Nehemiah and that Chronicles is the first part of the "Writings." Noel Freedman, "The Symmetry of the Hebrew Bible," *Studia Theologica* 46 (1992): 95–96.

8. 4QMMT Fragments 7–8, 10.

9. F. F. Bruce, *The Canon of Scripture* (Downers Grove, IL: InterVarsity, 1988), 39.

10. Ibid., 33.

11. For a thorough and nuanced discussion on the canon, see Lee M. MacDonald, *The Formation of the Christian Biblical Canon*, rev. ed. (Peabody, MA: Hendrickson, 1995).

12. These points are taken from John Goldingay, *Models for Scripture* (Grand Rapids: Eerdmans, 1994), 146–47. See also F. F. Bruce, *The Canon of Scripture*, 34–36.

13. These books include Tobit, Judith, Wisdom of Solomon, Ecclesiasticus (Sirach), and 1 and 2 Maccabees.

14. David C. Dunbar, "The Biblical Canon," in *Hermeneutics, Authority, and Canon*, ed. D. A. Carson and John D. Woodbridge (Grand Rapids: Zondervan, 1988), 310.

15. Jerome, however, did exclude Esther from the canonical collection, considering it "edifying but not canonical." See MacDonald, *The Formation of the Christian Biblical Canon*, 113.

16. Eusebius, *Ecclesiastical History* 3.25.

17. Lee MacDonald's *The Formation of the Christian Biblical Canon* tracks these questions in readable detail.

18. On this, see the discussion in Dunbar, "The Biblical Canon," 326.

19. For a helpful popular-level article on this, see Ben Witherington III, "Why the 'Lost Gospels' Lost Out," *Christianity Today*, June 2004, 29.

20. Dan Brown, *The Da Vinci Code* (New York: Doubleday, 2003). For a refutation, see Ben Witherington III, *The Gospel Code: Novel Claims about Jesus, Mary Magdalene, and Da Vinci*

(Downers Grove, IL: InterVarsity, 2004); see also Darrell Bock, *Breaking the Da Vinci Code* (Nashville: Nelson, 2004).

21. Eusebius, *Ecclesiastical History* 3.39.15; Irenaeus, *Against the Heresies* (Early Christian Writings, 2005), 3.1.2, http://www.earlychristianwritings.com/irenaeus.html. Irenaeus wrote: "These have all declared to us that there is one God, Creator of heaven and earth, announced by the law and the prophets; and one Christ the Son of God. If any one [does] not agree to these truths, he despises the companions of the Lord; nay more, he despises Christ Himself the Lord; yea, he despises the Father also, and stands self-condemned, resisting and opposing his own salvation, as is the case with all heretics."

22. Some of these comments taken from Wayne Grudem, *Prophecy in the New Testament and Today*, rev. ed. (Wheaton: Crossway, 2000).

23. *The Shepherd of Hermas*, trans. J. B. Lightfoot (Early Christian Writings, 2005), Mandate 4.3.1–6, http://www.earlychristianwritings.com/text/shepherd-lightfoot.html.

24. Ibid., Parable 9.1.1, http://www.earlychristianwritings.com/text/shepherd-lightfoot .html. Note the following quotation: "After I had written down the commandments and parables of the shepherd, the angel of repentance, he came to me and saith to me: 'I wish to show thee all things that the Holy Spirit, which spake with thee in the form of the Church, showed unto thee. For that Spirit is the Son of God.'"

25. Bruce, *The Canon of Scripture*, 259.

26. R. T. France, "Inerrancy and New Testament Exegesis," *Themelios* 1, no. 1 (Autumn 1975): 13.

27. Witherington, "Why the 'Lost Gospels' Lost Out," 30.

28. D. A. Carson, "Approaching the Bible," in *New Bible Commentary*, 6.

29. Ibid., 7.

Chapter 17 Isn't the *Gospel of Thomas* a Legitimate Source about the Historical Jesus?

1. Risto Uro, *Thomas: Seeking the Historical Context of the Gospel of Thomas* (Edinburgh: T&T Clark, 2003), 51–53.

2. Robert W. Funk and Roy W. Hoover, *The Five Gospels: The Search for the Authentic Words of Jesus* (New York: Macmillan, 1993).

3. Uro, *Thomas*, 135.

4. Elaine Pagels, *Beyond Belief: The Secret Gospel of Thomas* (New York: Random House, 2003), 57–58.

5. Ibid., 32.

6. John P. Meier, *A Marginal Jew: Rethinking the Historical Jesus*, vol. 1, *The Roots of the Probblem and the Person* (New York: Doubleday, 1991), 134.

7. On Eastern monism (and reincarnation), see Copan, "*That's Just Your Interpretation*," 49–68.

8. Meier, *Marginal Jew*, vol. 1, 126.

9. Karen L. King, *The Gospel of Mary of Magdala: Jesus and the First Woman Apostle* (Santa Rosa, CA: Polebridge, 2003).

10. Taken from the *Gospel of Thomas's* prologue.

11. R. T. France, *The Evidence for Jesus* (Downers Grove, IL: InterVarsity, 1986), 76.

12. Raymond E. Brown, "The Gospel of Thomas and St. John's Gospel," *New Testament Studies* 9 (1962–63): 173.

13. Wright, *Resurrection of the Son of God*. He cites, among others, sayings such as 21, 37, 29, 87, and 112.

14. Meier, *Marginal Jew*, vol. 1, 140–41. Meier also includes the *Gospel of Peter*. See also Joseph A. Fitzmyer, *The Gospel According to Luke*, Anchor Bible Commentary 28A (New York: Doubleday, 1985), 1157–58.

15. Pheme Perkins, "Pronouncement Stories in the Gospel of Thomas," *Semeia* 20 (1981): 121–32.

16. Wright, *The Resurrection of the Son of God*, 537.

17. Craig L. Blomberg, "Where Do We Start Studying Jesus?" in *Jesus Under Fire*, ed. Michael J. Wilkins and J. P. Moreland (Grand Rapids: Zondervan, 1995), 23. Blomberg adds: "*Thomas's* lack of historical narrative and lack of apocalyptic [such as the book of Revelation] reflects the Gnostic worldview, which cares nothing for God's acting in *history* to redeem the world" (ibid., 25).

18. Ibid., 24.

19. Robert E. Van Voorst, *Jesus outside the New Testament: An Introduction to the Ancient Evidence* (Grand Rapids: Eerdmans, 2000), 202.

20. John Meier, *A Marginal Jew: Rethinking the Historical Jesus*, vol. 2 *Mentor, Message, and Miracles* (New York: Doubleday, 1994), 333. For an expansion on this theme, see Christopher Tuckett, "Thomas and the Synoptics," *Novum Testamentum* 30 (1988): 132–57.

21. Meier, *Marginal Jew*, vol. 2, 333.

22. See Craig A. Evans et al., eds., *The Nag Hammadi Texts and the Bible* (Leiden: Brill, 1993).

23. Meier, *Marginal Jew*, vol. 1, 137.

24. Craig A. Evans, "Thomas, Gospel of," in *Dictionary of the Later New Testament and Its Later Developments*, ed. Ralph P. Martin and Peter H. Davids (Downers Grove, IL: InterVarsity, 1997), 1176.

25. N. T. Wright, *Jesus and the Victory of God* (Minneapolis: Fortress, 1996), 48, 62.

Paul Copan (Ph.D., Marquette University) is the Pledger Family Chair of Philosophy and Ethics at Palm Beach Atlantic University. He has lectured on many university campuses in the United States and internationally. He is the author or editor of various books, including *Creation Out of Nothing, "That's Just Your Interpretation," "True for You, but Not for Me," The Rationality of Theism,* and *Will the Real Jesus Please Stand Up?*

More **GREAT ANSWERS**
from Paul Copan!

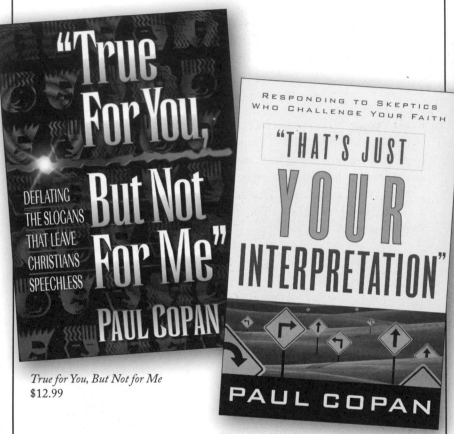

True for You, But Not for Me
$12.99

That's Just Your Interpretation
$14.99

Don't miss these other insightful apologetics resources
that offer incisive answers for defending the faith,
even when you're confronted with the toughest questions.